FREEDOMS STOLEN

FREEDOMS STOLEN

OUR COUNTRY IS DYING

BILL WHITLOW

Published by:
    CreateSpace Independent Publishing Platform
    North Charleston, SC, USA

ISBN: 978-1530035427
Library of Congress Control Number: 2016902814

4623

In memory of my wife
Wilma Jean Whitlow

A very loving wife and mother

Contents

Introduction

We have always been told that our Bill of Rights—the first ten amendments to the US Constitution—is a valuable guardian of our liberty. It protects our most fundamental rights against violation by the government. This is true—it should be the protector of our freedoms. But it is falling short in many ways because the federal courts have used their power to adjust, modify, interpret and revise these rights into a form that a court thinks is a better version on any particular day. The result is a Constitution that is different from what the Framers intended, having been modified, not through the legitimate amendment process, but through opinions written by a judge.

For example, the First Amendment guarantees our freedom of speech and of the press, saying that "Congress shall make no law . . . abridging the freedom of speech, or of the press . . . ." The Founders recognized that freedom of speech is essential for a republic such as ours, where the people, not a king, have the ultimate power. In order to exercise this power wisely, the people have to be informed about the issues of the day and about what their government officials are doing. But government officials and some special interest groups might be embarrassed if the people knew what they were doing, so they have found ways to silence speech that they didn't like. At various times, the federal courts have upheld laws making it illegal to criticize the government. During the Civil War, some military commanders arrested politicians and closed newspapers for criticizing the government. People have gone to jail for mailing political leaflets. The FBI and IRS have been used to harass organizations that disagreed with government policy.

Our freedom of religious expression is also supposed to be guaranteed by the First Amendment. Our Founders knew that religion was essential for our system in which the people are supposed to govern themselves. As John Adams, our second president, said, "Our constitution was made only for a moral and religious people. It is wholly inadequate to the government of any other." So the Founders tried to encourage religion, and it was widely recognized at the time that this was the duty of the government, and also was completely in accordance with the First Amendment. Church services were held in the Capitol Building. Religious instruction was an important part of many of the early schools and public universities. In response to a question, Congress issued a report saying, "At the time of the adoption of the Constitution and the amendments, the universal sentiment was that Christianity should be encouraged." The government issued millions of bibles to soldiers during World War II. The Supreme Court has stated that "This is a Christian nation."

But, in the last century, the courts have totally reversed this thinking, and are making every possible effort to prevent any religious expression in the public square. This is an absolute betrayal of the Founders' thinking and intention. This has reached such an absurd state that a federal court in Pennsylvania refused to allow schools to encourage students to "keep an open mind" about evolution. Teachers at some schools are not allowed to say "Merry Christmas." A US House committee conducted an investigation, and concluded that the Obama administration had grossly discriminated against the Catholic Church in its selection of grant recipients.

The Fourth Amendment used to give us protection against illegal searches by the government. But the courts, over the years, have so watered down and distorted this protection that it is almost unrecognizable. A search warrant based on probable cause was once required before the police could perform a search. But the courts have created so many loopholes and exceptions that police can now get a search warrant based on little more than a hunch and a rumor. And there are many situations where a warrant is no longer even required.

The protection against double jeopardy was considered so important to the Framers that they put it in the Fifth Amendment. A person has the right to be tried only once—not multiple times—for the same offense. The basic idea is that the State with its great resources and power, should not be allowed to keep trying over and over again to convict a person until that person is worn down or bankrupted. It is reassuring to know that we have this protection. But, wait, wouldn't you know it, the government has found a way to get around that one, too.

There are now laws that permit the police to seize a person's cash and property just based on the police claiming that they suspect that the property might have been used in criminal activity, or is the proceeds of criminal activity. The problem here is that there does not need to be any evidence of a crime. The police don't need to get a warrant, or explain anything to a judge. In fact, in most of these cases, the owner of the property which was confiscated is never convicted of a crime. What makes it even worse is that much of the cash or property seized is given to the law enforcement agency that makes the seizure, so the law enforcement agency has a perverse incentive to look for opportunities to confiscate cash, even where there is no evidence to justify it.

The well-known right to a trial by a jury of one's peers is one of the foundations of our justice system, and a fundamental protection of a citizen against unfair prosecution by the State. As a member of a jury, an ordinary private citizen can stand up and say to the government "Stop! This prosecution is not fair, and I won't allow you to do it!" Unfortunately, we have moved to the point that today, most criminal defendants in the United States no longer enjoy the protection of a trial by jury. How did this happen? Over time, various rules and laws and court decisions have given a disproportionately huge amount of power to the prosecutor in a criminal case. Prosecutors use this power to put enormous pressure on a defendant to accept a plea bargain, with a guilty plea to a lesser offence. With all the charges the prosecutor can threaten to bring against him, a defendant cannot afford to take the risk of a trial and a possible greatly extended prison sentence, so he is forced to accept the plea bargain. When he does this, the defendant not only loses the protection of having a jury decide his fate, but he also loses the opportunity of having the prosecutor's arguments tested in court through cross examination and opposing witnesses. He also gives up his right of appeal, where a fresh set of eyes reviews his case for possible errors or injustices. Today, over 90 percent of criminal cases are settled by plea bargains. The search for truth is no longer a priority, and false confessions to fictitious crimes are the order of the day.

For hundreds of years, one of the rights of free men has been that a person should not be compelled to testify against himself. This freed us from the ancient practice of torturing a man until he confessed to whatever he was accused of doing. That right is incorporated into the Fifth Amendment of the US Constitution. But, just like many of our other rights, the Supreme Court has decided that it doesn't really mean what it says, and so maybe sometimes a person can be compelled to testify against himself. The Court has ruled that it can balance our Constitutional rights against the desire of the State for a more efficient way to get evidence.

Before the Constitution was written, each of the thirteen states had sometimes adopted tariffs or other trade barriers, in an effort to protect commerce in its own state. The Framers of the Constitution wanted to eliminate these restrictions on free trade between states. They did this by giving the US Congress authority over trade between the states, in what has come to be known as the "Commerce Clause." Article 1, Section 8, Paragraph 3 of the Constitution gives Congress authority "to regulate commerce with foreign nations, and among the several states . . . ." The meaning of that clause clearly does not include activity totally within a state, and that understanding was plainly stated in the discussions and writings of the Framers. However, our old friend, the Supreme Court, in it's never ending effort to move more power from the states to the federal government, has twisted the meaning of that clause to an unbelievable extent. The Court now claims that that clause gives the federal government control over any activity which is totally within a state, if that activity has any remote, indirect effect on interstate commerce. Of course, almost anything you do could be said to have some vague, unintended, incidental effect on some tiny aspect of interstate commerce, so the effect of that interpretation is to give the federal government control over virtually every facet of your daily life. This is a major reason why the federal government has grown without limit, and has written thousands of laws and regulations which affect our every move.

No one can possibly hope to know all of these laws and regulations, so people are frequently sent to prison for doing something that they did not know was illegal. We used to value the principle that no one should be subjected to criminal punishment for conduct that he did not know was illegal. The Supreme Court at one time said that "All are entitled to be informed as to what the State commands or forbids." There once was a requirement that the prosecutor prove beyond a reasonable doubt that the defendant intentionally committed a wrong act. Rational people understood that intent made the difference between a mistake, an accident, and a crime. But in many current situations, we have lost this valuable protection, and a person can be convicted without any proof that he had any intention to do wrong.

Why do the American people put up with this destruction of our freedoms? A large part of the answer is apathy and ignorance. Many people are so caught up in their own problems that they will not go to the trouble to think about our Constitution and our freedoms. But a large number of people simply do not know enough about how their government is supposed to work. The public schools have, in general, done a very poor job of educating students about how the government is structured, and how it should operate. Surveys have shown that most Americans are woefully ignorant about our government. Most of us don't know how the Constitution is supposed to protect our freedoms, and, therefore, we don't understand how the courts have stolen those freedoms.

How did we arrive at this deplorable situation, and what can be done about it? Read on.

Chapter One

Limited Government

This country was founded on the idea of freedom and liberty for the individual. The Founders had seen the horrible abuses of human rights in England and other countries, and were determined to avoid that as much as possible. They were willing to suffer and die to give us the gift of freedom. These extraordinary men created a truly remarkable document—the United States Constitution, which was based on several principles:

1. The primary power would be with the people, not the federal government.
2. The states, because they are closest to the people, would have most of the power.
3. The federal government would be given only a very limited amount of power—just enough to do the basic things that it had to do.
4. The federal government would be split into three branches, with checks and balances, so that no one branch could gain too much power and become a despot.

The country had been operating under the Articles of Confederation, but this had made the central government too weak, and it could not operate efficiently. The authors of the Constitution needed to create a stronger central government. But they did not want to make it too strong, because then it might become tyrannical. So, it was a delicate balancing act. When the Constitution was submitted to the states for ratification, a great debate ensued. Critics of the new Constitution complained that the federal government would be too strong. Since the Constitution explicitly stated that certain powers were denied to the federal government, they said, then it might be assumed that all other powers not mentioned were powers that the federal government could assume. The Tenth Amendment was enacted to unequivocally state that that was not true using the very definite words: "The powers not delegated to the United States by the Constitution, not prohibited by it to the states, are reserved to the states respectively, or to the people." Supreme Court Justice Samuel Chase stated it very clearly when he wrote, "The Constitution of the Union, is the source of all the jurisdiction of the national government; so that the departments of the government can never assume any power, that is not expressly granted by that instrument, nor exercise a power in any other manner than is there prescribed."[1]

The Framers of the Constitution were afraid of the federal government, and especially the Congress, getting too much power over the people and the states. The creation of the Constitution was an absolutely brilliant effort to protect individual liberty. The writers of our Constitution installed various checks and balances among the branches in order to prevent any one branch from becoming too powerful. For example, the President can veto an act of Congress. Thomas Jefferson summed up their distrust of arbitrary power in the hands of men when he said, "In questions of power, then, let no more be heard of confidence in man, but bind him down from mischief by the chains of the Constitution."[2]

Nobel Prize winning economist Dr. Milton Friedman explained that the authors of the Constitution "regarded concentration of power, especially in the hands of government, as the great danger to freedom. They drafted the Constitution with that in mind. It was a document intended to limit government power, to keep power decentralized, and to reserve to individuals control over their own lives."[3]

Diplomat and historian James Bryce wrote that "the aim of the Constitution seems to be not so much to attain great common ends by securing a good government as to avert the evils which will flow ... from any government strong enough to threaten ... individual citizens."[4]

Supreme Court Justice Louis Brandeis reminded us that "the doctrine of the separation of powers was adopted by the convention of 1787 not to promote efficiency, but to preclude the exercise of arbitrary power."[5]

There is no question that the Framers of the Constitution wanted a small federal government. Thomas Jefferson said, in the year 1800, that "the true theory of our Constitution is surely the wisest and best, that the states are independent as to everything within themselves, and united as to everything respecting foreign nations. Let the general government be reduced to foreign concerns only . . . and our general government may be reduced to a very simple organization, and a very inexpensive one; a few plain duties to be performed by a few servants."[6]

We all know it is normal for any government to try to increase its power and control. That is just the nature of the beast. In The Federalist No. 48, James Madison recognized the inclination of every legislature toward "extending the sphere of its activity, and drawing all power into its impetuous vortex."[7] That is why the Framers were so careful to try to limit that encroachment. It is well known that power corrupts, and eventually leads to abuse and then to tyranny. As expected, over the years, the Congress gradually found one excuse after another to increase the scope of its power. It had an unexpected ally in this effort—the United States Supreme Court. The judiciary was supposed to be a check on the Congress, to keep them from abusing their authority. But now they have become partners in crime, so to speak. After all, the Supreme Court is a part of the federal government, so anything that makes the federal government more powerful helps both the Congress and the Court.

PROGRESSIVE MOVEMENT

One factor was the growth of the "progressive" movement in the early twentieth century. This movement embraced concepts such as social justice, redistribution of wealth and generally left-leaning policies. They wanted government to have more power to regulate significant portions of the American economy. Of course, they realized that the checks and balances built into the Constitution would make it more difficult for them to achieve their goals. The idea that the President, for example, would have only the powers specifically granted to him in the Constitution would severely limit his authority. Instead, as Theodore Roosevelt said, a progressive President should assume that he has indefinite powers, "limited only by specific restrictions and prohibitions appearing in the Constitution or imposed by the Congress."[8]

The Progressive strategy usually meant having a bureaucracy of government "experts" making more decisions. Former President Teddy Roosevelt reflected this view when, in a speech, he said that personal property is "subject to the general right of the community to regulate its use to whatever degree the public welfare may require it." In that same speech, he also said that if you honestly earn a fortune "we should permit it to be gained only so long as the gaining represents benefit to the community. This, I know, implies a policy of a far more active governmental interference with social and economic conditions in this country than we have yet had, but I think we have got to face the fact that such an increase in governmental control is now necessary."[9]

Progressives were very successful in influencing the public education system, with education "experts," rather than parents, having more control. Part of their program was to use the schools to indoctrinate children toward the progressive way of thinking. Whatever the reasons, many people's attitudes have gradually shifted away from the idea of a Christian nation with a limited federal government, to the concept of a more powerful government that would do more to solve the problems of the people. If the government is going to take care of more of your problems, that means it will have to have more control over your life, which means you will have to give up some of your rights.

Another part of the Progressive philosophy was a diminished appreciation for the structural forms which the Framers put into the Constitution in order to protect our freedom—things like separation of powers, checks and balances, and federalism. Progressives called these part of a "mechanical" system, which was obsolete and unnecessary. This should be replaced, they said, by a more flexible "living" system, which could be more responsive to the needs of the people.[10] This system of checks and balances is a terrible idea, thought Woodrow Wilson. He said: "No living thing can have its organs offset against each other, as checks, and live. On the contrary, its life is dependent upon their quick cooperation, . . . their amicable community of purpose."[11]

STATES' RIGHTS

The drafters of the Constitution considered and debated the idea of giving the federal government a veto power over state laws. At the Constitutional Convention in Philadelphia, Charles Pinckney and James Madison proposed that scheme, but most of the delegates absolutely rejected that concept. When the Bill of Rights was being debated in Congress, Madison again tried to give the federal government power over the state legislatures, with an amendment which listed certain things that the states could not do. This again was soundly rejected. The Framers were very much concerned about states' rights.[12]

During the debates when the Constitution was being ratified by the states, Fisher Ames said that "the state governments represent the wishes, and feelings, and local interests of the people. They are the safeguard and ornament of the Constitution . . . they will afford a shelter against the abuse of power, and will be the natural avengers of our violated rights."[13]

One of the most basic principles of our Constitution is that the people have the ultimate power. The Supreme Court should, therefore, give extreme deference to laws enacted by the people's elected representatives in the state legislatures. In the case of *Roe v. Wade*[14], for example, most of the states had passed laws restricting abortion. This was obviously the clear will of the people. By ignoring this fact, the Court violated the most bedrock feature of our Constitution—the supreme power of the people.

The ultimate reason for protecting states' rights is to guard the liberty of the individual. Supreme Court Justice Sandra Day O'Connor emphasized this point when she said: "The Constitution does not protect the sovereignty of States for the benefit of the States or state governments as abstract political entities, or even for the benefit of the public officials governing the States. To the contrary, the Constitution divides authority between federal and state governments for the protection of individuals. State sovereignty is not just an end in itself: Rather, federalism secures to citizens the liberties that derive from the diffusion of sovereign power."[15]

The general police powers have always belonged to the states. The states existed before the federal government, and the states already had those police powers. They are not listed in the enumerated powers in the Constitution, so the states never intended to relinquish those powers to the federal government. At one time, the Supreme Court recognized that fact when, in the 1911 case of *House v. Mayes*, it said that the states' "police power, is not granted by or derived from the federal Constitution, but exists independently of it, by reason of its never having been surrendered by the state to the general government."[16]

Alexander Hamilton wrote in The Federalist No. 26, "The state Legislature, who will always be not only vigilant but suspicious and jealous guardians of the rights of the citizens, against encroachments from the Federal government, will constantly have their attention awake to the conduct of the national rulers and will be ready enough, if anything improper appears, to sound the alarm to the people . . . ."[17] In The Federalist No. 32, Hamilton said that "State Governments would clearly retain all the rights . . . which were not by that act exclusively delegated to the United States."[18] The sovereignty of the states was recognized by James Madison when he wrote in The Federalist No. 39 that "each State, in ratifying the Constitution, is considered as a sovereign body, independent of all others."[19] Madison wrote in The Federalist No. 40 that the federal powers "are limited, and that the States in all unenumerated cases, are left in the enjoyment of their sovereign and independent jurisdiction."[20] The original intention, as explained by Madison in The Federalist No. 45, was that "the states will retain under the proposed Constitution a very extensive portion of active sovereignty"[21] and also that:

> The powers delegated by the proposed Constitution to the Federal Government are few and defined. Those which remain in the State Governments are numerous and indefinite. The former will be principally external objects, as war, peace, negotiation, and foreign commerce; with which last the power of taxation will, for the most part, be connected. The powers reserved to the states will extend to all the objects, which, in the ordinary course of affairs, concern the lives, liberties and properties of the people; and the internal order, improvement, and prosperity of the state.[22]

That was the original genius of our Constitution, but that principle is under relentless attack by the federal government.

When the courts have the final authority to interpret the Constitution, this interpretation could have the effect of changing the Constitution. Since the states alone have the power to ratify changes to the Constitution, the states should play some role in any process that changes the Constitution. This is also a conflict of interest, because it allows the national government to interpret its own laws as it sees fit, with no input from the ratifying power (the states). There are no checks and balances against the Judiciary; the judges are appointed for life, and they are not accountable to anyone.

Many of the most egregious examples of federal legislation in areas where they had no Constitutional authority were accepted by the public because people generally agreed with the goals of the program. After all, who could be against clean water, education, energy conservation, etc.?

Unfortunately, many people do not have an appreciation for the history of our country, and are not aware of how important it was to the Framers to preserve states' rights and the separation of powers. The authors of the Constitution realized that without these protections the federal government was likely to accumulate too much power, and to move toward dictatorial authority. That is exactly what is happening now. It's all about control. The federal government continues to amass control over more and more of our lives. One place the federal government did not initially have a lot of control was over the state governments. Of course, this was seen as a problem, and Washington finally found one way that it could gain more control over the states. The method that it found was through bribery:

- Although the federal government has absolutely no authority to set the minimum drinking age for the states, in 1984 Congress passed the National Minimum Drinking Age law, which permitted the secretary of transportation to deny federal highway money to states with a minimum drinking age lower than twenty-one years.[23]
- The federal government decided that we should lower our highway speed limits to 55 MPH in hopes that that would reduce gasoline consumption. It forced the states to do that by enacting the Emergency Highway Energy Conservation Act, in 1974, which prohibited the Secretary of Transportation from giving any highway construction funds to states having a speed limit in excess of 55 MPH.[24]
- The Federal Highway Beautification Act restricted the use of outdoor advertising signs in certain areas near primary highways. This was enforced by making compliance a requirement for the receipt of federal highway construction funds.
- Megan's Law is a federal law that requires states to create a sex offender registry and to release certain information about these offenders. Any state that fails to do this in compliance with federal standards will face a reduction in some of their federal grant money.[25]

Bribing the states with federal funds has become a popular method of coercing the states to do something where Congress concedes that it has no power to regulate under the Constitution. We are sadly moving away from our constitutional system of a limited federal government, with its listing of certain enumerated delegated powers. Congress is being given the power to regulate areas which are nowhere even hinted at in the powers granted in the Constitution. Why would state governments be motivated to accept the multitude of federal grants, which usually have strings attached and give the federal government control over state actions, which violates the principle of federalism? The answer is that they do it because they want the money. And state officials know that their citizens will often support the acceptance of these grants, being ignorant of the fact that they undermine federalism as a system.

Of course, the Supreme Court has upheld this practice of bribing the states. In the case regarding the drinking age, Justice Brennan recognized how outrageous this was, and he dissented from this ruling, saying, "Since States possess this constitutional power, Congress cannot condition a federal grant in a manner that abridges this right."[26] Unfortunately, he was in the minority. One way for the states to regain some of their independence would be for the federal grants to the states to be greatly reduced. There are always strings attached to these grants. And not all of the money paid by taxpayers gets back to the states, because Washington skims off some of the money for their cut. So let's eliminate the middle man, and have the states just tax their own citizens directly for some of these projects.

The EPA issued regulations requiring schools to remove asbestos, which involved enormous costs of millions of dollars. The EPA later realized that removal of asbestos from a building was not a good idea, because, if a building contains asbestos, it is safer to leave it in place than to remove it. The process of removing asbestos from a building stirs up fibers and gets them airborne, which is more dangerous to human health than just leaving the asbestos alone.

The federal government passed laws stating that a person under a restraining order, or one who is a convicted felon, cannot possess a gun. This is obviously an issue that should be handled under the state police power. But the federal government claimed this authority under the Commerce Clause. How is this justified under the government's power to regulate interstate commerce? The Supreme Court came up with the feeble excuse that this could be justified because the guns have previously traveled in interstate commerce. Under this logic, Congress could enact any arbitrary regulation regarding any product you might possess, as long as that product has previously traveled in interstate commerce. It is hard to believe that Supreme Court justices would be so brazen as to twist the meaning of words to get such a ridiculous interpretation. That absolutely defies all common sense and reason, but these laws have been upheld by federal courts.[27]

In the case of *Fry v. United States*, the US Supreme Court upheld a law allowing the federal government to control wages for state employees.[28] Another law required the states to implement certain policies for their electric utility companies.[29] The federal government was allowed to dictate regulations for mining companies operating entirely within a state.[30]

The federal government can fix minimum prices for milk that is produced and sold within a state. The reason is that it might compete with some milk that did travel in interstate commerce. This was upheld in the Supreme Court case of *United States v. Wrightwood Dairy Co.*[31]

In the case of *United States v. Darby*[32], the Court agreed that the government had the authority to fix minimum wages and maximum hours for a manufacturer merely because some of the products being manufactured may be sold in interstate commerce. Supreme Court Justice Lewis Powell expressed his concern very eloquently when he wrote: "by usurping functions traditionally performed by the States, federal overreaching under the Commerce Clause undermines the constitutionally mandated balance of power between the States and the Federal Government, a balance designed to protect our fundamental liberties."[33]

It appears that for many years, the majority on the Supreme Court has been inclined to look with disdain on certain traditional norms of sexual morality. The Court sees itself as the protector of the right to live according to the new emerging sexual immorality, against those who would like to retain the old traditional morality.[34] This is evident in the pattern of decisions on abortion, pornography, nudity and vulgar language. The result is that the states have been deprived of the power to maintain even a minimum level of decency and civility.

It would be reassuring to think that we could depend on our elected officials to be diligent in enforcing federalism. Experience has shown, however, that this is not a safe assumption. Officials at both the state and federal level are frequently willing to sacrifice federalism in order to achieve some short term objective, which will benefit themselves or their departments. Even the Supreme Court has acknowledged this reality, when it stated:

> If a federal official is faced with the alternatives of choosing a location [for a nuclear waste dump] or directing the states to do it, the official may well

prefer the latter, as a means of shifting responsibility for the eventual decision. If a state official is faced with the same set of alternatives— choosing a location or having Congress direct the choice of a location—the state official may also prefer the latter, as it may permit the avoidance of personal responsibility. The interests of public officials thus may not coincide with the Constitution's intergovernmental allocation of authority.[35]

There are many instances of this effect at work. For example, the Violence Against Women Act certainly encroaches on state authority. But taking a position against that law, when that position can be portrayed as hostile to women, may be seen by a state official as a disadvantage in his reelection campaign. He can get away with supporting the Act because most of his constituents are not conscious of federalism, or do not give it a high priority in their thinking.

Likewise, members of Congress have limited incentive to protect federalism. Each member of Congress knows that his reelection is largely dependent on his satisfying his individual constituents. So his legislative actions are often directed to that end, rather than what is best for the nation as a whole. His interest in defending federalism takes a back seat to his need to pander to the selfish desires of individuals or interest groups.

Besides the words of the Constitution, there is another good reason to give the states more latitude and authority to craft their own laws. In this way, the states would in effect be 50 "laboratories," which may try different things in different ways, being able to experiment and innovate. The benefit would be to gain real life experience with various approaches to problems, so everyone could see what strategy worked best. Supreme Court Justice Louis Brandeis approved of this idea when he said, "A single courageous State may, if its citizens choose, serve as a laboratory; and try novel social and economic experiments without risk to the rest of the country."[36] It is to be expected that when you experiment, you will probably make some mistakes. So, as part of the process, it is likely that some states might enact some laws which will prove to be unwise. But soon it will be obvious that these laws are ineffective or oppressive, and other states are doing it differently with better results. Therefore, the states with poor laws will revise them to emulate the more successful states. This could be done without the heavy-handed top-down control of the arbitrary and ever-changing federal judiciary. As one example, the states which had established state religions had all eliminated them before the Civil War, without any coercion from the federal government.

If the states want to demonstrate that they are deserving of more freedom, they need to strengthen their own state constitutions to provide more protections for, not only the rights covered in the federal Bill of Rights, but also in other areas such as property rights and economic freedom. Most states today have laws that exhibit blatant cronyism, favoritism and protectionism to benefit certain businesses or special interests. One example is the racket of occupational licensing laws, which now govern entry into about 20 percent of all jobs in America. For most of these, there is absolutely no justification for the licensing requirements except to restrict entry in order to reduce competition.[37]

THE DEFINITION OF "EQUAL"

The Framers believed in a written set of laws so that everyone knew what the laws were, and could plan their actions to comply with those laws. This would be better than the arbitrary and ever changing rulings of a monarch or dictator. The goal was maximum personal freedom to act within these laws (based on our Constitution). Another important concept was equal opportunity, so that everyone has a fair chance to succeed. It is true that, under this system, some people will do better than others. But two centuries of experience have proven that this arrangement has produced the most prosperous and most powerful country in the world. Even most of the so-called poor people in America are better off than the average person in many other countries. So who is it that is trying so hard to change our system? Some people see that we have some very wealthy people and some very poor people in this country. They say that this proves that our system is not fair. Something needs to be done to give the poor people more, even if that means that the wealthy might have less. This would make our country more "fair," they say, and they are working to change our government to make that happen.

The supporters of free enterprise say that the goal of giving everybody an equal amount of "stuff" is an impossible one. But the reformers say that they could do it, or at least come close. They admit that it is a complex and difficult task, so it would require putting an elite group of people in charge, and giving them the power to make all the decisions necessary. Can you accept their claim that "I'm smarter than you, and so I know better than you what is good for you?"

In order to accomplish this, our system of written laws would have to be modified to allow much more flexibility, so that the elites could make all the decisions. Part of their strategy for "modifying" these laws is for judges to read their own meanings into the words of the Constitution. The original intent of the Framers can be ignored, they say, if we think that a different interpretation would be "better."

There is another problem with this proposed solution. If we give a group of elites the power necessary to exert so much control over the minute details of everyone's life, then ordinary people will necessarily have to surrender much of their own personal freedom. This is not important, say the reformers, because the real problem is that we are defining "freedom" incorrectly. We say that everyone has the freedom to buy a Mercedes Benz if he wants to, but if some people can't afford to buy a Mercedes Benz, then they don't really have the freedom to buy that car. True freedom does not mean freedom from government interference in your life. True freedom includes economic freedom, so when everybody has equal "stuff," then they will have equal freedom. Legal scholar and philosopher Ronald Dworkin said that "a more equal society is a better society, even if its citizens prefer inequality."[38] Of course, those who still value personal liberty have a much different viewpoint.

Many of the people promoting this theory are not deliberately setting out to create a dictatorship. They just want to make everyone more "equal." But when a group of people get enough power to do that, then we are moving toward tyranny.

The Framers were most concerned about personal freedom and liberty, and were very aware of the dangers of concentrating power in a small group. We were supposed to have a government of laws and not of men. We are, however, now moving toward an entirely different vision, which is more focused on economic and social equality, even if it means reduced freedom of choice for the common man. Economist Milton Friedman expressed it well when he said:

> A society that puts equality—in the sense of equality of outcome—ahead of freedom will end up with neither equality nor freedom. The use of force to achieve equality will destroy freedom, and the force, introduced for good purposes, will end up in the hands of people who use it to promote their own interests.[39]

This is a dangerous trend, which could give us a country much different from the America which has long been a shining example of freedom for the entire world.

SUMMARY

The Founders of this country gave us an absolutely magnificent gift—our freedom. We should be eternally grateful for their wisdom, their determination, and their selfless sacrifice. To protect us against tyranny, our Constitution created an explicit limitation on the government's power, and checks and balances to further restrict the accumulation of excessive authority. This worked pretty well for about the first century and a half. The United States grew prosperous, and became very powerful. And we were an example to the world regarding human rights and personal freedom and opportunity.

But now we have seen, over a period of time, more and more power concentrated in the federal government. One word which comes to mind to describe this situation is "statism." As constitutional attorney John Whitehead wrote: "It was statism that the framers feared. It was statism that brought them in conflict with Great Britain. Now statism has reared its head in our time, and is finding its expression in varying forms through the state and its agencies. The courts, as agencies of the civil government, have in large part transformed the loose confederation of states, which once existed in America, into a highly centralized bureaucracy where, instead of law, the ever-changing opinions of men reign supreme."[40] This reminds us so much of the philosophy of the divine right of kings, wherein the king's word was law. Except now it is not the king, but the Supreme Court instead, issuing these decrees.

The explosion of growth in the United States government is nothing less than astounding. From 1913 to 2009, the federal government's share of the nation's economy grew from less than 2% to over 28%. In that same period, the number of federal laws and regulations has increased by 3000%. This is ten times the rate of population growth.[41]

Judicial activism is now an established principle. The decrees of the courts are now reaching into every facet of our lives. Areas which were, and should still be, the responsibility of legislatures and the people, are reeling under the heavy intrusion of the courts. It is tragic that most of the American people seem to have accepted this new reality, with the courts making laws. But what is even worse is that their elected congressmen have also allowed it, and will not do anything to reverse course.

There are several key phrases in our Constitution that are broad enough so they can be interpreted in different ways. If these phrases are interpreted narrowly, that would limit the kinds of powers that the federal government could exert under the Constitution. These phrases could also be interpreted very broadly to give the federal government much more power to get involved in innumerable activities. The most basic consideration in drafting the Constitution was the desire to limit the power of the federal government. If it was given too much power, it would abuse that power, and become tyrannical. Everyone involved was aware of this, and it is also obvious from reading the Constitution. Since the overriding objective of the Constitution was to limit the power of government, the courts should have taken this into account and should have interpreted the Constitution narrowly so as to continue the theme of trying to limit the power of government. However, they failed to be true to the spirit of the Constitution, and gave a broad interpretation where possible in order to give the government (and themselves) increased power and authority.

One of the most heartbreaking examples of judicial tyranny was when the Supreme Court allowed the American military, during World War II, to herd 70,000 Japanese Americans, many of whom were American citizens, into concentration camps.[42] This included elderly persons as well as children. Up until this time, no resident Japanese Americans had been convicted of sabotage or espionage. But still, we saw the Supreme Court reacting to a national concern about Japanese living on the Pacific coast. Yale law professor Eugene Rostow wrote that:

> They were held under prison conditions in uncomfortable camps, far from their homes, and for lengthy periods—several years in many cases. If found "disloyal" in administrative proceedings, they were confined indefinitely, although no statute makes "disloyalty" a crime.[43]

Since the word of the Supreme Court is final, and there is no appeal from their verdicts, there was no way to stop this horrible injustice.

It is truly frightening to realize that many of the most important issues of the day are being decided by five unelected justices on the Supreme Court. The original intent of the

Constitution was that the people themselves, through their elected representatives, would make these decisions. But that is no longer being done. This power has been taken away from the people. Even if the people decided that they did not like one of these rulings, and wanted to change it, it would not matter—the people have absolutely no power to do anything about it. The only way currently available to improve this situation is the lengthy and tedious process of voting for a president and senators who will appoint judges who will follow the original meaning of the Constitution.[44]

It is ironic that many of the problems we are seeing in the twenty-first century were anticipated back in the days when the Constitution was being written and ratified. Of course, there is Benjamin Franklin's famous remark that this new constitution has given us "A republic . . . if you can keep it."[45] He was acknowledging how difficult it was for a government such as ours to remain true to its original principles, given the realities of politics and human nature. When the Constitution was submitted to the states for ratification, Pennsylvania was the first state to hold a ratifying convention. During that convention, skeptics pointed to the General Welfare Clause and the Necessary and Proper Clause to show that Congress possessed unlimited authority under the Constitution. If ever a dispute arose over whether Congress had overstepped its authority, the federal government, armed with the Supremacy Clause, would make the final decision. How could the states or the people expect fair treatment when their federal rulers possessed all power, and were to be the final arbiters in disputed cases?[46] But these concerns were ignored, and Pennsylvania's convention voted 46 to 23 to ratify the Constitution. When Rhode Island ratified the Constitution, it submitted several proposed amendments, including the idea of a federal guarantee of state sovereignty.[47] When the Bill of Rights was being debated in the House of Representatives, Elbridge Gerry of Massachusetts proposed to add the word "expressly" to what became the Tenth Amendment, so it would read "The powers not *expressly* delegated by this Constitution...are reserved to the states . . . ."[48] But this was not adopted.

When the states were considering whether to adopt the new Constitution, James Madison tried to reassure those who were afraid that the federal government would become too powerful. He said, in The Federalist No. 46, that the people as a whole and also those sent to Congress would have a stronger loyalty to their respective states than to the federal government, and therefore the states would have the advantage in any dispute. This would, he claimed, mean that the new federal government would be "disinclined to invade the rights of the individual States." It is tragic that this turned out to be so far off the mark.[49]

We have a situation where what is called "constitutional law" has gotten away from the words of the Constitution, and instead consists primarily of the words spoken by the Supreme Court. We are also seeing that judicial power is more and more acknowledged to be legislative in nature. This has made our judicial system a morass of confusion, contradictory and inconsistent decisions, arbitrary and ever changing standards, and incoherent and unpredictable rulings. It is no wonder that polling data shows that public trust of the federal government is at an all-time low.

Chapter Two

Freedom of Speech
First Amendment

The First Amendment says, "Congress shall make no law . . . abridging the freedom of speech, or of the press; or the right of the people peaceably to assemble, and to petition the Government for a redress of grievances." This seems pretty clear, but it is amazing to see the games that have been played over the years by people trying to justify exceptions and different interpretations and reasons it doesn't apply in certain situations. It was anticipated that Congress and the President might abuse their authority, and try to silence embarrassing critics of these officials and their policies. The First Amendment says they cannot do that. That is one reason why an independent judiciary was established, to provide a check on the other branches, to make sure they followed the Constitution.

Freedom of speech is not only a valuable individual right for the people, but it is an essential requirement for a republic such as ours, which is supposed to be governed by the people. Since the people are ultimately responsible for making the important decisions that control the path of the nation, the people must be informed and knowledgeable so they can make intelligent decisions. It is important that they be allowed to hear both sides of a debate, so they can judge the arguments for themselves. It is helpful if people are exposed to a variety of opinions and ideas. Supreme Court Justice Louis Brandeis put it well when he said:

Those who won our independence believed . . . that
the greatest menace to freedom is an inert people;
that public discussion is a political duty; and that this
should be a fundamental principle of the American
government.[1]

The people also need to have information about what their
government and their elected officials are doing, even if it might
embarrass the officials. Government secrecy has a long history of
abuse, and people are naturally suspicious that government
officials are trying to conceal fraud, kickbacks, favoritism, poor
judgment, and broken promises. For a free government, such as
ours, to function effectively, it requires the confidence of the
people. Every instance where the government is suspected of
unjustified secrecy damages that confidence. The most effective
instrument for sustaining that confidence is a free and critical
press. A citizen's right to criticize the government, or individual
officials, is "the heart of what the First Amendment was meant to
protect," according to Justice Scalia.[2] We must do everything
possible to protect our freedom of speech and of the press in
matters related to the free exchange of ideas and information, and
open debate about policy.

To understand what our "freedom of the press" is really
supposed to mean, we should start by examining what it meant to
our Founders, who actually wrote this amendment. From their
writings, and also by the laws they enacted, we can see that this
freedom did not protect pornography, public nudity, obscenity and
libel. Oliver Ellsworth, a delegate to the Constitutional
Convention and later chief justice of the Supreme Court, wrote, "I
heartily approve of our laws against drunkenness, profane
swearing, blasphemy, and professed atheism."[3] One very
important function of the press was critiquing the government
and informing the people, so during the Founding Era the press
was filled with vigorous discussion of all sorts of topics.

Since the Constitution means just what a majority on the
Supreme Court says it means, this is unfortunately subject to
change over time. Justices might change their minds based on
their feelings, current events, public opinion, political pressures,
or dozens of other influences. And as new justices are added to the
Court, they will have different viewpoints, priorities, and biases.
One of our most important and fundamental rights, our freedom
of speech, has a long history of tortuous distortions and abuses,
with the Supreme Court bearing a large share of the blame. Here

are some examples of the wild swings in Court rulings attacking the freedom of speech:

In the 1919 case of *Shaffer v. United States*, the Court of Appeals ruled that your speech could be punished if it might have a "tendency" to produce an unlawful action, even if you don't specifically advocate anything illegal or dangerous.[4] Such a loose standard could be twisted by a judge to cover almost anything.

Then the Supreme Court ruled, in the case of *Brandenburg v. Ohio,* in 1969, that speech could not be suppressed unless it advocates an imminent lawless action.[5] That sounded like it might be an attempt to give more protection to the First Amendment. But in later court decisions, we see that the same old vague and ambiguous criteria are still being used as excuses to punish speech. For example, in 1972, the Supreme Court, in the case of *Grayned v. City of Rockford*, upheld an ordinance which prohibits "a noise or diversion that disturbs or tends to disturb the peace or good order of the school session."[6] So now we are back to the vague standard of something that "tends to disturb."

The case of *Dennis v. United States* involved some leaders of the Communist Party USA who were charged with conspiring to advocate the overthrow of the United States government by force.[7] Their conviction was upheld in 1951 by the Supreme Court which laid down the requirement for a "judicial balancing" to weigh the gravity of the danger against the invasion of free speech. Such an ambiguous standard makes it impossible for anyone to predict what speech will be allowed or not allowed. Even Justice Hugo Black was uneasy with the situation, and, in his dissent, he said that he hoped that "in calmer times, when present pressures, passions and fears subside, this or some later Court will restore the First Amendment liberties to the high preferred place where they belong in a free society."

The courts have held that speech is not protected by the First Amendment unless it is on a "matter of public concern," which of course is an ambiguous standard subject to change and varying interpretations. And even if it passes that test, this speech may still be punished based on some kind of "balance" between the interests of the State and the interests of the speaker in exercising his First Amendment rights. This was stated by the Supreme Court in the case of *Pickering v. Board of Education,* in 1968,[8] and again as recently as 2012 in the case of *Mosholder v. Barnhardt* from the Sixth Circuit Court of Appeals.[9] These balancing tests are primarily for the convenience of the judges, giving them ample flexibility to superimpose their own policy choices on the Constitution. Supreme Court Justice Hugo Black pointed out the hazards of any doctrine "that permits constitutionally protected rights to be 'balanced' away whenever a majority of this Court thinks that a State might have interest sufficient to justify abridgement of those freedoms."[10]

In Massachusetts, a 2007 law prohibited any person from having any contact with any other person within thirty-five feet of an abortion clinic. In 2009, a federal appeals court upheld the law, because it is "content-neutral." It restricts all speech regardless of the content. Obviously the intent of the law was not content neutral—it was clearly designed to impede the anti-abortion demonstrators. But this alleged "neutrality" gives the Court the excuse it needs in order to restrict speech of which it disapproves. In the mysterious, ever-changing world of Supreme Court jurisprudence, laws that are deemed to be "content-neutral" can be given a lower level of scrutiny. Under these rules, the government need only establish a "significant," rather than "compelling," reason to suppress speech. That makes it much easier for judges to uphold laws that happen to advance their personal agendas.[11]

In the 1971 case of *New York Times Co. v. United States*, the government attempted to bar the publication of the "Pentagon Papers" by the New York Times newspaper. This was a secret Department of Defense study of the United States' political and military involvement in Vietnam. The Supreme Court refused to enjoin the publication in this case, but seven of the nine justices indicated that prior restraint could be justified under certain conditions.[12]

A US District Court judge issued an order forbidding the media from interviewing jurors regarding their deliberations in a just completed trial. This gag order was intended to last forever—it never expired. The US Court of Appeals affirmed the order[13] and the Supreme Court refused to hear the case.[14]

The new progressive censors have found yet another form of expression that is too dangerous to be tolerated: jokes. In 1995, the Montana Human Rights Commission ordered the city of Great Falls to pay damages based solely on off-color jokes and cartoons distributed by city employees. The Montana Commission ruled that the dirty jokes were a form of sexual harassment, even when not directed at any particular employee. "Harassment" is the new magic word that renders the First Amendment powerless. This crusade has spread like wildfire, being picked up by many cities and states, and, of course, by the federal government. The US Department of Labor produced a pamphlet that tells employees that they have suffered harassment if "someone made sexual jokes or said sexual things you didn't like." Under the original understanding of the First Amendment, speech must be protected no matter how hateful the speech. In fact, it is only unpopular speech that even needs protection. There would be no challenge to speech that everyone agrees with, so it would need no protection. Even the Supreme Court stated that the First Amendment means that "we must tolerate insulting, and even outrageous, speech."[15] But when it is necessary to stamp out politically incorrect speech, the Supreme Court will find a way, hiding behind words like "harassment" and "hostile environment."[16]

There were some protestors at a Barrack Obama fundraiser in the San Francisco Bay area in 2011. A reporter for the *San Francisco Chronicle* posted a video of the protestors on the internet. In retaliation, the White House first blacklisted that particular reporter. Later, they threatened retribution to the *Chronicle* if it reported on the banishment. Then the White House changed their story again and said that the reporter would not be banned.[17] Unfortunately the bullying and intimidation of the press by the government has become all too common.

Supreme Court Justice Hugo Black thought that the words "Congress shall pass no law..." means exactly what it says. He felt that there should be no restrictions on the freedom of speech. In the case that allowed newspapers to publish the Pentagon Papers, he wrote:

> In the First Amendment the Founding Fathers gave the free press the protection it must have to fulfill its essential role in our democracy. The press was to serve the governed, not the governors. The Government's power to censor the press was abolished so that the press would remain forever free to censure the Government. The press was protected so that it could bare the secrets of government and inform the people. Only a free and unrestrained press can effectively expose deception in government.[18]

He also said: "My own belief is that no legislature is charged with the duty or vested with the power to decide what public issues Americans can discuss. In a free country, that is the individual's choice, not the state's. . . . I do not agree that the Constitution leaves freedom of petition, assembly, speech, press or worship at the mercy of a case-by-case, day-by-day majority of this Court. I had supposed that our people could rely for their freedom on the Constitution's commands, rather than on the grace of this Court on an individual case basis."[19] And in another opinion, he said, "An unconditional right to say what one pleases about public affairs is what I consider to be the minimum guarantee of the First Amendment."[20]

The bottom line is that we cannot depend on the federal judiciary to be effective or consistent in defending free speech. Since the Constitution is just what the judges say it is, the meaning is subject to change with the mood of the times. The words "Congress shall make no law . . ." is very clear in its meaning, definite and absolute. Yet Congress and the Supreme Court treat these words as a flexible admonition, merely a suggestion, to be applied with varying degrees of permissiveness. Of course this is totally alien to our claim to be a nation of laws, but this is the monstrosity that has been created by the Supreme Court. Laws punishing dissent are very appealing to public officials because they are relatively inexpensive, create the illusion of decisive action, and enable politicians to silence their critics in the guise of serving the national interest.

YOU ARE CRAZY

It has long been a practice of totalitarian regimes to eliminate their critics by declaring them mentally ill, and locking them up in psychiatric wards. The old Soviet Union used psychiatric hospitals as prisons in order to isolate political prisoners from the rest of society and discredit their ideas. This is also a common practice in China today. It is surprising to many people to find out that this is beginning to happen here in the USA:

- Adrian Schoolcraft was a NYPD officer who made allegations of wrongdoing within the police department. He made recordings of conversations that he said were evidence of corruption, arrest quotas, wrongful arrests, and fudging of crime statistics. In October 2009, a police team abducted him from his apartment and took him in handcuffs to a psychiatric ward, where he was held against his will for six days. In March 2012, the *Village Voice* published an article discussing an unpublished report from June 2010 of the NYPD internal investigation of Schoolcraft's case, which vindicated him, finding evidence of quotas and underreporting of crimes.[21]
- Brandon Raub is a decorated Marine veteran, who has served tours in Iraq and Afghanistan. One day in

August 2012, a swarm of police and federal agents came to his home, handcuffed him and transported him against his will to a medical center. What was his crime? He had posted some song lyrics and personal political views on his Facebook page. In a hearing, he was sentenced to up to 30 days further confinement in a VA psychiatric ward where he was forced to undergo psychological evaluations. Within days of Raub's ordeal, news reports started surfacing of other veterans having similar experiences.[22]

- In the 1970s, Martha Beall Mitchell, wife of US Attorney General John Mitchell, was diagnosed with a paranoid mental disorder for claiming that the administration of President Richard M. Nixon was engaged in illegal activities. Many of her claims were later proved correct.[23]

PORNOGRAPHY

The First Amendment protected freedom of speech and the press in order to safeguard the free exchange of ideas, and the right to criticize the government without fear of retribution. Certain disagreeable forms of speech were not considered essential to this free exchange of ideas, and therefore were not considered to be protected. This category included obscenity, fraud and libel.

Most people recognize that obscene material is not only depraved, but is also damaging to society as a whole, and does not deserve free speech protection. For almost two centuries after the beginning of this country, this material was restricted. In fact, as late as 1942, a unanimous Court said that prohibiting "the lewd and obscene, the profane" had "never been thought to raise any Constitutional problem" because "such utterances are no essential part of any exposition of ideas, and are of such slight social value as a step to truth that any benefit that may be derived from them is clearly outweighed by the social interest in order and morality."[24] However, later Supreme Court rulings have so narrowed the legal definition of obscenity that it is almost impossible for a prosecutor to get a conviction for selling it. That is why our country is flooded with pornography today, and communities have lost their legitimate right to set minimum standards for decency.

SCHOOL

For many years in this country, students had essentially no First Amendment rights when they were in school. They had to do whatever their teacher told them to do. And if a dispute ever got into the legal system, the courts would usually support the school in its dictatorial authority over the student.

For example, in 1913, Earl Wooster was a senior at Fresno High School in Fresno, California. The school had called a meeting of the entire student body to discuss a recent situation where the school had prevented a planned fight among students. At this meeting, Wooster stood up before the student body and said, "If the school board was so interested in keeping the bones of the students from being broken, probably they'd put some fire exits on the assembly hall." This seems pretty mild to us today, but some of the school officials then were so incensed at this criticism that they suspended Wooster from school, and refused to give him his diploma. Wooster filed a lawsuit, and the California Court of Appeals sided with the school in the case of *Wooster v. Sunderland*.[25]

In this repressive atmosphere, school officials even had the power to punish students for actions outside of the school. In 1906, two sisters who were students at the high school in St. Croix Falls, Wisconsin, took a poem written by one of their classmates and submitted it to the local newspaper. The poem was about their school, mocking school rules and satirizing a teacher. After the newspaper published the poem, the school principal was not amused, and he decided to expel the two sisters. He said that the poem caused "defiance toward the proper control and management of the school." The sisters sued in the case known as *Dresser v. District Board*, and the Wisconsin Supreme Court ruled against them.[26]

The concept of giving First Amendment rights to students appeared in the 1943 Supreme Court case of *West Virginia State Board of Education v. Barnette*. Gathie and Marie Barnette were raised by their father as Jehovah's Witnesses. The family believed in the teachings of Jehovah's Witnesses that it was wrong to salute the flag, because that was a form of idolatry. At the Slip Hill Grade School in Charleston, West Virginia, which the girls attended, all students were ordered to salute the flag and recite the Pledge of Allegiance. The girls refused to salute the flag, and the response of the principal was to send them home. The family filed a lawsuit in federal court, and eventually the US Supreme Court ruled in the students' favor. In his majority opinion, Justice

Robert H. Jackson wrote, "If there is any fixed star in our constitutional constellation, it is that no official high or petty shall prescribe what shall be orthodox in matters of politics, nationalism, religion or other matters of opinion or force citizens to confess by word or acts their faith therein." This court decision established that public school students have First Amendment rights. It also created the "compelled-speech doctrine," which holds that the government cannot compel individuals to engage in certain speech.[27]

There was still some confusion about exactly how far these new student rights would extend. One important court case developed out of the civil rights movement in Mississippi in 1964. Some students at the all-black Booker T. Washington High School in Philadelphia, Mississippi, started wearing "Freedom Now" buttons with the slogan "One Man, One Vote." The school principal objected to the buttons out of fear that they "would cause commotion" and possibly violence. He told the students to remove the buttons, and suspended the ones who refused. Three parents filed suit in federal court. The Fifth Circuit Court ruled in favor of the students in the case of *Burnside v. Byars*, and identified one key factor that wearing the buttons did not cause any disruption or disturbance. The court crafted an important legal test, which would prove to be critical in many similar cases in the future, when it wrote, "They [school officials] cannot infringe on their students' right to free and unrestricted expression as guaranteed to them under the First Amendment to the Constitution, where the exercise of such rights in the school buildings and schoolrooms do not materially and substantially interfere with the requirements of appropriate discipline in the operation of the school."[28]

This "substantial disruption" test was a major factor in a case in Iowa. This case was extremely important in solidifying students' rights because it went all the way to the Supreme Court, and therefore was applicable to the entire country. In 1965 the growing war in Vietnam had inspired anti-war protests and demonstrations. Two families in Des Moines, Iowa, the Eckhardts and the Tinkers, wanted to find a way to protest the war. Someone suggested the idea of wearing black armbands to school. Their teenage sons, Christopher Eckhardt, who attended Theodore Roosevelt High School, and John Tinker, who attended North High School, liked the idea, and began spreading the word around their schools. When school officials heard about the plan, they collectively issued a ban on black armbands for several of the schools in the area. The boys wore the armbands to school anyway, and were suspended from school. The case known as *Tinker v. Des Moines Independent Community School District* finally wound its way to the Supreme Court. On February 24, 1969, the decision in favor of the students was issued, in which Justice Abe Fortas famously wrote "it can hardly be argued that either students or teachers shed their constitutional rights to freedom of speech or expression at the schoolhouse gate." He emphasized that student expression could be suppressed only when school officials can show a reasonable forecast of substantial disruption.[29]

This seemed like a very practical way to approach First Amendment questions, to say that speech will not be censored unless it causes a disturbance. The trouble with this policy is that disruptive kids get to decide what speech will be censored. All they have to do is act up whenever the unwelcome message appears, and they've given officials the evidence they need to justify restricting the speech.[30] This "heckler's veto" presents a real dilemma. Schools should adopt a policy that the hecklers, and not the speaker, are causing the disruption, and will be punished. If the school cannot control the situation, it should make every effort to allow the speaker to deliver his message at another time in a more suitable forum that still protects his First Amendment rights.

In 2002, Joseph Frederick was a high school senior in Juneau, Alaska. He and some classmates decided to do an experiment in free expression. What he did was to unfurl a fourteen-foot banner bearing the strange message "BONG HITS 4 JESUS." The school principal was not happy. She confiscated the banner and told Frederick to come to her office. She told him that his banner violated school policy because it encouraged illegal drug use, and she gave him a five-day suspension. Frederick sued in federal court in the case known as *Morse v. Frederick*.[31] In June 2007, the Supreme Court issued its opinion in favor of the school. So one more exception to the freedoms established in the *Tinker* decision was created. Schools are allowed to censor student speech that they claim advocates illegal drug use. This exception poses the very real danger that other courts will use this philosophy to justify further limitations on student speech. In fact, the Fifth Circuit Court, in the 2007 case of *Ponce v. Socorro Independent School District*, applied the *Morse* decision to find that school officials can restrict student speech by claiming that it poses a danger to school safety. This could allow schools to apply zero-tolerance policies to a wide range of student speech.[32]

Mathew Fraser was a senior at Bethel High School in Pierce County, Washington. In April 1983 he delivered a speech in a school assembly nominating a classmate for student body vice president. The speech was filled with sexual innuendo and vulgar language. The school punished him with a three-day suspension, and by removing him from a list of possible student speakers at graduation. Fraser sued in federal court. Two lower courts ruled in the student's favor. But when the case got to the Supreme Court, the ruling was for the school. The case is *Bethel School District No. 403 v. Fraser*.[33] One of the tasks of a school is "teaching students the boundaries of socially appropriate behavior," the Court said. So school officials are allowed to prohibit "lewd, indecent or *offensive* speech and conduct."[34]

This ruling gave school officials and courts an open door to censor speech which was not only lewd, but might be *offensive to anyone*. This is obviously not a reasonable criterion, because anybody could claim to be offended by almost anything. A student in Ohio wore a shirt to school with pictures and slogans of shock rock star Marilyn Manson. School officials didn't like the shirt, and they suspended the boy. A Sixth Circuit Court panel upheld the school, quoting *Fraser* as a basis.[35]

The Mexican holiday known as Cinco de Mayo was being celebrated by some students at the Live Oak High School, in Morgan Hill, California. The school approved the celebration, and allowed students to wear clothing with the colors of the Mexican flag. On the same day, some students decided to wear T-shirts that displayed the American flag as a statement of their patriotism. School officials ordered these students to turn their American flag T-shirts inside out, claiming that they might offend some of their Mexican students.

In 2006, the Ninth Circuit Court of Appeals ruled that a school could prohibit a student from wearing a T-shirt with a message critical of homosexuality.[36] A student in Florida was suspended for having a small Confederate flag at school. The Eleventh Circuit Court of Appeals ruled for the school district, citing *Fraser* as the applicable standard.[37]

Justice William Brennan Jr. made an excellent point when he wrote, "The case before us aptly illustrates how readily school officials (and courts) can camouflage viewpoint discrimination as the 'mere' protection of students from sensitive topics."[38]

We would do well to remember the words of Justice Abe Fortas in the *Tinker* decision:

Any departure from absolute regimentation may cause trouble. Any variation from the majority's opinion may inspire fear. Any word spoken, in class, in the lunchroom, or on the campus, that deviates from the views of another person may start an argument or cause a disturbance. But our Constitution says we must take this risk . . . and our history says that it is this sort of hazardous freedom— this kind of openness—that is the basis of our national strength and of the independence and vigor of Americans who grow up and live in this relatively permissive, often disputatious, society.[39]

Through these and subsequent cases, the basic parameters of (limited) student First Amendment rights came to be defined:

1. Student initiated and student controlled expression (such as armbands) could not be suppressed by the school without a reasonable basis to predict disruption.
2. In school sponsored or published materials (such as a school newspaper), the school would be allowed more control over content.[40]
3. Lewd, profane, indecent or offensive speech in school can be censored by the school.[41]
4. Speech can be censored if the school claims that it promotes illegal drug use or poses a danger to school safety.[42] Some fear that this ruling could be used to create other new categories of restricted speech.
5. A student can be punished for making a perfectly innocent drawing or poem that is in any way related to violence or the military.[43]

VIOLENCE THEMED ART AT SCHOOL

School shootings such as the one at Columbine High School shocked the entire nation. In hindsight, some people remembered that some of the school shooters had written stories, essays, plays and poems with shockingly violent themes prior to their rampage. Many school officials decided that the way to prevent another Columbine was to look for writing and art with violent themes done by their students. Many adopted a zero tolerance mindset toward any student expression related to violence. Students were unjustly punished for sketches, essays, poetry and other perfectly innocent works that could be interpreted as being related to violence, weapons or the military.

A juvenile court judge ordered a middle school student in Texas to spend several days in jail for a Halloween essay for which he received an A from his teacher. A high school honors student in Kansas was expelled for writing a poem about seeking revenge against someone for killing her dog. In Florida, two boys, ages nine and ten, drew a crude stick figure showing a classmate being stabbed. For this, they were charged with felonies, taken away from school in handcuffs and suspended from school. A fourteen-year-old middle school student in New Jersey was suspended for five days for drawing a stick figure of a US Marine shooting at a Taliban fighter. The boy, whose father is in the military, said the picture was "patriotic." A five-year-old boy was suspended from kindergarten for three days for playing cops and robbers at school, pretending his finger was a gun. A federal court sided with the school. When a state evaluator was inspecting a pre-school facility in North Carolina, he deducted five points from its high rating because plastic toy soldiers were found in the play area. The grandfather of one of the students said "I don't think children should be taught that the military are bad guys." A student at a Cleveland, Ohio, high school received two Saturdays of detention for wearing a sweatshirt stating: "Abortion is Homicide." In Washington, a vice principal tried to bully and threaten to suspend a fifteen-year-old girl for wearing the same message on a T-shirt. An eight-year-old in Arkansas was punished with detention for pointing a chicken strip at another student in the cafeteria while saying "pow, pow, pow."

A third-grade honor student in Louisiana had a relative serving in the US Army. He was proud of this relative, so he drew a picture of him in uniform. The picture showed the Army fort where he might be stationed, and some military weapons. When his teacher saw the drawing, the boy found himself suspended from school. The school principal said "We have zero tolerance for drawings with guns." The boy's father was worried that the school was teaching his son that his relative in the Army is bad and dangerous and violent. We should, instead, be teaching respect and honor for these soldiers, who sacrificed their lives to protect our freedoms.

A student in Louisiana with no history of violence was expelled from his high school in 2001 for a drawing that showed his school under attack. He sued the school district, and the Fifth Circuit Court of Appeals agreed that the school had overreacted. But they still found an excuse to rule in favor of the school by granting them qualified immunity because of the "unsettled nature of First Amendment law" in this area.[44]

A high school student in Washington wrote a poem about a school shooter. The principal expelled him for fourteen days. In the subsequent lawsuit, the US District Judge ruled for the student, stating that the school officials overreacted, and that the poem could in no way be considered a true threat to anyone. But when it was appealed to the Ninth Circuit Court,[45] it ruled that the school officials could reasonably forecast that the author of the poem might be "intending to inflict injury upon himself or others," so the punishment was justified.[46] Now these school administrators, who are not trained psychiatrists, can abuse students' freedom of speech just because they are afraid that anyone who writes about violence is mentally deranged.

The FBI produced a report called "School Shootings: What You Should Know," which analyzed some school shootings, and tried to give guidelines to school personnel and others to try to prevent future instances. The report cautions not to predict violence based only on a youngster's speech, writing, videos, or drawings without evaluating him closely in four areas of his life:

- His personal behavior
- His family relationships
- His school's dynamics
- His social interactions

In most of the cases, the school officials do not perform the measured, considered evaluation of each individual situation, but instead they act hastily to suspend the student. The FBI report criticizes this approach as possibly increasing the danger, because this may just deepen the anger of the student, and he does not get professional evaluation and treatment.[47]

ACTIONS AWAY FROM SCHOOL

In another area of controversy, school officials repeatedly try to punish students for their actions away from school. This continues to be unsettled legal territory, because in some cases the courts will allow the schools to get away with it.

In 1976 a high school student was outside a shopping mall in Indiana, Pennsylvania. He saw a teacher from his school, and loudly made the remark "He's a prick!" For this he was given an in-school suspension, and was not allowed to attend the senior class trip. A federal court upheld the actions of the school.[48]

The popularity of the internet has given students a much more powerful and pervasive forum for their expression, and school officials consequently feel much more threatened. It seems that we are seeing a tendency for courts to allow the schools more often to punish online student speech. An eighth grader named Justin Swindler created a webpage on his computer filled with vulgar and profane derogatory comments about his math teacher and his principal. When the principal found out about it, he gave Justin a suspension. A lawsuit was filed in state court, and in 2002 the Pennsylvania Supreme Court ruled for the school. The court accepted the school's contention that the website caused an actual disruption of the school environment. They also relied on the school's authority to punish lewd and vulgar speech, even though the speech had not occurred at school.[49]

Since court opinions have been so contradictory, this is still a murky area, and student rights continue to be violated frequently. In fact, in a 2008 case in Connecticut, a teenager was punished for offensive language on an online blog. The federal court ruled for the school because of the doctrine of qualified immunity, which means that the law concerning punishment of students for online speech is so ill defined that it would be unfair to impose monetary damages on school officials.[50]

SPEECH CODES

Many colleges and universities have instituted so-called speech codes, which prohibit or restrict certain kinds of speech. The schools claim that these restrictions are justified in order to combat discrimination, harassment, and hate speech.

The University of Connecticut prohibits "actions that intimidate, humiliate, or demean persons or groups." Athens State University in Alabama forbids "words or actions that are unwelcome or *offensive* to a person in relation to race, color, sexual orientation . . ." and other attributes. Kenyon College in Ohio threatens students with discipline for any conduct that "*offends* the sensibilities of others." Frostburg State University in Maryland prohibits "*offensive* or inflammatory speech" over campus computer networks. At Rogers State University, "any students or student organizations wanting to hold a peaceful protest must register with the Office of Student Affairs by filling out a 'Campus Expression Form' at least three (3) days prior to the event." New Jersey's Anti-Bullying Bill of Rights Act requires all of New Jersey's public colleges and universities to prohibit "harassment, intimidation, and bullying," which it defines as: "[A] *single incident* or a series of incidents that . . . has the effect of insulting or demeaning any student or group of students." The University of Central Florida suspended a professor on the basis of an in-class joke in which he likened his extremely difficult exam questions to a "killing spree."[51]

Many schools have "free speech zone" policies, which limit student demonstrations and other expressive activities to small or out-of-the-way areas on campus. Such policies are generally inconsistent with the First Amendment. For example, Longwood University in Virginia limits speeches, demonstrations, and literature distribution to one area, and requires the area to be reserved five days in advance

Most of these regulations are so vague that it is frequently difficult for a person to guess if his speech might bring him some kind of punishment. The First Amendment prohibits public (government supported) universities from interfering with freedom of speech. And, even though they are not required to by the First Amendment, most private universities explicitly promise freedom of speech to their students and faculty. Much of the speech prohibited by these speech codes should actually be protected speech. The federal Department of Education's Office for Civil Rights (OCR)—the agency responsible for the enforcement of federal harassment regulations in schools—issued a letter of clarification to all of America's colleges and universities. Then-Assistant Secretary of Education Gerald Reynolds wrote: "Some colleges and universities have interpreted OCR's prohibition of 'harassment' as encompassing all offensive speech regarding sex, disability, race or other classifications. Harassment, however, to be prohibited by the statutes within OCR's jurisdiction, must include something beyond the mere expression of views, words, symbols or thoughts that some person finds offensive."[52]

America's colleges should be leading the way, infusing their students with the principles of the search for truth, free exchange of ideas, and tolerance of differences of opinion. Instead, many are attempting to outlaw speech and expression that does not conform to the official line.

HATE SPEECH

In recent decades, some people have promoted the idea that, if a crime is motivated by prejudice or bias, then that makes the crime even worse than it would be otherwise, and the perpetrator should be punished even more severely than he would be if his bias were not present. This creates a new class of crimes called "hate crimes," where a person gets additional punishment based on his speech or his supposed thoughts. But these hate crime laws are a real threat to our rights of free speech. If a person can be punished for his speech or thoughts when associated with a crime, then it is only a small step to make the words themselves a crime, without any additional criminal activity. If the government can punish criminals for wrong thinking, then it can also punish law-abiding citizens for the same.

This has already happened in some places. We have seen the college speech codes which prohibit certain kinds of vaguely defined speech. The various "harassment" laws can suppress an unbelievable range of expression, including jokes, political statements, legitimate art, religious speech, and other constitutionally protected speech.[53] Other countries have gone even further in trying to outlaw offensive speech. A law in the United Kingdom declared that "a person who uses threatening, abusive, or *insulting* words or behavior, or displays any written material which is threatening, abusive, or *insulting*, is guilty of an offence" if a judge thinks that the material is "likely" to stir up racial hatred. A Canadian law prohibits any electronic communication "that is likely to expose a person or persons to hatred or contempt." And of course, many Muslim nations have severe penalties for anyone using language which is thought to be insulting to Islam or the Prophet.

The advocates of these measures say that our freedom of speech, which the Founders prized so highly, is now outmoded. It must be balanced, they say, against the psychological hurt that some particular speech might cause. Many would argue that our need to combat discrimination is more important than our right to free speech. We must reject these arguments. The freedom of speech enshrined in our First Amendment makes us unique among nations. Historically, this has always been recognized as one of the most fundamental elements of our liberty. We must recognize this most precious gift, and defend it against all challengers. The best remedy for hurtful speech is not censorship, but it is more speech. Bad speech should be countered by good speech. Censorship is a dangerous proposition. When we accept the premise that government agencies should monitor "hateful" speech, we must accept the possibility that one day, our own speech could be termed hateful, given the vagaries of public opinion.

Hate crime laws are frequently enacted as an emotional reaction to the publicity surrounding some particularly tragic crime. And like many emotional actions, they are often poorly thought out. These laws are not only unfair but they are also unnecessary. The laws on the books already carry severe enough penalties to punish people convicted of crimes. In fact, the United States has a higher percentage of its population incarcerated than any other country in the world. All of our hate crime laws should be revised to eliminate the enhanced punishment based on a person's bad thoughts. Prosecuting people for their opinions is not the hallmark of a free society.

Chapter Three

Freedom of Religion
First Amendment

In the seventeenth century, various enterprises were formed to bring settlers to the New World. Typically, the King of England would give a charter to a business or settlement company. This charter gave them the legal right to form a colony in America. The charter defined the objectives, the legal rights and responsibilities, the form of government of the colony, and the relationship of the colony to England. Sometimes a great deal of authority would be granted to the company, which, in turn, would decide the laws and form of government. Frequently, it would be stated in the charter that one purpose of the colony was to spread the Christian gospel.

For example, the first charter of Virginia, in 1606, stated that the colony would propagate the "Christian Religion to such People, as yet live in Darkness and miserable Ignorance of the true Knowledge and Worship of God, and may in time bring the Infidels and Savages, living in those parts, to human Civility, and to a settled and quiet Government."

Then, the second charter of Virginia, in 1609, was even more explicit in saying that "the principal Effect which we can desire or expect of this Action, is the Conversion and Reduction of the People in those Parts unto the true Worship of God and Christian Religion."

The charter of New England in 1620 specified that they hoped to "advance the enlargement of Christian Religion, to the Glory of God Almighty."

The charter of Massachusetts Bay in 1629 had an ambitious goal to "win and incite the Natives of Country, to the Knowledge and Obedience of the only true God and Savior of Mankind, and the Christian Faith, which in our Royall Intention, and the Adventurers free Profession, is the principal End of this Plantation."

When William Penn established the colony of Pennsylvania, his charter said that they wanted "to reduce the savage Natives by gentle and just manners to the Love of Civil Societie and Christian Religion."

The Rhode Island Charter of 1663 states their intention that the colonists "may be in the better capacity to defend themselves, in their just rights and liberties against all the enemies of the Christian faith."

The Mayflower is probably the most famous ship of all those that made the treacherous voyage to America. Instead of the adventurers and entrepreneurs who were typical of many of these expeditions, this ship carried people who were fleeing religious persecution by the English kings. These are the people who eventually came to be known as "Pilgrims." The Mayflower reached America in November of 1620. They had a charter to establish a colony in Virginia, but when they reached land, they discovered they were far from there, in what is now Massachusetts. This ship headed south, trying to reach Virginia. But they had numerous problems, their provisions were running low, and winter was fast approaching, so they decided to stay where they were. While they were still on the ship, they created a document called the *Mayflower Compact*. This is recognized as the first governing document of the colony they founded, which was called Plymouth Colony. The *Mayflower Compact* gives "advancements of the Christian faith" as one of the primary reasons for this voyage.

THE DECLARATION OF INDEPENDENCE

The men who founded this country believed that our most important rights came from God. If governments could give rights to men, then those same governments could take those rights away. They had seen that already in other countries. A widespread philosophy at that time was the Divine Right of Kings. This was the premise guiding most of the governments in Europe. This new country was going in a different direction—this would be a government based on law. The law came from the Word of God. And all men, even a king, were under the law and not above it. The Declaration of Independence spelled out the Judeo-Christian basis of this government, when it said "all men are created equal, that they are endowed by their Creator with certain unalienable Rights, that among these are Life, Liberty and the pursuit of Happiness. That to secure these rights, Governments are instituted among Men, deriving their just powers from the consent of the governed." That is the purpose of government—not to give men rights, but to *secure* those rights. The rights are given to us by God.

William Blackstone was the most widely read and revered legal authority of the day. In his book *Commentaries on the Laws of England*, he said that when the Supreme Being formed the universe he impressed certain principles upon that matter, from which it can never depart. These are the laws of human nature, which have been revealed by God.[1]

CHRISTIAN NATION

The Christian faith was very much in evidence at the founding of this country. Even many years after the founding, both government and society showed a high respect for Christianity, and this was known as a Christian nation.[2] When the earliest colonies came to the New World from England, they each had an official charter authorizing the enterprise, and stating its rights and duties. Many of these charters stated that one purpose of the colony was to spread the Christian gospel. Many of the early New England colonies had laws with religious references. The legal code adopted in 1641 as the *Massachusetts Body of Liberties* contains prohibitions against blaspheming the name of God, or worshiping other gods.[3]

When the government of the United States was formed, many of the principles in the Declaration of Independence and the Constitution came from the Bible:

- The Declaration of Independence states that governments are "deriving their just powers from the consent of the governed." And the US Constitution begins "We the People of the United States . . . do ordain and establish this Constitution for the United States of America." This means that the people are in charge, and have the right to establish the government, control the government, and select their leaders. This was a radical idea at the time, when most governments in existence were based on the divine authority of kings. But the concept of government based on the consent of the governed appears over and over again throughout the Bible. For example, God didn't want Israel to have a human king, but the people wanted a king, so the people got what they wanted (1 Samuel 8:22). The people were sometimes allowed to choose their kings (Judges 8:22, Judges 9:6, 1 Kings 12:20, 2 Kings 14:21) and their judges (Deut. 16:18).

- The Declaration of Independence declares that "all men are created equal." This is another concept from the Bible, which states that "God shows no partiality" (Acts 10:34), and "There is neither Jew nor Greek" (Galatians 3:28). The Old Testament judges were commanded not to be partial to either the rich or poor, or to take a bribe, or to "kill the innocent and righteous" (Exodus 23).

- The idea that a ruler should be limited in power did not originate with the Founders, but was decreed by God in Deuteronomy 17:16–20. When King Rehoboam was very strict and cruel to his people, the people rebelled against him and replaced him as king (1 Kings 12).

- Article 3, Section 3, paragraph 1 of the Constitution states that "No Person shall be convicted of Treason unless on the Testimony of two Witnesses to the same overt Act, or on Confession in open Court." Where do you suppose they got the idea of requiring two witnesses? That's easy. Deuteronomy 19:15 says that "One witness is not enough to convict anyone accused of any crime or offense they may have committed. A matter must be established by the testimony of two or three witnesses."

- In some countries not only a criminal would be punished, but also his family. This is the meaning of the term "corruption of blood." Sometimes this meant that the children of a criminal would not be allowed to inherit his property. Sometimes this meant that the entire family would be executed. Daniel 6:24 records that "the king commanded, and those men who had maliciously accused Daniel were brought and cast into the den of lions—they, their children, and their wives." Scripture tells us that God decrees that the criminal's family should not be punished for his crime (Deut. 24:16), and so the Framers put that into the Constitution, in Article 3, Section 3, Paragraph 2, which says "no attainder of treason shall work corruption of blood, or forfeiture except during the life of the person attained."

- Our Constitution repeatedly stresses that it is trying to protect our rights of "life, liberty and property." Sure enough, these too come straight from the Bible, where the rights to life (Exodus 20:13 says, "Thou shalt not kill"), liberty (Exodus 21:16 and Deut. 24:7 forbid kidnapping and enslaving a person), and property (Exodus 20:15 says, "Thou shalt not steal") are clearly important to God.

- The Bible acknowledges that the church and the civil government are two separate entities, and perform different functions. Jesus said, "Render to Caesar the things that are Caesar's, and to God the things that are God's" (Luke 20:25). King Saul was punished by God when he tried to perform sacrifices that only the priests were allowed to do (1 Samuel 13). But God made it very clear that it was the responsibility of the king (the government) to acknowledge God, and to encourage the people to worship God. There was big trouble when kings did not do this. For example, King Jehoshaphat "made [his nation] Judah go astray. . . . And after all this, the Lord struck him in his bowels with an incurable disease" (2 Chron. 21:11, 18). God said that King Baasha "made my people Israel to sin, provoking me to anger with their sins, behold, I will utterly sweep away Baasha and his house" (1 Kings 16:2-3). When a king led his people in the right direction, God was pleased: "And [King] Asa did what was good and right in the eyes of the Lord his God. He took away the foreign altars . . . and commanded Judah to seek the Lord" (2 Chron. 14:2-4). Our first president, George Washington, recognized this duty when he wrote in his first Thanksgiving Proclamation "Whereas it is the duty of all nations to acknowledge the providence of Almighty God . . . ." It is heartbreaking that our country has strayed so far away from this ancient truth.

Our founding fathers certainly did not believe that preachers should stay out of politics. At the time that our Constitution was being ratified, the clergy took an active role in politics. Forty-four clergymen from various denominations served as delegates to the ratifying conventions of eight states.[4]

FIRST AMENDMENT

The Founders of this country believed that everyone should be able to follow their conscience, and should be allowed to worship as they saw fit. Therefore, the First Amendment guarantees the free exercise of religion. The Founders were very familiar with the Church of England, and its horrible record of corruption and abuses of the rights of religion and speech. The Founders knew that they did not want an official national church here in America. In the First Amendment, Congress was prohibited from "an establishment of religion" (the "Establishment Clause"). This was generally understood to forbid the federal government from establishing a national church, instead leaving all policy regarding religion to the states, free from federal interference.

But on the other hand, the Founders wanted to encourage religion in general. It was widely recognized that this Republican form of government that they were forming was only suitable for a virtuous people. As John Adams, our second President, said: "Our constitution was made only for a moral and religious people. It is wholly inadequate to the government of any other."[5] Benjamin Franklin wisely observed "Only a virtuous people are capable of freedom. As nations become more corrupt and vicious, they have more need of masters." James Madison reinforced this feeling when, in The Federalist No. 39, he said that our form of government depended "on the capacity of mankind for self-government."[6] In his farewell address, George Washington wrote: "Of all the dispositions and habits which lead to political prosperity, religion and morality are indispensable supports. . . . Reason and experience both forbid us to expect that national morality can prevail in exclusion of religious principles." The distinguished author and educator Dr. Jedidiah Morse said:

> The foundations which support the interests of Christianity, are also necessary to support a free and equal government like our own. In all those countries where there is little or no religion . . . there you will find . . . arbitrary and tyrannical governments . . . In proportion as the genuine effects of Christianity are diminished in any nation . . . in the same proportion will the people of that nation recede from the

blessings of genuine freedom, and approximate the miseries of complete despotism . . . all efforts made to destroy the foundations of our holy religion, ultimately tend to the subversion also of our political freedom and happiness. Whenever the pillars of Christianity shall be overthrown, our present republican forms of government, and all the blessings which flow from them, must fall with them.[7]

The Founders of this country certainly were not indifferent to religion. But they were trying to achieve a delicate balance. They knew they had to encourage religion for the sake of the Republic, but they wanted to avoid giving too much support to any particular denomination. Naturally, finding this exact balance was very tricky. There was also some disagreement about exactly how to interpret the Establishment Clause.

WHAT DOES IT MEAN?

Some people claimed that the government should not do anything to promote religion. But professor and Supreme Court Justice Joseph Story saw it differently. He stated his view that "probably at the time of the adoption of the Constitution, and of the amendment to it now under consideration [First Amendment], the general if not the universal sentiment in America was that Christianity ought to receive encouragement from the State so far as was not incompatible with the private rights of conscience and the freedom of religious worship.[8]

The distinguished jurist Thomas Cooley, in his widely recognized treatise *Constitutional Limitations,* stated that "the American constitutions [*sic*] contain no provisions which prohibit the authorities from such solemn recognition of a superintending Providence in public transactions and exercises."[9]

George Washington wrote in his first Thanksgiving Proclamation, "Whereas it is the duty of all nations to acknowledge the providence of Almighty God, to obey his will, to be grateful for his benefits, and humbly implore His protection and favor . . ."[10]

Thomas Jefferson's 1801 remark about a "wall of separation between Church and State" has been incorrectly used by some to try to claim that he was opposed to the government helping religion. He was opposed to the concept of an established Church, and he did speak and work to disestablish the Church of England in Virginia. But Jefferson's biographers confirm that Jefferson never opposed the non-preferential encouragement of religion.[11] And Jefferson stated, "And can the liberties of a nation be thought secure when we have removed their only firm basis, a conviction in the minds of the people that these liberties are the gift of God?"[12] Thomas Jefferson was not involved in the drafting of the US Constitution or the Bill of Rights—he was in France at the time. So to find out the real meaning of this amendment, we should go back to the original authors of the bill.

James Madison was the primary author of the First Amendment, so we must try to determine his understanding of its meaning. When Madison first introduced his proposal for this amendment in the House of Representatives, on June 8, 1789, the language he used in his proposal was "nor shall any national religion be established."[13] This confirms that his own personal intent was to prevent the establishment of a national church. Supreme Court Chief Justice Rehnquist has done a thorough analysis of the recorded discussions related to this subject in the first Congress. He gives the result of this analysis in his dissent to a 1985 Supreme Court case *Wallace v. Jaffree*, where he says: "It seems indisputable from these glimpses of Madison's thinking, as reflected by actions on the floor of the House in 1789, that he saw the Amendment as designed to prohibit the establishment of a national religion, and perhaps to prevent discrimination among sects. He did not see it as requiring neutrality on the part of government between religion and irreligion."[14] As Law Professor Michael Paulsen has observed, "The very fact that the First Amendment protects the free exercise of religion means that the Constitution is *not* neutral with respect to religion. It gives religious belief and exercise special protection from government."[15]

Another thing that the first Congress did was to hire chaplains for the Congress, to be paid with public money. It also reenacted the Northwest Ordinance for the governance of the Northwest Territory. The Northwest Ordinance provided that "Religion, morality, and knowledge, being necessary to good government and the happiness of mankind, schools and the means of education shall forever be encouraged."[16] These were the men who wrote the First Amendment, and then voted to adopt it. If anyone knew what it meant, they certainly would have. This confirms that Congress did not mean that the Government should be neutral toward religion.

During the early years of our country's history, church services were held in the Capitol building, the Treasury building, and the Supreme Court.[17] There was no doubt that government support of religion was a cherished part of our heritage, and certainly violated no part of the Constitution.

OTHER CLUES TO UNDERSTANDING

The Bible was widely read in America, and these Bibles had been imported from England. As the American Revolution heated up, the importation of these Bibles was interrupted by the hostilities. In 1777, Patrick Allison, Chaplain of Congress, told Congress that something needed to be done about this. To assuage the problem, Congress authorized a resolution to import 20,000 copies of the Bible from another country. Then in 1782 Congress authorized Robert Aitken, a Philadelphia bookseller and printer, to print some Bibles.[18]

When the University of Ohio was first established, it was called Western American University. The original 1802 charter by the state creating this university stated its mission as "the instruction of youth in all the various branches of the liberal arts and sciences for the promotion of good education, virtue, religion, and morality . . ."

When Thomas Jefferson wrote the first plan of education adopted by the District of Columbia, he used the Bible and Isaac Watt's hymnal as the principal texts for teaching reading to students.[19]

As the United States moved from the eighteenth into the nineteenth century, Congress appropriated time and again public moneys in support of sectarian Indian education carried on by religious organizations. Typical of these was Jefferson's treaty with the Kaskaskia Indians, which provided annual cash support for the tribe's Roman Catholic priest and church.[20]

In a letter in 1822, Thomas Jefferson described how the churches in his village of Charlottesville used the court house as a place to hold church services. He had no problem with using a public building for religious services.[21]

Church leaders and politicians alike believed that conversion to Christianity would quickly, humanely, and permanently solve the Indian question. Indeed, in 1869, the Board of Indian Commissioners noted in its annual report that where assimilating Indians was concerned, "The religion of our blessed Savior is . . . the most effective agent for the civilization of any people."[22]

In 1854, the constitutionality of having chaplains in Congress and the military was challenged. In response, the Committee of the Judiciary in Congress made an investigation, and issued a report which contains the following: "At the time of the adoption of the Constitution and the amendments, the universal sentiment was that Christianity should be encouraged, not any one sect."[23]

The House of Representatives in 1854 passed a resolution proclaiming that "the great vital element in our system is the belief of our people in the pure doctrines and divine truths of the gospel of Jesus Christ."[24]

During World War II, the government issued seventeen million Bibles to the soldiers with a message in them from Generals Dwight Eisenhower and George Marshall. And many of the World War II posters printed by the government contained religious imagery.[25]

In the Library of Congress, the Main Reading Room contains a bronze statue of Moses holding the Ten Commandments. In addition, two scripture verses are inscribed on the walls. In 1998, the Library of Congress held an exhibit called "Religion and the Founding of the American Republic." The exhibit contained over two hundred artifacts, and explored the role of religion in the colonies from Jamestown until after the Revolutionary War. This exhibit demonstrated unquestionably that religion and morality were, in Alexis de Tocqueville's words, "indispensable to the maintenance of republican institutions."[26]

In *Zorach v. Clauson* (1952), the Supreme Court stated "The First Amendment, however, does not say that in every and all respects there shall be a separation of Church and State."[27]

The Congress in 1952 prescribed a "National Day of Prayer," and it was reaffirmed in legislation in 1998:

> The President shall issue each year a proclamation designating the first Thursday in May as a National Day of Prayer on which the people of the United States may turn to God in prayer and meditation at churches, in groups, and as individuals.[28]

In 1983, the practice of opening legislative sessions with prayers by paid chaplains (in the Nebraska legislature) was upheld by the Supreme Court in the case of *Marsh v. Chambers*. The Court said:

> In light of the unambiguous and unbroken history of more than 200 years, there can be no doubt that the practice of opening legislative sessions with prayer has become part of the fabric of our society. To invoke Divine guidance on a public body entrusted with

making the laws is not, in these circumstances, an "establishment" of religion or a step toward establishment; it is simply a tolerable acknowledgment of beliefs widely held among the people of this country.[29]

The United States Supreme Court ruling in the case of *Lynch v. Connelly,* in 1984, contained the statement, "There is an unbroken history of official acknowledgment by all three branches of government of the role of religion in American life from at least 1789."[30]

The First Amendment prohibits the establishment of a religion, but the acknowledgement of God is certainly not the same thing as an establishment of a religion. As Supreme Court justice Antonin Scalia said: "Historical practices thus demonstrate that there is a distance between the acknowledgment of a single Creator and the establishment of a religion. . . . Governmental invocation of God is not an establishment. . . . Acknowledgment of the contribution that religion has made to our Nation's legal and governmental heritage partakes of a centuries-old tradition. . . . Display of the Ten Commandments is well within the mainstream of this practice of acknowledgment."[31]

Down through the years, we seemed to have found a good practical balance for the Establishment Clause. Congress opened their sessions with prayer. Chaplains continued their work in Congress and in the military. Presidents proclaimed a national day of thanksgiving. Many schools opened the day with a prayer or Bible reading. Our coins say "In God We Trust." And never was there any serious threat of establishing a national church.

Our country prospered and grew strong, and it continued to maintain its basically Christian character. In 1892 the Supreme Court issued a ruling in the case of *Holy Trinity Church v. United States* that contained the statement "this is a Christian nation."[32] Then again, as late as 1952, in *Zorach v. Clauson*, the Supreme Court stated "We are a religious people whose institutions presuppose a Supreme Bring."[33]

So the First Amendment was never (until recently) seen as being hostile to religion. It was not an effort to protect us against religious influence. It was actually a statement about state sovereignty. The First Amendment made it clear that the states, and not the federal government, would have the primary authority to enact laws relating to religion. As Supreme Court Justice Clarence Thomas said, "It protects state establishments from federal interference but does not protect any individual right."[34] The states should be free to do what they wanted regarding religion, and the federal government would not have any power at all to interfere.

RECENT CHANGES IN DIRECTION

The attack on the traditional interpretation of the Establishment Clause, as described above, was escalated in 1947. In the case of *Everson v. Board of Education*, the Supreme Court ruled that: "The 'establishment of religion' clause of the First Amendment means at least this: neither a state nor the Federal Government can set up a church. Neither can pass laws which aid one religion, *aid all religions*, or prefer one religion over another."[35] To reach this ruling, the Court abandoned 150 years of precedent, declaring that the Establishment Clause could be used as a weapon against the states. Before 1947, states had been free from federal interference regarding the relationship between religion and civil government. After 1947, this was at the mercy of the whim of the Supreme Court.

In the *Everson* decision, the Supreme Court majority decided that the Fourteenth Amendment required them to enforce the Establishment Clause against the states. This was a surprise to many, since no one had ever noticed such a requirement in all the years since the Fourteenth Amendment was ratified. Those who ratified the amendment certainly did not understand it to destroy state authority over religion. The very clear wording of the amendment makes it obvious that it applies only to the federal government, to protect the states from interference from the national government. This was apparent because six of the states that ratified the establishment clause themselves established a state religion.[36] Supreme Court Justice Joseph Story wrote in 1833, "the real object of the First Amendment was . . . " leaving "the whole power over the subject of religion . . . exclusively to the state governments."[37]

The irrelevance of the Fourteenth Amendment was also demonstrated when, six years after the Fourteenth Amendment was ratified, there was a movement to adopt a constitutional amendment to prohibit the states from "establishing" religion. No one would have bothered promoting such an amendment if they thought the Fourteenth Amendment had already accomplished the same purpose[38]

The Supreme Court continued to try to solidify this new interpretation in the case of *Board of Education v. Allen* (1968), and then again in *Lemon v. Kurtzman* (1971). In both of these cases, the Court ruled that, for a law to comply with the Establishment Clause, "Its principal or primary effect must be one that neither advances nor inhibits religion."[39]

Religious instruction and prayer have always been a part of the public schools, from before the time the Constitution was written. The people who wrote and adopted the First Amendment not only knew this practice, but encouraged it. They knew this did not violate the Constitution, but in fact fulfilled the obligation of a nation to acknowledge our Creator, who is the source of all our rights.

In 1962 the Supreme Court, in the case of *Engel v. Vitale*, ruled that it is unconstitutional for a public school to compose and recite a prayer in school.[40] Since we had had prayer in schools for 200 years, why did it suddenly become illegal? Did the Constitution change? Was the Constitution amended? No. The only thing that changed was that these judges now felt bold enough to incorporate their personal beliefs and desires into a Supreme Court decision.

The Supreme Court continued this theme through several other decisions that banned reading of scripture in a school's opening exercises (*Abington School District v. Schempp*, 1963), prayer at high school graduation ceremonies (*Lee v. Weisman*, 1992), and prayer at high school football games (*Santa Fe ISD v. Doe*, 2000). Justice Potter Stewart was concerned because "A refusal to permit religious exercises thus is seen, not as the realization of state neutrality, but rather as the establishment of a religion of secularism."[41] The Court has discovered that it can get away with doing just about anything it wants to, and no one will hold it accountable. So it forges ahead, destroying rights that we have enjoyed for hundreds of years.

"By the turn of the twenty-first century," Professor Michael Paulsen explains, "the Court had almost entirely abandoned the idea that the First Amendment provides special protection of individual and group freedom of religious exercise from the sphere of government power."[42] Supreme Court Chief Justice Rehnquist said that the Court "bristles with hostility to all things religious in public life."[43]

All of these decisions were split decisions. There is no consensus here. This is a very contentious and divisive subject, and legal scholars are bitterly divided. Supreme Court Justice Antonin Scalia summed it up very eloquently when he wrote that the meaning of the First Amendment "is to be determined by reference to historical practices and understandings." He wrote that: "We must respect the understanding of the Founding Fathers, and what history reveals was the contemporaneous understanding of the First Amendment. The existence from the beginning of the Nation's life of a practice . . . is a fact of considerable import in the interpretation of the Establishment Clause . . . The history and traditions of our Nation are replete with public ceremonies featuring prayers . . . From our Nation's origin, prayer has been a prominent part of governmental ceremonies and proclamations."[44]

The Supreme Court's hostility toward religion was further illustrated by a change in the rules regarding "standing." A citizen generally does not have the right to bring a suit in federal court unless the person has a specific and direct loss at issue, such as the loss of money or liberty. But in 1968 in the case of *Flast v. Cohen*, the Supreme Court created the entirely novel rule that taxpayers can sue under the establishment clause to prohibit federal expenditures aiding religious schools. The Court refused to allow similar suits to be brought under other parts of the Constitution. Thus, every single provision of the Constitution except one is immune from taxpayer or citizen enforcement. That exception is the one used to attack public manifestations of religion. This has led to the outrageous spectacle of lawsuits by persons whose only complaint is that they are "offended" by seeing a religious symbol or display.[45]

Here is more evidence of the Court's inexplicable paranoia whenever it suspects that anything might give even the slightest hint of support to a concept that might be remotely related to anything religious. In 2005, a federal court in Pennsylvania invalidated a school policy of requiring biology teachers to recite a statement encouraging students to "keep an open mind" about both evolution and intelligent design. So just a suggestion to "keep an open mind" is sufficiently religious to cause the Court to conclude that the school is trying to "establish" an official religion. For any rational, objective person this is absolutely beyond comprehension, but for the federal courts, it is just business as usual.[46]

As constitutional attorney John Whitehead observed, the removal of prayer in schools may well have "contributed to the apparent deterioration in the quality of American public education. Such deterioration is certainly consistent with the removal of the moral and ethical force for good, which had been present in the form of prayer, Bible reading, and the recognition of man's relationship to God."[47]

BLACKLIST

During the Cold War, we were looking for Communists under every rock. Those were the days of the blacklists. If a person was even suspected of having any sympathy or any relationship to a Communist organization, his name would go on a list. And if a person's name was on that list, then he might have trouble getting or keeping a job in some fields. The education and entertainment industries showed particular enthusiasm for purging the offenders. A blacklisted writer, actor, or director would find getting work in Hollywood to be very difficult. The National Education Association voted to bar Communists as members or teachers. Many teachers and college professors were fired based on their opinions or friendships. Even when there was no hard evidence of any criminal act, Congressional investigating committees would use accusations, innuendo, gossip, hearsay and rumors to expose a person to public embarrassment and destroy his reputation. Eventually the excesses involved in this witch hunt were exposed and discredited, and the country moved back toward more protection of individual rights.

But now a new generation has forgotten the shame of that era. The same old tactics are back. We now have a new blacklist. A person might find himself on this new blacklist if he questions any of the current doctrines of the left. If he supports traditional marriage between a man and a woman, for example, he may find himself attacked from multiple quarters, with his reputation ruined and his career destroyed. While diversity of races is mandatory, diversity of thought and opinion is not to be tolerated. Look what happened to Brendan Eich, the CEO of the software company Mozilla. Even though he was one of the founders of that company, when it was discovered that he believed in traditional marriage, the company forced him to resign. He was never accused of engaging in any discrimination toward his employees or customers, but just his beliefs were justification for his persecution. In this brave new world, if your beliefs don't match the current orthodoxy, and you try to exercise your freedom of speech, many hateful people will say that you deserve to have your career ruined and your reputation demolished. If you don't toe the line, then you are not even worthy to be able to earn a living.

Multiple wedding cake bakers have been sued, fined, or, in some cases, forced out of business, when they did not want to participate in a gay wedding (or commitment) ceremony. Photographers were fined by the New Mexico Human Rights Commission because they declined to photograph a gay wedding due to their religious convictions. Several different enterprises that rent out facilities for weddings have been punished for not wanting to support a gay wedding. A florist in Washington State was sued for declining a gay wedding assignment. A company in Kentucky is under legal attack for not printing "gay pride" designs on a T-shirt, even though they offered to have another company do the printing. The Catholic Church has been forced to shut down adoption agencies in several states because it opposes adoption by homosexual couples. Therapists have been prohibited by law from helping young people overcome unwanted same-sex attractions. More and more of these kinds of problems are being seen all over the country. If any jurisdiction has added "sexual orientation" to its list of legally prohibited discriminations, it is time to rethink this policy, and consider removing that phrase from the statutes. This is causing more injustices than it is solving.

THE PLEDGE OF ALLEGIANCE

In 1954 Congress added the words "under God" to the Pledge of Allegiance. It now reads: "I pledge allegiance to the Flag of the United States of America, and to the Republic for which it stands, one Nation under God, indivisible, with liberty and justice for all."

At the time of this change, the House of Representatives issued an accompanying report, which said "from the time of our earliest history our peoples and our institutions have reflected the traditional concept that our Nation was founded on a fundamental belief in God."[48]

Since then, several people have actually filed lawsuits challenging these words in the Pledge, claiming that this violates the Establishment Clause. Of course, it is absurd to claim that these words are the same as establishing a national church. But as ridiculous as it seems, some lower court judges have actually tried to use this excuse to advance their attack on religion. However, the most recent court rulings at this writing reaffirm that these words are not unconstitutional:

- The United States Court of Appeals for the Ninth Circuit upheld the words "under God" in the Pledge of Allegiance in the case of *Newdow v. Rio Linda Union School District* in 2010. In this ruling, the court stated "The Founders did not see these two ideas—that individuals possessed certain God-given rights, which no government can take away, and that we do not want our nation to establish a religion—as being in conflict."[49]

- In 2010, the United States Court of Appeals for the First Circuit in Boston ruled that there was nothing wrong with the words "under God." The United States Supreme Court refused to hear an appeal of this case, allowing this ruling to stand.[50]

IN GOD WE TRUST

In 1955, Congress required the words "In God We Trust" to be placed on all US currency. These words had appeared on US coins for many years. Then in 1956, Congress ordained that this phrase "shall henceforth be the United States' national motto." Of course, this was challenged in the courts with the ridiculous claim that this is the same as establishing a national church. In the case of *Aronow v. United States*, the United States Court of Appeals for the Ninth Circuit ruled, in 1970, "It is quite obvious that the national motto and the slogan on coinage and currency 'In God We Trust' have nothing whatsoever to do with the establishment of religion."[51]

ATTACKS ON RELIGIOUS FREEDOM

We have seen an ever increasing effort at all levels of government—federal, state and local—to deny us our most basic rights:

Mr. Michael Salman and his wife Suzanne have been holding weekly bible studies at their home for family and friends for several years. One day, the police and city inspectors raided their home, and said that their bible studies put them in violation of the city's building codes. He was sentenced to 60 days in jail, and more than $12,000 in fines. It seems obvious they were targeted because of the religious nature of the gathering. If this had been a football party or a family reunion, nothing would have been said.

A security guard physically forced Emma Anderson—an 82 year old woman—off the Metrorail at the Brickwell Metrorail Station in Miami, Florida, for publicly singing spiritual hymns. According to the security guard, public singing, dancing, and playing music without a permit is against the Miami-Dade Transit rules.

A school in California had a gay and lesbian awareness day. Tyler Harper wanted to express his view, and he wore a shirt bearing the words "Homosexuality Is Shameful" and "Be Ashamed. Our School Has Embraced What God Condemned." The principal refused to let him attend class. He sued, and the Ninth Circuit Court panel ruled in favor of the school.[52]

Shirley Elliot sold produce at Thibodaux Farmer's Market at the Jean Lafitte National Historical Park in Louisiana, and provided free Bibles on her table to anyone that wanted one. When a park ranger discovered the Bibles, he demanded that Ms. Elliott remove the Bibles from her table because "they were on federal property."

A street preacher in Cincinnati, Ohio, was threatened with arrest and denied the right to speak on the public square around the Capitol building because he didn't have a permit. He sued, and eventually a federal court ruled that individuals cannot be required to get a permit to speak in a public place.

Teachers and students at Boulevard Heights Elementary School in Fort Lauderdale, Florida, were told that they may not say "Merry Christmas." The school recommended "Happy Holidays" as an alternative.

In 2011 the Department of Veterans Affairs issued a decree that banned any mention of Jesus Christ during burials at Houston National Cemetery.[53]

Two students at Roosevelt High School in Des Moines, Iowa, wore T-shirts to school with the message "Abortion Kills Kids." School officials told them to cover their shirts or face punishment.

The US Army revised its guidelines for Walter Reed Medical Center in 2011 to read: "No religious items (i.e., Bibles or reading materials) are allowed to be given away or used during a visit."[54]

The United Caring Shelter (UCS) in Evansville, Illinois, allowed anyone who wanted to pray before the free meal provided by the shelter to do so. The prayers were open to all and were not mandatory. The US Department of Agriculture, however, demanded that UCS stop the prayers or stop accepting federal assistance to feed the homeless. The UCS now permits only a moment of silence before meals.

A park ranger at George Wyth State Park in Iowa displayed his privately-owned cross in his personal home situated in the park. An atheist group complained about having to look at the cross when and if its members ever ventured near the home. It conceded that the park ranger could display personal religious items inside his home, but asserted that his religious freedom stopped at his front doorway, and demanded that he remove his personal religious item from outside his home. The Iowa Department of Natural Resources yielded to the demands, and ordered its employee to remove the cross.

When a pastor in Chandler, Arizona, complained that a public library display excluded Christmas, and only included Hanukkah and Kwanzaa, the library took down the entire display rather than add any information about Christmas.

Teachers in Boulder, Colorado, refused to allow Elizabeth Johnson, an eleven-year-old student, to give her book report presentation on the Book of Exodus, and then told her that she could not bring her Bible to school. Their reason was that the Bible might be "offensive" to members of other religious faiths.

Reunion Church leased an empty high school on Sunday mornings for services, but the Dallas Independent School District evicted the church in the middle of the lease, claiming that renting their facilities to a church violates school board policy. Reunion Church filed a lawsuit challenging their eviction, and the school district reversed its decision.

Matthew Reynolds, the valedictorian at HLV Junior-Senior High School in Victor, Iowa, wished to express his faith and attribute his success to faith in Jesus Christ in his graduation speech. Although Matthew planned to begin by clarifying that his views were not the views of the school or the administration, the school principal told Matthew that he must make his speech "secular."

In November 2011, the House of Representatives investigated charges that the Obama administration, in its selection of grant recipients, had been discriminating against Catholic institutions. The majority on the House Oversight and Government Reform Committee concluded that Obama had grossly discriminated against the Catholic Church.[55]

A fourth-grade student at Karns Elementary School in Tennessee was stopped by school officials from holding Bible studies with his peers during recess. The United States Court of Appeals for the Sixth Circuit ruled in favor of the school.[56]

A group of Christians had assembled at a local festival in Phoenix, Arizona, to publicly express their Christian faith. They also were giving away cold bottles of water to the people on a public sidewalk on that very hot day. A city official informed them that they were violating the city code by passing out free bottles of water without a vendor's permit.

A public school in Washington State prevented students from forming a Bible club, stating that the club's requirement that club members possess a true desire to grow in a relationship with

Jesus Christ would exclude non-Christians and violate the school's nondiscrimination policy.

These cannot be viewed as isolated incidents. They are part of a widespread and determined pattern of discrimination against Christians fueled by a relentless campaign of propaganda and brainwashing by the media, educators, political elite, and progressives.

We can see that this country is and always has been a Christian nation. The evidence is overwhelming. But in the last hundred years or so, many of us seem to have forgotten that. We have not been diligent in standing up for our rights. Modern Christianity, in order to avoid controversy and criticism, has tried to be accommodating to the secular world. That is a mistake. The secular world does not accommodate. Instead, it tries to destroy all opposition. Christianity must not be accommodating; it must stand up and speak the truth.[57]

The churches have a duty to inform their congregations about these threats to our freedom of religion. As long as churches continue to remain silent, the forces hostile to God will increase their influence in our government and our culture, and we will continue to see our religious freedoms erode. The churches could make a difference—they have the influence and the numbers. It is so sad that they are abdicating their responsibilities in this vital arena.

Chapter Four

Keep and Bear Arms
Second Amendment

A well regulated Militia, being necessary to the security of a free State, the right of the people to keep and bear Arms, shall not be infringed.

Second Amendment to US Constitution

One of our great rights that is very much under attack today is the right to keep and bear arms. The Founders thought that this was such an important right that they included it in the original Bill of Rights, and even gave it a separate amendment all by itself. Their respect for this right was based in part on years of experience in the colonies, where personal protection from outlaws and Indians was a matter of life and death. Another factor were the abuses committed by King George's army, and the political control that England exerted over the colonies without giving them any representation in the Parliament. The Founders also had the knowledge of many decades of experience in England, where monarchs had used their power to oppress the people.

The authors of our Constitution were strongly influenced by English history, with which they were very familiar. In order to get a better understanding of the meaning of this Amendment, it is important to go back and review some of the history behind its writing.

SEVENTEENTH AND EIGHTEENTH CENTURY ENGLAND

From the time of the Middle Ages, the typical Englishman was understood to have a duty to help to preserve the peace. It was natural for him to want to protect himself and his friends and loved ones, but he was also required by law to help to protect his community and even his country. Serving in the militia was a part of this obligation. He was also required to take his turn keeping watch at the town gates. A man was expected to provide his own weapons in order to fulfill these responsibilities.

In England, hunting had become a popular amusement of the upper class. The aristocracy was so jealous of their privileges in this regard that they tried various ploys to restrict the common folk from participating. Several laws were passed with the stated purpose of preserving wildlife, but actually were intended to prohibit persons who failed to meet certain property or income requirements from hunting. Some of the game laws also made significant changes to the royal forests by expanding their boundaries and restricting the uses of the land. This caused severe hardship for many poor people living on these lands. This resulted in massive protests, riots, destruction of forest enclosures, and poaching. The king became even more suspicious of his subjects, and concerned about their easy access to firearms.

The mid seventeenth century was a tumultuous time in England, with a series of civil wars. This was in addition to the long running conflict between Catholicism and Protestantism. The king was distrustful of the Parliament, the people, and the citizen militias. One of the disputes centered on the king's efforts to form his own army, which he felt would be more loyal to him than the militias would be. The people, on the other hand, liked the idea that the general militia members would often be sympathetic to their interests, which gave the people more leverage over the king.

In 1660 Charles II became King, and soon began an effort to clamp down on firearms. The Militia Act of 1662 authorized any Lord Lieutenant of the militia to disarm anyone they "judge[d] dangerous to the Peace of the Kingdome," and many guns were confiscated. A proclamation was issued forbidding transport of arms or ammunition into the countryside without permission.[1] Then, in 1671, a new game act was enacted which, for the first time in English history, removed from the common people the privilege of owning firearms.

When Charles II died in 1685, his brother James became King. James was a Catholic, and he had some justifiable anxiety about his reception in Protestant England. He quickly began efforts to solidify his hold on the country by removing Protestant officeholders and army and militia leaders, and replacing them with Catholic ones. He moved to disarm the militia in Ireland, and to remove funding from the militia in England, diverting those funds to his army. Many in Parliament balked at this move, however, given their long standing distrust of a standing army. James had been trying for several years to disarm more of the population, using the Militia Act of 1662 and the Game Act of 1671. The people finally had enough, and in 1688 several prominent Englishmen invited William of Orange to bring an invasion force from Holland to England and take over the Crown. He did this, and King James, realizing that he did not have popular support, fled to France.

Before officially agreeing to turn the throne over to William, the Parliament realized that they had an opportunity to negotiate with the new monarch, and possibly regain some of their rights which had been taken away by recent kings. They formed a convention that drafted a "Declaration of Rights" or "Bill of Rights." Two of the rights included in this list were the prohibition against keeping a standing army in time of peace without the consent of Parliament, and the right of Protestant subjects to have arms. The right to keep arms was obviously an individual right, for the militia was not even mentioned.

The need for self-defense was always an important consideration in the English right to keep arms. While service in the militia was seldom mentioned, the right of self-defense was frequently invoked as justification for being armed. A court case in 1704 agreed that constables could seize guns, dogs, nets and other items used for illegal hunting, but cautioned that "none of her Majestie's Protestant subjects were to be by virtue hereof disturbed in keeping arms for their own preservation."[2] Another court ruling, in 1739, agreed with the defense that a man's gun could not be seized because "a gun is necessary for defence of a house."[3] Even back in the seventeenth century, when there was fear of a Catholic counter-revolution and Catholics were being disarmed, Catholics were still allowed to keep arms "for the defence of his house or person."[4]

The English judge William Blackstone was highly respected in the eighteenth century, and his work *Commentaries on the Laws of England* became the great authority on English Law. In this book, he explained that keeping arms was necessary both for the "natural right of resistance and self-preservation," and "to restrain the violence of oppression."[5] In other words, that was the people's last resort if their government became tyrannical. Another prominent eighteenth century writer was Jean-Louis de Lolme, whose famous book *The Constitution of England* was influential, not only in England, but for the authors of the American Constitution. In this work, he asked what would happen if the ruler went outside the Constitution and tried to force his will on the people. The answer, he said, was "resistance . . . The question has been decided in favour of this doctrine by the laws of England" which expressly guaranteed to the people "being provided with arms for their own defence."[6]

THE COLONIES

Colonial law required that each man was not only required to have arms, but, in some cases, to actually carry weapons. In Newport, Rhode Island, a law required that "noe man shall go two miles from the Towne unarmed." In both Virginia and Georgia, men were required to bring their gun when they went to church.[7]

As people migrated from England to America, they expected that they would retain all the rights of English subjects. A guarantee to that effect was written into the charters of some of the colonies. One feeling that the colonists brought with them was the strong English distrust of standing armies. As time went on, the colonists were becoming more and more apprehensive about the intentions of King George III. The British had stationed a sizable military force in America, not only on the frontier where increased dangers were obvious, but also in the cities. The commander of the British army had vast authority to take over command of the local militia, and even to disarm it at his discretion. A clergyman, Simeon Howard, expressed the fears of many when he said, "To have an army continually stationed in the midst of a people, in time of peace, is a precarious and dangerous method of security." Tensions increased as the British imposed a series of taxes and penalties, and committed a multitude of abuses against the people. The people became more and more vocal in their protests, until finally in Lexington in 1775 the shooting started.

The Declaration of Independence tried to summarize many of the complaints against King George. These items were specifically listed in the Declaration:

- He has kept among us, in times of peace, Standing Armies without the Consent of our legislatures

- He has affected to render the Military independent of and superior to the Civil power
- Quartering large bodies of armed troops among us

Our first attempt at a national Constitution, the Articles of Confederation, continued the theme of trying to limit standing armies. It specifically forbade any state (with the Declaration of Independence, the colonies had become independent sovereign states) from maintaining a standing army in peacetime except as authorized by Congress. But the states were each required to keep a "well-regulated" militia.[8] The militia consisted of all able-bodied men in the state, who were required to be armed and ready to serve when called upon.

After we declared ourselves independent from Great Britain, each state had to write a constitution for itself. They recognized the importance of the English Bill of Rights of 1689, and many of the states included in their constitution their own bill of rights. Most of them had a statement that the people had a right to be armed, or made that necessary by requiring a general citizen militia. Several of the state constitutions actually used the language "a well-regulated militia."

THE CONSTITUTION

When the convention met in 1787 to draft a new Constitution, the colonies had been through the experience of fighting a very grueling war, and they saw the difficulties under the Articles of Confederation of raising and financing an army. When they approached the task of writing a constitution, they realized the need for a stronger federal government. They also had learned from experience that it would be worthwhile to make some provisions for a permanent professional army, rather than depending entirely on the militias.

The authors of our Constitution still retained their ingrained skepticism about a standing army, and they tried to create in the Constitution some checks and balances that could prevent misuse of military power. In an attempt to divide authority, they decided that the President would be commander-in-chief of the army, but Congress was given the power "to raise and support armies." To maintain civilian control over the army, appropriations of money for the military were limited to a maximum period of two years. The power to declare war was taken away from the President and given to Congress.

When the Constitution was submitted to the States for ratification, many in the state ratification conventions complained about the government's power to keep a peacetime army. The standing army, they said, was very dangerous, and a threat to the liberty and freedom of the people. But others responded that the fact that the people would be armed would be their protection against oppression.

Many were concerned that the Constitution did not have a Bill of Rights to protect the rights of the people. The cry for a Bill of Rights became so powerful that the Constitution was ratified only with assurances that a Bill of Rights would be added.

THE SECOND AMENDMENT

When the first Congress of the United States convened on March 4, 1789, James Madison was present as a congressman from Virginia. Although initially opposed to the idea, he was sensitive to the universal desire of the people for a Bill of Rights, and in response he drafted and introduced his proposed amendments. His version of the amendment regarding arms stated, "The right of the people to keep and bear arms shall not be infringed; a well-armed, and well-regulated militia being the best security of a free country; but no person religiously scrupulous of bearing arms, shall be compelled to render military service in person."[9] The amendments were discussed, debated and revised in a committee, in the House, and then in the Senate, to finally yield the present version: "A well regulated Militia, being necessary to the security of a free State, the right of the people to keep and bear Arms, shall not be infringed."

The Senate considered a motion to add the phrase "for the common defense," but rejected this in order to recognize that this was an individual's right to have weapons for his own defense, rather than just for collective defense.[10] In fact, the objective of guaranteeing an individual right to have arms, rather than a collective right, is repeatedly validated in historical evidence in the Constitutional debates, the state constitutions, colonial practice, and even back to the English Bill of Rights in 1689. The American right was even more sweeping than the English one. In the English Bill of Rights, the right to have arms was limited to Protestants, and was given to subjects "suitable to their Conditions and as allowed by Law." The Second Amendment did away with these qualifications, and forbade any *infringement* on the right of the people to keep and bear arms.

Thomas Jefferson recognized the value of being armed when he wrote (quoting Cesare Beccaria)[11] "Laws that forbid the carrying of arms...disarm only those who are neither inclined nor determined to commit crimes.... Such laws make things worse for the assaulted and better for the assailants; they serve rather to encourage than to prevent homicides, for an unarmed man may be attacked with greater confidence than an armed man."[12]

Some have tried to claim that the clause about the militia proves that this amendment was intended to limit ownership of arms to militia members. As the English history indicates, this was not the case at all. The purpose of this phrase was to express the preference for a militia over a standing army. Many were still concerned about the standing army, and this was another chance to reinforce the feeling that the militia had many advantages over the army in peacetime. During the ratification of the Constitution, five states had urged an amendment to restrict the standing army. The language in the Second Amendment stated that it was the militia, not the army that was necessary for the security of a free state. The Philadelphia Federal Gazette newspaper ran an article explaining each of the proposed amendments. It explained this amendment this way: "As civil rulers, not having their duty to the people duly before them, may attempt to tyrannize, and as the military forces which must be occasionally raised to defend our country, might pervert their power to the injury of their fellow-citizens, the people are confirmed . . . in their right to keep and bear their private arms."[13]

CONSENT OF THE GOVERNED

One of the hallmarks of a free people is a government which rules with "the consent of the governed." If a free people don't like what their government is doing, they have the ability to try to change its direction through protests, debate, the courts, actions of the legislature, and elections. If all of these prove ineffective, the people who are armed have the option of armed resistance available as a last resort. This is a truly free people, where the people are in charge of their government and not the other way around. This was well understood and accepted in the eighteenth and nineteenth centuries.

Theodore Sedgwick of Massachusetts thought it impossible that the army could enslave a people "who know how to prize liberty and who have arms in their hands." Noah Webster stated that "before a standing army can rule, the people must be disarmed; as they are in almost every kingdom in Europe."

Michigan jurist Thomas M. Cooley, in his treatise on constitutional law, noted that the purpose of the Second Amendment was to allow the people to provide a check against potential governmental usurpation of power.[14] In The Federalist No. 46, James Madison wrote, "Let a regular army, fully equal to the resources of the country, be formed; and let it be entirely at the devotion of the federal government: still it would not be going too far to say, that the State governments, with the people on their side, would be able to repel the danger." The federal army, he said, could not prevail against "citizens with arms in their hands . . . fighting for their common liberties." We are fortunate to have "the advantage of being armed, which the Americans possess over the people of almost every other nation."[15] Supreme Court Justice Joseph Story wrote:

> The right of the citizens to keep, and bear arms has been justly considered, as the palladium of the liberties of a republic; since it offers a strong moral check against the usurpation and arbitrary power of rulers; and will generally, even if they are successful in the first instance, enable the people to resist, and triumph over them.[16]

Is our government really willing to accept the idea that the people should retain the ultimate authority? And is the government prepared to trust its people? One test of how well any government adheres to those principles is its willingness to allow the people to be armed. Unfortunately, most governments throughout the world are determined to retain all power within the government elite, and do not trust the people enough to allow them to be armed.

ATTACKS ON THE RIGHT TO BEAR ARMS

The Second Amendment stands for the principle that the people should have ultimate authority over their government, and if the time comes when the government is not meeting the needs of the people in a fair and reasonable manner, then it is the right of the people to remove that government and install a new one. The fact that the people are armed gives them a better chance to be able to remove the government if it comes to the point where it is necessary to resort to violence to accomplish that. Naturally, the government does not like the idea of the people violently overthrowing the government, so this sets up a potential conflict of interest. This is especially true in modern times, when our government seems to be no longer focused primarily on serving the people, but instead has as its top priority the perpetuation of its own power and the reelection of its members.

One notable excuse for regulation of guns arose during the prohibition era. The criminal gangs involved in the sale of bootlegged liquor engaged in open warfare with each other in some cities using automatic weapons. The exploits of some famous criminals, such as John Dillinger and George "Machine Gun" Kelly, also got a lot of publicity in the 1930s. These events inspired the National Firearms Act of 1934, which restricted so-called gangster weapons, such as machine guns and sawed-off shotguns. The law did not provide an outright ban on these weapons, since the administration conceded at the time that a ban would probably be unconstitutional.[17]

The gun control advocates finally got enough support in 1968 to pass federal legislation that actually restricted the purchase of several types of firearms. In 1994, Congress enacted a 10 year prohibition on the sale of so-called "assault weapons," which were defined as certain weapons having particular cosmetic features that made the gun look scarier, but did not make it more dangerous. This was evidence of the success of a publicity campaign to stir up public hysteria about guns. This assault weapon ban had no discernible effect in reducing gun violence, and therefore was not renewed in 2004.

The right to bear arms has been diminished in multiple ways through legislation and interpretations by the courts. The "Progressive" political faction that would like to see increased power in the federal government and reduced power for individuals is pushing the assaults on the Second Amendment at every opportunity. Since the Amendment mentions the militia, some have tried to claim that the right described is not an individual right, but is a collective right only as the function of an organized military organization. Under this theory, an individual's right to have arms could be drastically limited without violating the Constitution. As more and more serious scholarship and research was produced on this subject, we began gradually moving toward the recognition that the Second Amendment produced a right for individuals, not a collective right. In 1982, the Senate Judiciary Committee issued a report supporting the individual rights view. Four years later, the federal Firearms Owners Protection Act contained a statement declaring that the Second Amendment was an individual right. In 1989, the prominent Constitutional law scholar and liberal law professor Sanford Levinson published an article supporting the individual rights view. The US Attorney General, in 2004, issued a formal memorandum confirming the individual rights interpretation. This memorandum was notable for its detailed analysis of the history and recent scholarship related to the Second Amendment.[18] Then finally in 2008, in the case of *District of Columbia v. Heller*, the Supreme Court held that the Second Amendment protects an individual's right to have a firearm, unconnected with service in a militia.[19]

Scholarly research has found that guns in the hands of civilians are used much more often to prevent crime than to commit crime.[20] Many lives have been saved by guns used by private citizens. But, in spite of these facts, continued emotion-driven attacks on this right are likely in the future. And any new progressive Supreme Court justice could potentially pose a major threat to this and other rights.

Chapter Five

Search and Seizure
Fourth Amendment

The right of the people to be secure in their persons, houses, papers, and effects, against unreasonable searches and seizures, shall not be violated, and no Warrants shall issue, but upon probable cause, supported by Oath or affirmation, and particularly describing the place to be searched, and the persons or things to be seized.

Fourth Amendment to US Constitution

In colonial America in the 1760s, the British customs officials used a document called a "Writ of Assistance." This was, in effect, a general search warrant, which allowed officials to search a colonist's home or business for smuggled goods. The problem was that these writs were so broad that they allowed agents to search anybody's home anywhere for any reason without any evidence of a crime, and without obtaining a specific warrant. The colonists were very angry about these writs, and considered them a violation of their rights as Englishmen. Some feel that this was a major factor in pushing the colonies toward independence from Great Britain. It was certainly an obvious inspiration for the Fourth Amendment prohibiting unreasonable searches.

The first ten amendments to our Constitution were supposed to be a solid guarantee and protection that our rights would not be violated by the federal government. The authors of our Bill of Rights had lived under the rule of the oppressive British government, and they had personal experience with government abuse. They were determined to give us every possible protection against another potential domineering government. Over the years, however, we have lost our fear of tyrannical government.

The Supreme Court has watered down our rights by one ruling after another, saying that our rights could not be violated *unless there was a good reason to violate them*. This makes a mockery of the concept of "rights," and has led to the severe erosion of those rights. In recent years, we have seen the government moving more and more in the direction of oppression and abuse of power, and we should be more concerned that our rights are fading away. The Fourth Amendment provides a good example of how this process has unfolded.

REASONABLE

The Fourth Amendment requires that a search be "reasonable," and the Supreme Court, at one time, believed that one "governing principle" is that "a search of private property without proper consent is unreasonable unless it has been authorized by a valid search warrant."[1] In order to get a search warrant, the Fourth Amendment required probable cause to suspect criminal activity. This philosophy used to provide a fair degree of protection of our rights. But then the exceptions began to appear.

At one time, the Supreme Court required that, when the police received a tip, there must be some reason to believe the credibility of the informant in order to get a valid warrant. But in the case of *Illinois v. Gates*, the Court relaxed that requirement, and said that a warrant could be issued based on the "totality of the circumstances."[2] Such a vague and ambiguous standard is really no standard at all, and so the police are given a blank check to get a warrant based on little more than a hunch and a feeling.

Somehow the Supreme Court created the idea that owners of commercial property are entitled to receive less constitutional protection than owners of residential property. Then came the "administrative search warrant," which would be issued for a search based on some administrative standard for conducting an inspection, such as a routine inspection of the physical condition of a property. This was claimed to be a "less hostile intrusion" than a policeman's search for criminal evidence, so there was no need for a showing of probable cause that a violation is occurring.[3] Of course, this excuse turned out to be deceitful, for soon the police were using these routine administrative inspections as pretexts for searching for evidence of criminal activity.[4]

In one early Supreme Court case,[5] the Court ruled that the Fourth Amendment requirements for a valid warrant applied only in criminal cases, and did not apply in a civil matter.[6] The

Supreme Court ruled in the case of *Carroll v. United States* that police were allowed to search an automobile without a search warrant.[7] In the case of *Oliver v. United States,* the Court decided that the Fourth Amendment protected your house from unreasonable searches, but not the land around your house.[8] In 1986, the Court decided that the police could fly over your house in a helicopter and look into your fenced back yard, and that did not violate the Fourth Amendment.[9] When you put your trash out for collection, the Fourth Amendment does not prohibit the police from searching through it without a warrant.[10] You are not protected by the Fourth Amendment against searches of any records held by a third party, such as your bank or phone company.[11] The embarrassing and intrusive pat-down searches at airports has been ruled not to be a violation of the Constitution.[12] The government now even has the right to require that a person undergo drug testing, even when there is not even any suspicion of any illegal drug activity.[13]

We can see from all the exceptions and loopholes that the balance has shifted relentlessly toward the government, and away from protecting the rights of citizens. The police have always wanted the right to search cars at random without having to bother with showing probable cause, or even suspicion. The courts have said, however, that police needed at least some specific suspicion before searching an automobile. As you might expect, the police have finally found a way around that requirement. The solution is roadblocks. The police can set up roadblocks which are supposed to be designed to catch people drinking and driving. Once a car is stopped, the police have an opportunity to harass and intimidate any person or group they desire. They can and do use the stop to look for evidence of other crimes. In California, for example, communities have been using sobriety checkpoints to collect large fines and confiscate vehicles for violations which, most of the time, have nothing to do with drunk driving. It's a multi-million-dollar enterprise for local communities.[14]

Another place that probable cause is not required is at the border, or at an airport. Customs officers have the right to search any person or any item at a border. But the US Government has a very flexible definition of "border." For this purpose, the border ostensibly includes all the space up to 100 miles inland from a border or coastline. Border patrol agents can set up checkpoints and operate freely within this area. The ACLU calls this the nation's "Constitution Free Zone," and fully two thirds of Americans live within this zone. For example, such checkpoints are often set up along Interstate 91 near White River Junction,

Vermont, 97 miles south of the border with Quebec. People are frequently caught up in this dragnet, even though they have not crossed a border and had no intention of crossing a border.

The Fourth Amendment guarantee was weakened again when the Supreme Court created the theory that certain "closely regulated" industries were exempt from requirements for a search warrant. Originally, the idea was that businesses that traditionally were subject to extensive regulations should assume that the government would have more power over their activities, and this would justify warrantless searches. Over the years, however, the list of "regulated" industries subject to this exemption has expanded enormously, so that it could apply to almost any business, since all businesses are subject to some government regulation.[15]

The current judicial effort to give the police such broad and arbitrary power to decide if and how to make searches and seizures has encouraged officials to very brazen abuses of their discretion. In one example, a policeman stopped Gail Atwater for violating the seat belt law. Her two small children were also in the car. The policeman could have just given her a citation, but instead he "verbally berated her, handcuffed her, placed her in his squad car, and drove her to the local police station, where she was made to remove her shoes, jewelry, and eyeglasses, and empty her pockets. Officers took her mug shot and placed her, alone, in a jail cell for about an hour."[16]

The Supreme Court refused to rule this unconstitutional. In her dissent to this decision, Supreme Court Justice Sandra Day O'Connor said that Atwater's arrest "was a pointless indignity that served no discernible state interest . . . and yet [the Court] holds that her arrest was constitutionally permissible." Justice O'Connor said that this action

> defies any sense of proportionality and is in serious tension with the Fourth Amendment's proscription of unreasonable seizures . . . Giving police officers constitutional carte blanche to effect an arrest whenever there is probable cause to believe a fine-only misdemeanor has been committed is irreconcilable with the Fourth Amendment's command that seizures be reasonable. . . . Turek [the officer] was loud and accusatory from the moment he approached Atwater's car. Atwater's young children were terrified and hysterical. Yet when Atwater asked Turek to lower his voice because he was scaring

the children, he responded by jabbing his finger in Atwater's face and saying, "You're going to jail" . . . Having made the decision to arrest, Turek did not inform Atwater of her right to remain silent. . . . Atwater asked if she could at least take her children to a friend's house down the street before going to the police station. But Turek—who had just castigated Atwater for not caring for her children—refused and said he would take the children into custody as well. Only the intervention of neighborhood children who had witnessed the scene and summoned one of Atwater's friends saved the children from being hauled to jail with their mother . . . . With respect to the related goal of child welfare, the decision to arrest Atwater was nothing short of counterproductive. Atwater's children witnessed Officer Turek yell at their mother and threaten to take them all into custody. Ultimately, they were forced to leave her behind with Turek, knowing that she was being taken to jail. Understandably, the 3-year-old boy was very, very, very traumatized. After the incident, he had to see a child psychologist regularly, who reported that the boy "felt very guilty that he couldn't stop this horrible thing . . . he was powerless to help his mother or sister." Both of Atwater's children are now terrified at the sight of any police car. . . . Such unbounded discretion [given to the police] carries with it grave potential for abuse.[17]

In the case of *United States v. Sokolow,* the Supreme Court decided that an official may stop and search a person if they have "suspicion" of criminal activity; probable cause is not required.[18] But just how much "suspicion" is required to justify a warrantless search? As it turns out, not very much. Court decisions have approved searches using factors such as location (being in a "high crime area"), time (at night), and the officer's experience. The result is that just about anyone in a "high crime area" is subject to an impromptu search.

Assume a police car stops at a street corner in a poor African American neighborhood. The response of a young African American man standing nearby is to leave the scene. The police might interpret his quick departure as evidence of a guilty conscience, and as justification to pursue and search the man. This would be a very unreasonable action by the police, but this has been upheld in court. It is most likely that the young man fled, not because he was guilty of anything, but because he wanted to avoid the risk of an unfair and unpleasant confrontation with the police, including perhaps a strip search on a public sidewalk.[19] Not only does social science research verify this reality, but Supreme Court Justice John Stevens acknowledged this in a dissent in the case of *Illinois v. Wardlow*, where he said, "Among some citizens, particularly minorities and those residing in high crime areas, there is also the possibility that the fleeing person is entirely innocent, but . . . believes that contact with the police can itself be dangerous."[20]

The Supreme Court has fabricated yet another fantasy to justify warrantless searches. This is called the "consensual search." The theory is that the Fourth Amendment does not require a warrant for an officer to question a person and even request permission to do a search, as long as the encounter remains consensual. Two African American men were on a Greyhound bus when the bus made a scheduled stop at a bus station. The driver got off, and three police officers got on the bus. One stayed in the front of the bus, one stood at the rear of the bus, and the other one began questioning passengers. The police officer asked one of the men for permission to search him for weapons, and the man agreed. During the search, illegal drugs were found, and he was arrested. In court, the man claimed that he did not voluntarily consent to the search. The Supreme Court ruled that his consent was voluntary, because a reasonable person in that situation would have felt free to leave the bus and refuse the officer's request.[21] This is so far removed from reality as to be almost laughable. Most people in this situation would certainly not feel free to refuse the officers. This would especially be true for some minorities or poor people, who have every reason to be intimidated by even the most innocent contact with the police. Even a middle class white man might be hesitant to refuse such a request unless he had his attorney sitting next to him advising him. When an officer says, "May I please see your driver's license," we know that this is not just a request but a command. Even the Eleventh Circuit Court of Appeals in this case recognized that the search was not consensual, but the Supreme Court disagreed, and overruled the appeals court.

In the 2011 case of *Kentucky v. King*, the Supreme Court gave police more leeway to break down the doors of homes and apartments without a warrant. In this case, the excuse was that the police were looking for illegal drugs, which they said they feared might be destroyed by the suspects if the police followed normal procedures. In this specific instance, it actually turned out that the police were at the wrong apartment and found the wrong person, but the Supreme Court still sanctioned the warrantless raid in an 8-1 decision. Justice Ruth Bader Ginsburg was outraged at this travesty, and issued a dissent in which she said, "The warrant requirement . . . ranks among the fundamental distinctions between our form of government, where officers are under the law, and the police-state where they are the law. . . . In no quarter does the Fourth Amendment apply with greater force than in our homes, our most private space which, for centuries, has been regarded as entitled to special protection. . . . Home intrusions, the Court has said, are indeed the chief evil against which . . . the Fourth Amendment is directed. . . . How 'secure' do our homes remain if police, armed with no warrant, can pound on doors at will and . . . forcibly enter?"[22]

The Supreme Court has gradually destroyed the Fourth Amendment's objective, neutral requirement of probable cause by requiring in its place a subjective balancing test. In "weighing" the needs of the state against the rights of the individual, the question of whether a search is "reasonable" is left to a personal value judgment, because there are no longer any objective guidelines. We have long prided ourselves on being a nation of laws administered according to neutral principles, rather than a government of men operating according to their personal feelings. With this balancing test, the Fourth Amendment has been transformed from a rule of law into a rule of subjective opinion.[23]

EXCLUSIONARY RULE

In the 1914 case of *Weeks v. United States*, the Court created a policy which has become known as the Exclusionary Rule.[24] This rule requires that, if a search is declared to be illegal because it violates the Fourth Amendment, then any evidence collected in that search is not allowed to be admitted in court. Most people would think that, if the police did something wrong and violated the Constitution, the proper remedy would be to punish the responsible agency and the officers involved. But now we have the situation where, if the police commit a violation, the way to punish the police is to possibly allow the criminal to go free. Many thought this to be a foolish and dangerous approach. And so the Supreme Court began to carve out a series of "exceptions" to reduce the impact. In 1921, the Court ruled that if evidence was taken illegally by a private person, rather than a government official, then that evidence could be used in court.[25] If evidence was obtained illegally, but the prosecutor was able to convince a judge that that evidence probably would have been discovered eventually by lawful means, then that evidence could still be admitted in court.[26] In the case of *United States v. Leon*, the Court ruled that if a search warrant was defective, but the police acted in good faith thinking that the warrant was valid, then the evidence obtained should not be excluded from trial.[27]

There has been a lot of criticism of the Exclusionary Rule, primarily because it frequently has the effect of letting guilty persons go free. We need another remedy to prevent violations of the Fourth Amendment, and to provide redress for anyone who has suffered an unconstitutional search or seizure. Out of all the possible strategies for addressing this situation, the most attractive one would seem to be an action for damages against the responsible agency. This has been endorsed by Supreme Court Chief Justice Warren Burger and others. This would have several benefits:

- It would offer some measure of deterrence against future violations, because, theoretically, officials would be more careful to comply with the law in order to avoid paying damages.
- It would compensate the victims of a Fourth Amendment violation. This would also have the advantage of providing relief for *innocent* victims of police misconduct. The Exclusionary Rule is of no benefit to these people because, for an innocent person, there is no evidence to be excluded.
- It has an element of proportionality, because the amount of a judgment may be varied to reflect the seriousness of the violation.

In the eighteenth century, the victim of an unlawful search could bring suit against the officials, and have his complaint heard by a jury. If he was successful, he would receive damages. Over the years, though, the effectiveness of this approach has been almost totally destroyed. Through various court rulings and immunities, it has now become extremely difficult to get a judgment against a police officer.[28] It appears that new legislation would be useful which would facilitate this kind of suit, allowing the individual police officer to be punished, and the police department to pay damages. This would have the desired effect of discouraging future infringements.

DIGNITY

The Fourth Amendment has always been understood as an effort to protect the privacy of our homes, papers and person against unreasonable searches and seizures. We have seen that the evolution of Fourth Amendment jurisprudence has made it less and less effective in protecting our personal liberty. So much of our lives is stored on computers, and it has become much easier to access those computers, that our basic concept of privacy has changed. Other advances in technology have given authorities much greater capacity for intrusion, often even without our knowledge. The result is that protection of the limited amount of privacy we have left is no longer adequate to make us feel secure against government incursion on our lives. When the courts are evaluating the reasonableness of a police search, they need to consider another core value in addition to privacy in their analysis. That missing ingredient is human dignity.

Dignity and privacy are two separate values, and should be treated as such. The courts need to start making a serious and formal effort to protect dignity in Fourth Amendment cases. Part of the test of reasonableness must be the degree of the intrusion on an individual's dignity. Searches and seizures that infringe on a person's reasonable expectation of being treated with dignity are unreasonable, and in violation of the Fourth Amendment. There have been rare statements in cases such as *Schmerber v. California*, where the Supreme Court said, "The overriding function of the Fourth Amendment is to protect personal privacy and dignity against unwarranted intrusion by the State."[29] But this needs to be advanced to a consistent, recognized and fully integrated element of the court's analysis.[30] Once the authorities learn that personal dignity is an important element in applying the Fourth Amendment, we may see fewer cases like these:

- In Chicago, a fifteen-year-old boy, accused by an anonymous tipster of having drugs, was taken to a locker room by two security guards, a Chicago police officer, and a female assistant principal, and made to stand against a wall and drop his pants while one of the security guards inspected his genitals. No drugs were found.
- In the case of *Florence v. Board of Chosen Freeholders*, the Supreme Court ruled that a person arrested for a minor traffic offense could be subjected to an embarrassing, humiliating, and dehumanizing strip

search. In his dissent, Justice Stephen Breyer said, "In my view, such a search of an individual arrested for a minor offense that does not involve drugs or violence— say a traffic offense, a regulatory offense, an essentially civil matter, or any other such misdemeanor—is an unreasonable search forbidden by the Fourth Amendment, unless prison authorities have reasonable suspicion to believe that the individual possesses drugs or other contraband."[31]

- Sixty-nine-year-old Gerald Dickson was handcuffed and taken into custody after giving a ride to a neighbor's son, who police suspected of being a drug dealer. Despite Dickson's insistence that the bulge under his shirt was the result of a botched hernia surgery, police ordered Dickson to "strip off his clothes, bend over and expose all of his private parts." No drugs or contraband were found.

SUSPICIOUS ACTIVITY

It is normal for law enforcement agencies to maintain files of information on criminals and criminal suspects. But sometimes the police will collect the personal data of innocent people, and put it into criminal intelligence files, with little or no evidence of wrongdoing. As police records become more automated, and there is more effort to share information among different agencies, this information can easily end up in federal intelligence databases.

This situation is made even worse because the federal government is now encouraging various law enforcement agencies (federal, state and local), as well as the general public, to report to authorities anyone engaging in activities which could be considered "suspicious." Many agencies have developed formal programs to facilitate their Suspicious Activity Reporting (SAR) programs. They have even developed lists of "suspicious" activities that should be reported. The problem is that some of the activities included in these guidelines are perfectly innocent activities, having no connection to criminal activity, such as taking pictures, making sketches, taking notes, purchasing flashlights, using binoculars, and espousing extreme views. Not only does creating these files of innocent people involve serious privacy and civil liberties concerns, but it is actually counterproductive. Intelligence agencies are inundated with thousands and thousands of these useless reports which take up time they should use to evaluate the more serious information which might point to possible illegal activity. This is also one avenue whereby an innocent person's name could end up on one of the government's terrorist watch lists, causing him endless problems in his normal daily activities, and from which he has very little recourse.

Another way for a person to have the government label them as "suspicious" is to make a cash deposit or withdrawal at his bank. If a person makes a cash deposit above a certain amount, the bank is required to file a Currency Transaction Report with the government. Even if the transaction is absolutely legal, the government has been alerted to a "suspicious" deposit, and who knows what kind of inquiry, investigation, questioning, or harassment this might trigger. The Bank Secrecy Act requires this kind of reporting, and also gives the government access to a person's financial records at his bank. Many people feel that this violates the Fourth Amendment, including Supreme Court Justice William Douglas, who said, "One's bank accounts are within the 'expectations of privacy' category. For they mirror not only one's finances but his interests, his debts, his way of life, his family, and his civic commitments. . . . Delivery of the records without the requisite hearing of probable cause breaches the Fourth Amendment."[32]

SURVEILLANCE

The Foreign Intelligence Surveillance Act (FISA) was enacted in 1978. This law was intended to increase the judicial and congressional oversight of surveillance by US agencies. It established the Foreign Intelligence Surveillance Court, which was authorized to hold secret hearings to issue secret warrants for surveillance activities. This sounds like a good idea—to have a judicial body review the government's request to insure that an individual's rights are not being violated. Unfortunately, you can't depend on this court to protect your rights. That is because the FISA Court does not operate like the normal courts we are used to.

- First, its operations are entirely secret. Its proceedings are not public. Its rulings are not made public. Therefore, no one can evaluate the fairness of its actions. If a person's records are acquired, the holder of those records is not allowed to disclose the fact that those records were provided to the government. All of this excessive secrecy even makes congressional oversight difficult, and in many cases ineffective.

- Second, the proceedings are not adversarial. Only one side of the case (the government's side) is presented to the court. There is no one there to argue for the person being scrutinized and to make sure that his rights are protected. Does this sound like the deck is stacked against mister average citizen? Many people say that the FISA Court is little more than a rubber stamp for the intelligence community to do whatever it wants. We need to insist on more openness and transparency in this whole process.

In the atmosphere of fear and panic following the attacks of September 11, 2001, Congress also hurriedly passed the USA PATRIOT Act, which allows the government to monitor your e-mails, financial records, medical records, internet activity, and library records. All parts of the process are shrouded in secrecy. Many of its provisions were powers which had previously been requested by law enforcement agencies, but which Congress had refused to enact due to concerns about civil liberties. This law significantly increased the surveillance and investigative powers of law enforcement agencies, but did not provide the traditional checks and balances to protect personal freedom. This bill was introduced with great haste and passed with little debate, and without a House, Senate, or conference report. As a result, it lacks the typical very informative legislative history which accompanies most bills. Some congressmen wanted to take the time to incorporate some improvements and safeguards into the bill, but the Attorney General warned that further terrorist acts were imminent, and that Congress could be to blame for such attacks if it failed to pass the bill immediately

John Podesta, former White House Chief of Staff, expressed his concerns about possible abuses of this legislation when he observed that "many aspects of the bill increase the opportunity for law enforcement and the intelligence community to return to an era where they monitored and sometimes harassed individuals who were merely exercising their First Amendment rights. Nothing that occurred on September 11 mandates that we return to such an era."[33] After many years of experience with the PATRIOT Act, Senator Ron Wyden of Oregon complained that while there are many different interpretations of how the PATRIOT Act works, the official government interpretation of the law remains classified. "There is a gap between what the public thinks the law says and what the government secretly thinks the law says," Wyden said.[34]

Under this law, the FBI is authorized to request a secret court order "requiring the production of any tangible things" (including books, business records, medical records, educational records, library records, personal documents, and other items). The radical departure from previous practice is that there is no requirement to show "probable cause" that a crime has been committed, or that the items sought are evidence of a crime. Instead, the government only needs to claim that the records may be related to an investigation. The people targeted do not have to have any link to a terrorist organization, or be suspected of being terrorists. And whoever is served with this warrant requiring the records is not allowed to disclose, under penalty of law, the existence of the warrant, or the fact that records were provided to the government. So if your doctor is forced to give your medical records to the government, your doctor is not allowed to even tell you that he gave them your records.

The PATRIOT Act also lowered the standards for National Security Letters. Using these documents, the FBI can secretly demand a variety of records without even bothering to get a court order. And the holder of the records is not allowed to disclose this action to anyone. This could allow the FBI to compile vast dossiers of sensitive information about innocent people. Not surprisingly, many abuses of National Security Letters have been documented.[35]

A so-called "sneak-and-peek" warrant allows law enforcement to enter and search a suspect's house without notifying the subject. A large majority of the times this authority has been used, the purpose of the raid had nothing to do with terrorism, but was for other issues.

The official definition of terrorism was greatly expanded by the PATRIOT Act, so that many domestic groups that engage in certain types of civil disobedience could very well find themselves labeled as terrorists. This law also allows the government to seize the assets of an individual or organization without prior notice or hearing, if the government says that they are planning an act of "domestic terrorism." Using this power, the government could effectively bankrupt an organization with which it disagrees. Some of the PATRIOT ACT expired in 2015, but most of it was renewed by the USA FREEDOM ACT.

The National Security Agency (NSA) has been monitoring and collecting massive amounts of data about innocent

Americans, including telephone records, e-mails, telephone calls, and other forms of communications. In fact they are accumulating so much information, they had to build an enormous new data center in Utah just to store all the data. Does all this spying on ordinary citizens violate the Fourth Amendment which is supposed to protect us against unreasonable searches? Of course it does. But, as we have seen before, when the government wants to do something, it will find all manner of excuses why it is okay "just this one time" to violate some of our rights.

Much of this extensive spying can be done without showing probable cause, and without getting a search warrant. The person being monitored does not even have to be suspected of any wrongdoing. All that is necessary is that someone in the government thinks that his information might be "relevant."

Telecommunications and internet companies are collaborating with the government in this massive collection of information. Some of the major telecommunications switching facilities have secret monitoring rooms, controlled by the NSA, where the agency taps into the communications networks. In fact, the FISA Amendments Act of 2008 gave private companies immunity from legal action when they cooperate in these efforts.

Another type of data is collected by mobile phone networks: they register a phone's location continuously as long as it's turned on, even when it is not in use. It has become very common for law enforcement agencies to obtain this data from the phone companies, which they can do without a search warrant. These records can be extremely enlightening. They can reveal, for example, if a person went to a pro-life rally or a fundraiser for a conservative politician, or just how many times he went to church. Just think how valuable this information would be to an administration that is putting together an enemies list.

On March 12, 2013, the US Director of National Intelligence, James Clapper, testified before the Senate Select Committee on Intelligence that the NSA does not wittingly collect any type of data on millions of Americans. Clapper later admitted the statement was false. On June 8, 2013, Clapper released a fact sheet providing information about the program. Senators Mark Udall and Ron Wyden subsequently criticized the fact sheet as being inaccurate, and NSA Director Keith Alexander acknowledged the problems, and the fact sheet was withdrawn from the NSA's website.

The arrogance of the government in being willing to ignore our Fourth Amendment rights is illustrated by some internal memos generated by John C. Yoo, in the office of the Attorney

General. After the attacks of September 11, 2001, he wrote that "the government may be justified in taking measures which in less troubled conditions could be seen as infringements of individual liberties." He also said, "It appears clear that the Fourth Amendment's warrant requirement does not apply to surveillance and searches undertaken to protect the national security from external threats." In another memo he wrote "Our office recently concluded that the Fourth Amendment had no application to domestic military operations."[36]

All this is certain to have a chilling effect on public discourse. As constitutional attorney John Whitehead reminds us, "When citizens—especially those espousing unpopular viewpoints—are aware that the intimate details of their personal lives are pervasively monitored by government, or even that they could be singled out for discriminatory treatment by government officials as a result of their First Amendment expressive activities, they are less likely to freely express their dissident views."[37] If people think that their conversations and their e-mails and their reading habits are being monitored, they will feel less comfortable saying what they think, especially if what they think is not what the government wants them to think.

As if the intrusive searches at airports weren't bad enough, now teams are fanning out all over the country to do random security sweeps at bus stations, train stations, concerts, and other locations. Even though there is no specific threat, people are being patted down, and luggage and vehicles are being searched. What is accomplished by these random warrantless searches? This scattershot effort is certainly not likely to catch many terrorists. But what it will do is to inculcate and condition citizens to a culture of submissiveness towards authority, and regularize intrusive, suspicionless searches as a facet of everyday life. We are being taught to accept this normalization of police state tactics so that government agents are permitted to trample Americans' constitutional rights with impunity. We are all suspects now. The government sees ordinary citizens as the enemy. No government that truly respects or values its citizens would subject them to such intrusive, dehumanizing, demoralizing, suspicionless searches. The TSA's motto, posted at its air marshal training center, tells a lot: "Dominate. Intimidate. Control."[38]

Of course, all this is being done in the name of "national security." It has long been known that ignorant and frightened citizens will be willing to give up some of their liberty in exchange for a questionable promise of a little more security. And that is being exploited to the fullest. We are also used to the idea that a president might need expanded powers during a war to be able to deal with the emergency. We are now told that we are in a "war on terrorism," and we should be willing to give the government more power so they can deal with this temporary emergency. But as we learn more about this "war," it looks like this may be a more or less permanent "war" without end. Therefore, the government's "temporary emergency" powers are looking more and more like they might be an unending expansion of powers. This is not looking good.

Another frightening result of all this secret surveillance is that the names of many innocent Americans end up on bloated and inaccurate watch lists—lists of people supposedly thought to pose a danger to the country. We are not told that our name is on such a list, and we do not have an effective way to make inquiries, or to challenge the information. As a result, a person may someday find himself the subject of unusually intensive scrutiny at an airport, and not know why. Someone whose name is on one of these lists may have trouble opening a bank account or getting a loan or numerous other things. Part of the background check run on some job applicants involves checking the name against one of these terrorist watch lists. The potential for harm being done to innocent persons is mind boggling. And the actual experiences of real people have shown that this does happen many times.

Does anyone doubt that the government would use these powers to attack its political opponents? There is no question about that, because it has been done over and over again. In the Nixon, Clinton and Obama administrations, major scandals arose upon disclosure that the government had improperly used FBI and IRS capabilities against people and groups that disagreed with the president. According to a US Senate committee, the government conducted surveillance of hundreds of thousands of Americans, and "permitted, and sometimes encouraged, government agencies to handle essentially political intelligence."[39]

We now have to live in fear that if we express any disagreement with the administration—a letter to the newspaper, a donation to an opposition candidate, or attending a rally—the government may try to punish us in some way. Remember what President Obama said, shortly before the 2010 midterm elections, "We're gonna punish our enemies, and we're gonna reward our friends."[40] This is not America the land of liberty. It seems more like some kind of oppressive totalitarian dictatorship. It is absolutely dangerous and foolish to give the government this much power to abuse our rights. Our liberty is much too valuable to allow it to be taken away in exchange for the hope of a little additional security.

We are reminded of the words of former Justice Department Counsel John Lord O'Brian, who wrote that one of the principal dangers to democracy is the "craving for security at any price." He also warned that violations of our liberties are made possible by the creation of an "atmosphere of unreasoning fear," an atmosphere generated, nurtured and "seized upon by unscrupulous politicians" for partisan ends.[41]

Supreme Court Justice William Douglas expressed his concern in this way: "The privacy and dignity of our citizens is being whittled away by sometimes imperceptible steps. Taken individually, each step may be of little consequence. But when viewed as a whole, there begins to emerge a society quite unlike any we have seen—a society in which government may intrude into the secret regions of man's life at will."[42]

We need to remember that the Supreme Court itself said that the "basic purpose of this Amendment, as recognized in countless decisions of this Court, is to safeguard the privacy and security of individuals against arbitrary invasions by government officials."[43]

Chapter Six

Fifth Amendment

No person shall be held to answer for a capital, or otherwise infamous crime, unless on a presentment or indictment of a Grand Jury, except in cases arising in the land or naval forces, or in the Militia, when in actual service in time of War or public danger; nor shall any person be subject for the same offence to be twice put in jeopardy of life or limb; nor shall be compelled in any criminal case to be a witness against himself, nor be deprived of life, liberty, or property, without due process of law; nor shall private property be taken for public use, without just compensation.

Fifth Amendment to US Constitution

DOUBLE JEOPARDY

The Supreme Court has explained that "the constitutional prohibition against double jeopardy was designed to protect an individual from being subjected to the hazards of trial and possible conviction more than once for an alleged offense. . . . The underlying idea, one that is deeply ingrained in at least the Anglo-American system of jurisprudence, is that the State, with all its resources and power, should not be allowed to make repeated attempts to convict an individual for an alleged offense, thereby subjecting him to embarrassment, expense and ordeal and compelling him to live in a continuing state of anxiety and insecurity, as well as enhancing the possibility that, even though innocent, he may be found guilty. In accordance with this philosophy, it has long been settled under the Fifth Amendment that a verdict of acquittal is final, ending a defendant's jeopardy, and, even when not followed by any judgment, is a bar to a subsequent prosecution for the same offence."[1]

The exact origins of this concept are unclear, but it is certainly one which has a long history. Supreme Court Justice

Hugo Black wrote: "Fear and abhorrence of governmental power to try people twice for the same conduct is one of the oldest ideas found in western civilization. Its roots run deep into Greek and Roman times."[2] The General Court of the Massachusetts Bay Colony, in 1641, enacted the "Body of Liberties." Paragraph 42 of this document stated that "no man shall be twise sentenced by Civill Justice for one and the same Crime, offence, or Trespasse." Connecticut also adopted a similar provision in 1652. After the Revolutionary War, the state of New Hampshire, in its constitution of 1784, provided that "no subject shall be liable to be tried, after an acquittal, for the same crime or offence." Before the Bill of Rights was added to the Constitution, all thirteen states had adopted guarantees against double jeopardy in their state constitutions.

The language in the Fifth Amendment states that this applies when a person is "put in jeopardy of life or limb." The courts, however, have settled on the interpretation that this protection applies to any criminal prosecution, not just where capital punishment is a possibility.

Even though the Supreme Court claims to consider the right against double jeopardy "fundamental," there is a serious weakness in its application. The Supreme Court has ruled that a person could be tried and acquitted of a crime in a state court, and then that person could be tried again, based on the same act, in a federal court. This is based on the "dual sovereignty" doctrine, which states that since the state government and the federal government are separate sovereigns, with separate laws, then the same action produced two different offenses (state and federal), and so the person was not being tried twice for the "same" offense. Technically, perhaps there is some perverted logic to this argument, but the practical effect is that an individual is being tried twice for the same act. This is what the Fifth Amendment was trying to prevent.

This issue did not arise very often before the twentieth century because Congress had not created many criminal offenses. But in the last few decades, there has been an explosion of federal criminal law which, in many cases, overlaps with state law covering the same subject. As a result, many more defendants now potentially face successive state and federal prosecutions for the same act.

Although not in the majority, some Supreme Court Justices have disagreed with this philosophy. Justice John McLean wrote that "There is no principle better established by the common law—none more fully recognized in the federal and state constitutions—than that an individual shall not be put in jeopardy twice for the same offense. This, it is true, applies to the respective governments, but its spirit applies with equal force against a double punishment for the same act by a state and the federal government."[3] He also said that "it is no satisfactory answer to this to say that the states and federal government constitute different sovereignties, and consequently may each punish offenders under its own laws. It is true the criminal laws of the federal and state governments emanate from different sovereignties, but they operate upon the same people, and should have the same end in view."[4]

Justice Hugo Black stated that "the Court apparently takes the position that a second trial for the same act is somehow less offensive if one of the trials is conducted by the Federal Government and the other by a State. Looked at from the standpoint of the individual who is being prosecuted, this notion is too subtle for me to grasp. If double punishment is what is feared, it hurts no less for two Sovereigns to inflict it than for one."[5] Another factor that shows the indefensibility of the dual sovereignty concept is the fact that when the two sovereigns are a city and state government, the Supreme Court has agreed that only one prosecution is permitted for a single act.[6]

Much of our legal heritage was based on English law, so it is interesting to note that people were protected against double jeopardy under English common law. An English subject did not lose this protection just because there were two separate sovereigns involved. If a person had already been tried for a crime in France, for example, then English law would not allow him to be tried again for the same crime in England. So the American dual sovereignty approach to double jeopardy is at odds with the longstanding English common law. In fact, most free countries have accepted a prior conviction elsewhere as a bar to a second trial in their jurisdiction.[7]

The explosion of federal criminal laws in recent history makes this problem even more severe. This was recognized by Guido Calabresi, senior judge on the US Court of Appeals for the Second Circuit, and the former Dean of Yale Law School, when he wrote in 1995:

> Since its very first application in Lanza, the dual sovereignty doctrine has been strongly criticized. . . . These criticisms, echoed and supplemented by more recent ones, have emphasized both the doctrine's weakness from an originalist point of view and its

jurisprudential flaws. Thus, the doctrine has been called unfaithful to the Fifth Amendment's historical roots . . . When *Bartkus* and *Abbate* were decided in 1959, the scope of federal criminal law was still very narrow, and the overlap of federal and state criminal jurisdiction was quite small. The risk to individual rights posed by successive prosecutions by state and federal officials was therefore necessarily limited. . . . In recent years, however, the scope of federal criminal law has expanded enormously. And the number of crimes for which a defendant may be made subject to both a state and a federal prosecution has become very large. . . . It follows that today defendants in an enormous number of cases can be subjected to dual prosecutions. . . . [P]ermitting successive state-federal prosecutions for the same act appears inconsistent with what is a most ancient principle in western jurisprudence—that the government may not twice place a person in jeopardy for the same offense.[8]

One way for this unfairness to be corrected would be for the Supreme Court to revise its interpretation to protect an individual against dual prosecutions in federal and state courts. Since this seems unlikely, another avenue would be the legislative remedy. A federal law would provide that no federal case should be tried when there has already been a state prosecution for substantially the same act. Corresponding legislation at the state level has already been adopted by several states. One example is Alaska's law, which states, "When an act charged is within the jurisdiction of the United States, another State, or a territory, as well as of this State, a conviction or acquittal in the former is a bar to the prosecution for it in this state."

Some people argue for allowing both federal and state prosecutions based on the idea that sometimes the result of a state trial may not seem "fair." A good example is the trial of the Los Angeles police officers accused of beating Rodney King. A jury acquitted the officers in the state trial. The federal government did not like that verdict, and so the officers were tried again in federal court. A state cannot always be trusted to provide perfect justice, the argument goes, so the federal government needs the power to step in and produce what it thinks is a "correct" verdict. This is based on the assumption that the people in the federal government are always smarter than the people in state government, which is very questionable. The basic premise of this book is that the federal government has grown too large and powerful, and a new balance needs to be restored. This leads to the conclusion that the individual deserves complete protection against double jeopardy, and two trials for the same action, whether by two states or by state and federal, should be prohibited.

WITNESS AGAINST HIMSELF

John Lambert may have been one of the first on record to claim the right against self-incrimination in an English court. Lambert was on trial for heresy in 1532 when he argued that it was illegal to force a man to accuse himself. He may have been inspired by the very influential writings of William Tyndale, who was the first to translate the New Testament into English. In his English Bible, which was first printed in 1525, he commented that "neither ought a judge to compel a man to swear against himself . . ."[9] Actually, this concept appeared centuries earlier in the Talmud, which is the ancient Jewish law, based on the first five books of the Bible. The Talmudic criminal procedure provided that "no one can incriminate himself."[10]

Soon, the refusal on the part of suspected heretics to accuse themselves became more commonplace, and this gradually became more widely accepted in the legal community. Sir Anthony Fitzherbert's manual for justices of the peace, published in 1583, stated that the law assumes that no man is obliged to accuse himself. William Lambard wrote the very popular book *Eirenarcha: or of the Office of the Justices of Peace*, which became a standard legal text. The second edition of this book, published in 1588, restated this concept, spreading the word to every lawyer in England.[11] In their zeal to ferret out heretics and Catholics, however, Parliament was slow to incorporate this "right" into their statutes. An act of 1593, for example, provided that any person suspected of being a Jesuit or priest, and on examination refused to answer whether he is a Jesuit or priest, should be imprisoned without bail until he did answer.[12]

The right against self-incrimination in England struggled for recognition for many years. A most remarkable man then appeared on the scene. In 1637, a young man named John Lilburne was arrested for printing and circulating unlicensed books. He was only twenty-three years old, but he proved to be a skilled and flamboyant advocate for the fundamentals of liberty. He had an incomparable ability to dramatize himself and his cause. He was a master of the arts of propaganda, and he produced a flurry of brilliant political pamphlets, even while he was in prison. During his multiple trials, he could debate and argue with the judges in a most persuasive manner.

Lilburne paid dearly for his principles—he spent most of his adult years in prison. Yet he was so successful at inspiring his followers that he was recognized as the primary and most effective leader in the fight for the right against self-incrimination. After his lifelong crusade, this right was an established, respected rule of English law. The book *Examen Legum Angliae: Or, The Laws of England Examined*, published in 1656, affirmed that a man was not obliged "to confess the truth against himself."[13]

The right against self-incrimination was one of the rights the American colonies borrowed from the English common law. Not only is it enshrined in our Bill of Rights, but most of the state constitutions also have some version of this right. The Fifth Amendment says that "no person . . . shall be compelled in any Criminal Case to be a witness against himself." That sounds pretty clear, but just like with so many of our rights, the Supreme Court has found a way to say that it doesn't actually mean what it says. The Court has decided that, well maybe sometimes a person CAN be compelled to be a witness against himself. This could happen if the Court thinks that the State's desire to find a more efficient way to gather evidence in a criminal case is more important than a citizen's constitutional rights. It's the old balancing test again.

The government can force a person to testify against himself if they offer to give him a limited form of immunity.[14] They have to agree that his testimony will not be used directly or indirectly in criminal prosecutions against him. The Supreme Court justifies this by pretending that this is just as good as if this person exercised his Fifth Amendment right to keep silent. Of course, the problem is that this is NOT just as good as if a person remained silent. There are several reasons why this represents a serious reduction in a person's protection and liberty:

- Once the prosecutors have a person's incriminating testimony, who knows what benefit this might be to help them in making a case against him? This might provide different leads to follow, or people to interview, that they did not know about previously. If they do decide to prosecute this person, the government will say that their evidence was discovered independently, without use of the testimony. And how would the defendant ever prove that

that was not true? Supreme Court Justices Douglas and Marshall understood this, and stated in dissenting opinions that at the very least, the prosecutors should be required to agree that they will never prosecute the person for that crime.[15]

- If a person is compelled to give incriminating testimony in a state court, in exchange for immunity from prosecution, that immunity is only good in the courts of that particular state. That testimony could still be used as a basis for prosecution in a federal court. Likewise, immunity in the federal courts does not protect a person from prosecution in a state court.

- Even if this immunity reduces the possibility of criminal prosecution, it does not remove the penalty of infamy. After his compelled incriminating testimony, the witness may suffer disfavor among his friends and neighbors, ostracization, disgrace, and embarrassment. In fact, throughout history, infamy has been considered to be punishment as effective as fine and imprisonment.

- When a person's past questionable behavior becomes public knowledge, he might suffer other, more subtle penalties, such as difficulty getting a job, a bank loan, a scholarship, etc. At one time, people were forced to testify whether they belonged to the Communist Party. Once it was known that they did, federal law made them ineligible for employment in the federal government and in defense plants.

- Justice Douglas protested that immunity did not protect a person's "conscience and human dignity and freedom of expression."[16] Justice Field argued that there is an "essential and inherent cruelty" in forcing self-accusation.[17]

The right not to be a "witness against himself" used to apply to the self-production of any adverse evidence that would cause disgrace or embarrassment. This understanding was illustrated by a case in Pennsylvania. The Pennsylvania constitution contained a similar protection against a man being compelled to give evidence against himself. In the first case involving this clause, the state Supreme Court in 1802 ruled that this protection would not be "confined to cases where the answers to the questions proposed would induce to the punishment of the party. If they would involve him in shame or reproach, he is under no obligation to answer them."[18] In a New York case, *People v Herrick*

(1816), the court ruled that "It is against a fundamental principle, that a party shall accuse himself, and propagate to the remotest period his own infamy." Over the years, however, the courts have gradually whittled away at this right, and now courts will generally not allow a witness to refuse to testify due to infamy.

The right against self-incrimination has been destroyed in many areas of our modern environmental law. In this field, it could be a crime not to report a crime. The information that the EPA and other authorities use comes almost entirely from self-reporting requirements. Elaborate environmental regulatory systems include extensive reporting and recordkeeping requirements. Whenever a regulation is violated, those responsible are required to reveal their identities. Should a business executive fail to confess regulatory violations in a timely manner, the penalties for that failure can be quite serious. Ordinary criminal suspects enjoy the constitutional option of remaining silent during an official inquiry, but environmental criminal suspects have no choice but to cooperate with regulators in their investigations. The EPA, for example, has the authority to subpoena any report, paper, or document desired. The EPA can even subpoena answers to questions. Such prosecutorial powers are unheard of outside of the regulatory context.[19]

What could be done to restore the Fifth Amendment protection to suspected polluters? In general, the reporting requirements are valuable, so that spills and industrial accidents can be reported without delay. This allows cleanup operations to begin, and quick public dissemination of this information could reduce injuries. But the Fifth Amendment should prevent the government from criminally prosecuting an individual or company for something it reports. The laws must be rewritten to include this protection, and the courts must recognize this defense in their analyses.

Giving prosecutorial immunity to polluters does not mean that they will escape the consequences of their actions. The government would still be able to pursue an irresponsible polluter for cleanup costs under civil law. And anyone who is harmed by pollution would also be able to sue polluters for damages. So there is no conflict between the privilege against self-incrimination and workable environmental policies.[20]

The courts have gradually become more and more skeptical about confessions induced by coercion, threats and promises. The Supreme Court made an effort to ensure that any statement was entirely voluntary by ruling, in 1966, that before the police could interrogate a suspect, they had to clearly inform him that he had the right to remain silent and to have an attorney present during questioning.[21] This became the famous "Miranda warning," which has now become a routine part of everyday police procedure. This was certainly a giant step forward in protecting the rights of suspects against abusive and aggressive interrogation techniques used by the police. However, as with many of our rights, the courts have, over time, created many exceptions and conditions and loopholes that compromise the right to remain silent. For example:

- If the police tell a person that he has "the right to remain silent," he would typically understand that he has a constitutional right to remain silent so he does not have to say anything to the police. However, if he does simply remain silent, the Supreme Court has ruled that he will not have that protection, and the police are allowed to continue to threaten, abuse, and bribe him to try to provoke a statement. For him to take advantage of his Fifth Amendment protection, he has to know the right words to say. He cannot just remain silent, but he has to actually state that he wants to invoke his right to silence. An ignorant or confused person may not think to do this, and may be taken advantage of by unscrupulous police interrogators. Supreme Court Justice Sonia Sotomayor recognized the unfairness of this policy of construing "ambiguity in favor of the police." This ruling, she said, "invites police to question a suspect at length—notwithstanding his persistent refusal to answer questions."[22]
- The requirement for a Miranda warning does not apply unless a person is in "custody." Of course, this is a legal term, the subtleties of which will not be obvious to a layman. It does not apply, for example, when a policeman stops a person on the street for questioning, or when a person is stopped for a traffic violation. The courts have shown such flexibility in defining this term that an inmate in prison is not considered in "custody," and, therefore, is not entitled to the Miranda warning.[23]
- A person in jail talking to an undercover police officer is not entitled to a Miranda warning.[24]

Most people find it hard to believe that anyone would admit to a crime that he did not commit. Yet this happens all too often, usually under the stress of police interrogation. Many times the victims are children, the mentally ill or retarded, and people under the influence of drugs or liquor. But frequently mature adults of normal intelligence also can be led into false confessions. Many people are susceptible to suggestion, eager to please authority figures, desperate to end the unpleasant stress of aggressive questioning, easily confused, disconnected from reality, or unable to defer gratification. Ignorance of the law and of constitutional rights is a factor in many cases, as is fear of violence, the threat of a harsh sentence, and just misunderstanding the situation.

The Innocence Project[25] is doing some great work in reversing unlawful convictions. In one tabulation of 271 convictions reversed through their efforts, false confessions figured in about 20 percent of those cases. In these specific situations, the conviction occurred years after the Miranda warning was required, so it has not stopped false confessions. Even when the Miranda warning is read to a suspect, the police are very skilled at convincing a suspect to waive his right to remain silent. Formal training programs teach police to use manipulation and trickery to keep a suspect talking. During questioning, the police themselves are permitted to lie by pretending to have evidence or eyewitnesses, or by denying that the interview is being recorded. Experiments have shown that adults who are told convincing fictions have sometimes actually had doubts about their own memories. A large majority of those who are not guilty will sign the Miranda waiver and keep talking in the belief that their refusal would look suspicious, and that their innocence will free them.

Even when a confession contains inconsistencies, or sounds suspicious, juries and judges are still inclined to accept the confession. They just don't want to believe that a person would confess to a crime that he didn't commit. Another problem with a false confession is that it influences the police and prosecutors. Once they have a confession, they tend to treat it as a fact, and it colors their interpretation of the evidence, leading them to discredit anything that points away from that suspect. Police typically close the investigation and make no effort to pursue other possible leads, even if the confession is filled with errors and contradictions.

Coercion and intimidation by the police used to be frowned upon. In a case in 1897, the Supreme Court said that a confession "must not be extracted by any sort of threats or violence, nor obtained by any direct or implied promises, however slight. . . . Any doubt as to whether the confession was voluntary must be determined in favor of the accused."[26] Since that time, however, courts have largely disregarded that opinion, giving police more and more leeway. Finally, in 1991[27] the Court explicitly stated that such a stringent test was no longer required.[28]

Given the surprising number of innocent people sent to prison where false confessions were a factor, some changes in procedures would certainly be justified to reduce this number. These would move our justice system closer to the ideal goal of obtaining the truth, rather than just trying to obtain a conviction:

- Police should be prohibited from lying to suspects by pretending to have evidence that doesn't exist.
- Return to the 1897 standard against getting confessions through threats or promises.
- No child should be questioned without a parent and a lawyer present.
- The entire interrogation must be videotaped from beginning to end. Many jurisdictions have already adopted this policy, with favorable results.
- Confessions must be backed solidly by independent evidence. Some states have recognized the wisdom of this policy, and have required "corroborating" evidence for a conviction. This requirement needs to be made universal.
- Post-conviction appeals and challenges to confessions should be assigned to different prosecutors and judges. The original prosecutors are normal human beings, not eager to admit to their mistakes. They are naturally going to be hesitant to concede that they put the wrong person behind bars.[29]

TAKING

Property rights have always been considered very important in English and American legal thinking. The free ownership and use of property was considered indispensable for both liberty and economic growth. So our Constitution and Bill of Rights contain important provisions designed to restrain legislative incursions on property rights. Of course, these rights, like all of our rights, are at the mercy of the whims of the Supreme Court. And the Court has had a very uneven record of protection for property rights. In the 1930s, some of the New Deal legislation that was upheld by the Supreme Court marked an enormous expansion of government power at the expense of property rights.

An important protection for property rights is the "Takings Clause" of the Fifth Amendment, which says, "nor shall private property be taken for public use, without just compensation." For many years, this was interpreted using common sense and plain English to mean that

- The government could take your property if it needed it for some public use, such as a school or highway. It could not take your property just to give it to a developer who might someday pay higher property taxes.
- If the government did need your property for some public use, it had to pay you a fair price for that property.

The Supreme Court recognized this meaning, and in 1798 wrote that "a law that takes property from A and gives it to B" would be void because such a law would be a "flagrant abuse of legislative power . . . against all reason and justice."[30] Somehow, though, this common sense interpretation has been abandoned, and the Supreme Court now is not willing to protect our property rights against the aggressive efforts of some state and local authorities, who would be willing to sacrifice the rights of their citizens in exchange for some benefit for their city. A city might want to take property away from one private owner and give it to a different private owner who the city thinks might create a more desirable development, or one which would pay more in property taxes. One excuse that is sometimes used for this confiscation is "blight." A property may not actually be blighted, but the city could claim that it is in order to justify condemnation. This has happened frequently. One example is the Five Points district in Denver, where 246 properties were declared blighted, including some well-maintained Victorian homes. The city had commissioned a blight study, which admitted that there were very few building code violations, but identified a small number of properties with some defects, and used this to justify condemnation of an entire neighborhood.

Another blatant example of this abuse was in the case of *Kelo v. City of New London* (2005), where the Supreme Court upheld a city development plan under which land acquired from residents by eminent domain would be transferred to private parties for the construction of new homes and stores.[31] The motivation of the city was the hope of increased tax revenue from the new projects. Dissenting Justice Sandra Day O'Connor objected that "Under the banner of economic development all private property is now vulnerable to being taken and transferred to another private owner." Justice Clarence Thomas, in a separate dissent, complained that "I do not believe that this Court can eliminate liberties expressly enumerated in the Constitution. . . . In my view, the Public Use Clause, originally understood, is a meaningful limit on the government's eminent domain power. Our cases have strayed from the Clause's original meaning."

In a New York case where the housing authority wanted to acquire land to build a low income housing project, the Court of Appeals decided that this was a "public use" because it benefited the public. The court said "The law of each age is ultimately what that age thinks should be the law."[32] This is a frightening, but all too common, attitude.

Until the Supreme Court can be forced to return to respecting the Constitution, the only remedy might be for states to revise and interpret their own statutes and constitutions to provide greater protection for property rights. And some states have made efforts to do just that. For example, in 2004 the Supreme Court of Michigan refused to allow the condemnation of property for transfer to another private party in the case of *County of Wayne v. Hathcock*. And in 2006, after the *Kelo* decision, 80 percent of the voters approved an amendment to the Michigan state constitution that prohibits "the taking of private property for transfer to a private entity for the purpose of economic development or enhancement of tax revenues." The amendment also makes it more difficult to use "blight" as an excuse to condemn large parcels of land for private development.

Florida is another state that moved rapidly to strengthen property rights. Florida passed a law that requires localities to wait 10 years before transferring land taken by eminent domain from one owner to another—effectively eliminating condemnations for private commercial development. This law also forbids the use of eminent domain to eliminate so-called blight. They then passed an amendment to the Florida Constitution that requires a three-fifths majority in both legislative houses to grant exceptions to the state's prohibition against using eminent domain for private use. South Dakota passed a law that prohibits government agencies from seizing private property by eminent domain "for transfer to any private person, nongovernmental entity, or other public-private business entity." Many states have responded to the outrageous *Kelo* decision by passing laws to enhance private property rights related to eminent domain. There are many states that still have weak laws, however, so much work remains to be done.

Citizens are subjected to a host of government actions, restrictions, regulations, and prohibitions that reduce the use and value of our properties, including laws relating to wetlands, endangered species, energy conservation, economics, zoning, licensing, global cooling (in the 1970s), and now global warming. If the government does something that significantly reduces the value of your property, it has in effect "taken" that property, and the owner should be entitled to compensation under the Fifth Amendment. In 1871, a landowner challenged a Wisconsin law authorizing the building of a dam that flooded his property, and the Supreme Court ruled for the landowner. The Supreme Court said "It is not necessary that property should be absolutely taken, in the narrowest sense of that word, to bring the case within the protection of this constitutional provision. There may be such serious interruption to the common and necessary use of property as will be equivalent to a taking, within the meaning of the Constitution."[33] This was recognized again by the Supreme Court in 1922, when it stated "while property may be regulated to a certain extent, if regulation goes too far, it will be recognized as a taking."[34]

As it has in many other areas, however, the Supreme Court has, over the years, watered down this part of the Fifth Amendment beyond recognition. In one case[35], the Court has replaced the text of the Fifth Amendment with a "balancing test" involving several factors.[36] In most cases, these balancing tests usually wind up favoring the government. In recent cases, it has been decreed that, if the government is not taking title to the land, they are not required to compensate the owner, even though the government actions may have made the land almost worthless. If the government regulations make the land completely valueless, then the government must pay full compensation. But if the value of the land is reduced by 90%, then the government does not have to pay any compensation. That is ridiculous and illogical, of course. The only sensible policy would be: the more you take, the more you pay. Another rule says that the government does not need to compensate when it can claim that the health, safety, morals or general welfare would be promoted by prohibiting particular contemplated uses of land. That rule frequently produces unfair results, because it does not take into account the fact that the owner may be innocent of any bad motives or actions.

A way must be found, either through legislation or a constitutional amendment, to require federal departments and agencies to reimburse individuals and enterprises for the costs associated with regulations that compromise the use of their property.[37] The compensation paid must also cover relocation costs where applicable, and any legal expenses incurred by the owner. When a family or an entire community is disrupted by government action, their compensation should also include the recognition of the relational interests that are being destroyed. This includes things like business, personal, religious, social, and recreational associations built up over the years.

STRUCTURING

If a person deposits more than $10,000 cash in a bank, this is considered by the government to be a "suspicious" transaction, and the bank is required to file a Currency Transaction Report with the government. Even if this deposit is perfectly legal, most people would like to avoid being reported to the government as suspicious, with the resulting government investigation, questioning, delay, suspicion, intimidation, slander and risk of complications. It would appear that one way to avoid this would be to keep deposits below $10,000. A person might deposit $9,000 today and then another $9,000 tomorrow, and another $9,000 the next day. However, the law is written so that, if the government can claim to have even the slightest suspicion that you are doing this in order to avoid the reporting requirement, they can seize all the money involved, even though there is no other illegal activity. This is defined as the crime of structuring, and the result has been the seizure of large amounts of money from perfectly innocent people.

This has happened to several farmers and small businesses, including Taylor's Produce Stand in Maryland. The government seized about $90,000 from their bank account. Even though this law was supposed to be used against criminals, Taylor's Produce was not charged with any other crime. There is no evidence that they were doing anything wrong. They just happened to run afoul of one of the technicalities in our laws. But this business was pressured into a settlement agreement where the government kept about half of the seized money. Our justice system used to be related to common sense—if you were not trying to do something wrong, you had nothing to worry about. But now, if you inadvertently violate one of the thousands of obscure regulations on the books, the government may decide to prosecute you, even if there is no evidence of criminal intent. Perhaps it makes the prosecutor look good to have a long string of convictions. Or maybe if he can seize more money from his victims, it will help fatten up his department's budget.

There are often legitimate business reasons for making deposits below $10,000, but just making such deposits are often enough to lead to a seizure, without having to show any intent of wrongdoing. The law discourages banks from telling their customers that these deposits may generate suspicion. "We're not allowed to tell them anything," said the fraud and security manager for one bank.[38] There is no reason that a bank deposit of any amount should be a crime. If a person is suspected of committing other crimes, then the authorities should charge him based on those crimes. But in many of the structuring cases, no other illegal criminal activity was alleged. The so-called crime of "structuring" has a long history of unjust application to innocent people, and should be repealed.

ASSET FORFEITURE

There are laws that permit law enforcement offices to seize a person's cash and property under the assumption that this property is either the proceeds from illegal activity, or the tools used in the commission of a crime. The problem with this is that there does not need to be any proof or even any hard evidence of a crime. The officers don't need to get a warrant or prove anything to a judge. All they have to do is to say they had a suspicion of possible criminal activity. In fact, one study estimates that 80 percent of civil forfeitures do not result in criminal conviction.[39] It is easy to see how such a system could be misused. What makes it even worse is that much of the cash or property seized is given to the law enforcement agency that makes the seizure. This obviously gives the law officers a perverse incentive to maximize the amount of cash and stuff that they confiscate, even where there is little or no evidence to justify it. In fact, many agencies have come to depend on asset forfeiture for a portion of their operating budget. The US Attorney General stated in 1990 "We must significantly increase forfeiture production to reach our budget target."[40]

Such loose standards are certainly an invitation to corruption and abuse. And it is clear that there is a lot of abuse.

In 2005, Javier Gonzalez was driving to Brownsville, Texas, to make arrangements for his aunt's funeral. He carried $10,000 in cash to pay for her burial. The police pulled him over for having an improperly attached license plate. When officers found the cash, they handcuffed him and seized his money. A search revealed no drugs or contraband, but the officers refused to return his money. There was no evidence of any criminal activity, but the police told him that he could either sign away his legal right to the cash or face money laundering charges. Gonzalez had to hire a lawyer to fight this injustice, and it took him three years to get his money returned.

Donald Scott owned a rugged 200 acre estate in Malibu, California. His property was located adjacent to a federal park, and for years the Park Service had said that they would like to acquire that property. A Los Angeles deputy sheriff heard rumors about marijuana plants on the property, so he planned a raid knowing that if they could find any drugs, the property would be forfeited. Before the raid, the police discussed the idea that the property could be forfeited. They researched the value of the property, and bragged that if only 14 marijuana plants were found, they could seize the estate. In order to get a search warrant, someone flew over the property in an airplane and claimed to have seen some marijuana plants, although a subsequent investigation said that that was likely not true. Early one morning, a large task force broke down the door, entered the house and shot Mr. Scott dead. Of course, the subsequent search of the property did not find any illegal drugs or marijuana plants.

An African American man, Shukree Simmons, was driving to Atlanta after selling his Chevy Silverado truck for $3,700. The police stopped him and questioned him and searched his car. They found no evidence of any illegal activity. A drug sniffing dog could not find any indication of drugs in his car. Simmons was never charged with any crime. But the officers still confiscated the $3,700 in cash. He was told that he would need to file a legal claim to get his money back.

In Putnam County, Indiana, Anthony Smelley was pulled over for an unsafe lane change. The officers found $17,320 in cash that he was planning to use to buy a car, and they confiscated the money. He was able to prove that the money was part of a settlement he had received from a recent car accident. And the police found no evidence of any illegal activity. But the police still insisted on keeping the money. After a tremendous legal battle, Smelley's money was finally returned to him thirteen months after the incident. But Smelley will not be reimbursed for his time, interest on the money, or attorney's fees.

Generally laws allow the confiscation of property that is used to "facilitate" the commission of a crime. There is much debate about exactly what it means to "facilitate" the commission of a crime. Courts have naturally favored expansive definitions, allowing the seizure of property with a questionable connection to an actual crime. And many questions have arisen when someone borrows or rents some property, and uses that property in a criminal act. What if the property owner does not know that his property is being so used? Can the government confiscate the innocent owner's property, just because a third party has used that property in the commission of a crime? That would obviously be very unfair to the property owner. On the other hand, if this type of seizure were not allowed, the state and federal governments would lose out on a lucrative bonanza of millions of dollars' worth of property confiscated from innocent owners. So the Supreme Court has said that they will allow the seizure of property from innocent owners.

Billy Munnerlyn owned a small air-charter company. One day he agreed to fly an old man and four locked blue plastic boxes from Little Rock, Arkansas, to Ontario, California. After the plane landed, DEA agents arrested Munnerlyn and hauled him off to jail. His passenger turned out to be a convicted cocaine dealer, and the blue boxes contained about $3 million in cash. After 71 hours in jail, Munnerlyn was released. No drugs were found on the plane. No charges were filed against him. But the government confiscated his airplane and the $8,300 flight fee. Munnerlyn spent three years fighting for the return of his 1969 Learjet, incurring more than $120,000 in legal bills. He had to sell his other three planes and his office equipment to pay his debts. Finally he got his airplane back. But, as Munnerlyn learned, the government has no obligation to maintain or safeguard the property in its custody—despite charging him storage fees. His plane had been ripped apart in a futile search for drugs. The Learjet Co. told him it would cost more than $100,000 for repairs and maintenance to pass a federal airline inspection. Eventually, he declared bankruptcy.

It is typical in these proceedings that the government holds most of the advantages, the police are assumed to be correct, and the property owner must go to court to make his case. Many of the perfectly innocent victims of this rip-off do not ever get their money back because:

- They are intimidated by the police.
- They are not aware of the complex legal procedures required to challenge the seizure.
- They can't afford to hire an attorney to fight for them.
- It would cost more for the attorney than the value of the property taken.

In the East Texas town of Tenaha, the police had turned this racket into a long term money making business for the police department. Over a period of at least two years, many people passing through town were stopped by the police and searched. If any valuables or money was found, the police would confiscate it, usually without charging anybody with a crime. The victims were given the choice of signing over their belongings to the town, or facing felony charges of money laundering or other serious crimes. They also faced the prospect of having to hire a lawyer and returning to Tenaha multiple times. In one case, a couple gave up $6,000 after police threatened to seize their children and put them into foster care. The ACLU filed a class action lawsuit, and finally reached a settlement with the town, which agreed to observe rigorous new rules governing traffic stops.

The asset forfeiture con game has stripped us of many of our core rights: the right to be considered innocent until proven guilty, the right not to be punished until guilt is proven beyond a reasonable doubt, the right to be free from unreasonable searches and seizures, the right not to be deprived of property without due process of law, the right to be free from excessive and disproportionate punishment, and the right to the assistance of counsel.[41] An owner's property can be seized if a trespasser or visitor, unbeknownst to the owner, does something illegal on the property. It is then up to the owner to prove that she is innocent. The property owner is effectively guilty until proven innocent. This is the exact opposite of the dictum "innocent until proven guilty," which used to be the foundation of our justice system. What makes it even more unfair is that the standard of proof is extremely low. "Probable cause" is the lowest standard used for forfeiture, meaning that the government only has to claim to have probable cause that the property was used in a crime, rather than the much higher "beyond a reasonable doubt" standard used in criminal cases. This lowest standard of probable cause is the standard used in 14 states. Twenty-seven states and the federal government use a "preponderance of the evidence" standard—still a very low standard and inadequate to protect citizens' rights.[42]

These laws were initially justified as part of the "war on drugs," but have been expanded to cover many areas not related to drugs, and are now obviously out of control. Such a low burden of proof and prejudicial financial incentives almost guarantee the severe corruption and abuse that have been evident. The value of forfeited property at the federal level is over one billion dollars a year. And state and local efforts add millions more to that. When such enormous amounts of money are available, many law enforcement agencies will succumb to the temptation to focus on looking for property that can be seized, instead of the neutral administration of justice. Logically, law enforcement should be prioritized based on the danger posed by various criminal activities. But the potential for asset forfeiture causes these priorities to become distorted, and the focus is shifted to revenue generation. More resources are directed toward nonviolent "vice" offenses, such as drug dealing or illegal gambling, which offers the possibility of seizing large amounts of cash or other valuable property.

Asset forfeiture laws at the state and federal level need to be either repealed or seriously modified to prevent abuses. Two former directors of the Justice Department's Asset Forfeiture Office, Brad Cates and John Yoder, have publicly stated that the program has so much corruption and abuse that "it should be abolished." They said that "civil forfeiture is fundamentally at odds with our judicial system and notions of fairness," and that it has led to "law enforcement efforts based upon what cash and property they could seize to fund themselves, rather than on an even-handed effort to enforce the law."[43] Another approach would be to establish the rule that no asset could be forfeited except to pay a lawful fine, imposed by verdict of a jury, by selling at public auction. Otherwise, some revisions that are absolutely necessary would require that before property can be seized:

- A suspect must be charged and convicted of a crime.
- Police must go before a judge and justify the forfeiture.

Some other changes must be made to these unfair laws:

- All forfeiture laws must be modified to disallow seizure of assets where the owner had no knowledge of the illegal activity. The principle of "innocent until proven guilty" must be restored by putting the burden on the government—instead of the property owner—to show that the owner had knowledge that his property was used in criminal activity.

- Increase the burden of proof by requiring the government to prove property is subject to forfeiture by "clear and convincing evidence"—a higher standard than is currently required.
- After the authorities move to seize an asset, require prompt hearings to allow the owner to contest the seizure.
- The value of the property seized must have a reasonable relationship to the scope of the criminal activity. In one case, a yacht was seized after one marijuana cigarette was found aboard.[44]
- When it is claimed that property was used to "facilitate" the commission of a crime, it must be proven that the forfeited property had a direct, essential, and substantial role in the commission of the crime.
- The practice of giving seized money and property to the law enforcement agencies cannot be allowed to continue.
- Provide legal counsel, paid by the government, to citizens and small business owners in all civil forfeiture proceedings.
- In any situation where the government wrongly uses civil forfeiture, not only should the assets be returned but the government must pay all legal expenses for the victim, must pay for any damage to the asset, and must also pay three times the value of the seized assets as punitive compensation.
- States must be required to collect data on their forfeiture practices to bring some transparency to this situation.

ASSET FREEZE

The government has found yet another way to use its overwhelming power and resources to threaten and intimidate its citizens. Without a trial or a conviction, the government can freeze a person's bank account so that he doesn't have the use of his money to operate his business, or to pay his defense lawyer. This can obviously place enormous pressure on an individual to yield to government desires. One notable example of this type of abuse was an attempt to compromise one of the most ancient and prized elements of basic fairness and justice in our legal system—the attorney-client privilege. The confidentiality of communications between an attorney and his client has long been held to be essential so that a person's lawyer could properly defend him.

During the trial of Charles H. Keating, in the Lincoln Savings and Loan Association case, the government claims that his law firm, Kay, Scholer, Fierman, Hays & Handler, should have revealed confidential information given to them by Keating. To put pressure on the law firm, the government filed a lawsuit against them for $275 million, and put a freeze on the assets of, not only the law firm, but also each of the partners individually. Of course, this came close to putting the firm out of business, and forced them to settle by paying the government $41 million. Since the firm settled without fighting the lawsuit, the precedent has been established that this outrageous use of raw power can be used to pressure, not just a law firm, but any business or citizen.

The New York City Bar Association thought that this was a gross misuse of power by the government. The Bar Association said that the asset freeze order is "of questionable constitutionality," and that it "clearly went beyond a reasoned response." The unilateral power to freeze assets without a judicial hearing, the Bar Association said, destroys the "chief guarantee of our liberties, due process and judicial review of government power." In fact, a New York appellate court later exonerated Peter Fishbein, the Kaye, Scholer partner whose alleged misconduct was the basis for the government's action.

The Code of Professional Responsibility provided at that time that "a government lawyer . . . should not use his or her position, or the economic power of the government, to harass parties or to bring about unjust settlements or results." University of Chicago law professor Daniel Fischel stated that the government's "unilateral and unjustified imposition of the asset freeze . . . was a clear violation of this ethical principle."[45]

Chapter Seven

Right to a Fair Trial
Sixth Amendment

In all criminal prosecutions, the accused shall enjoy the right to a speedy and public trial, by an impartial jury of the State and district wherein the crime shall have been committed, which district shall have been previously ascertained by law, and to be informed of the nature and cause of the accusation; to be confronted with the witnesses against him; to have compulsory process for obtaining witnesses in his favor, and to have the Assistance of Counsel for his defence.

Sixth Amendment to US Constitution

We have seen many abuses of the justice system by prosecutors whose careers depend on a large number of convictions, and who have therefore relegated the pursuit of justice to a secondary role. In the search for the truth, the prosecutor should protect the rights of the defendant, and should not withhold evidence or suborn perjury. In many courtrooms, this high ethic has been replaced by a win-at-all-costs mentality. Former Deputy US Attorney General Arnold I. Burns warned in 1998 that "it is time for a sober reassessment of the power we have concentrated in the hands of prosecutors and the alarming absence of effective checks and balances to prevent the widespread abuse of that power."[1]

Prosecutors have many opportunities to create crimes and frame innocent people by paying criminals for their testimony, which may or may not be true. Helmut Groebe, a German criminal wanted in four countries, was hired by federal prosecutors. He was paid with protection from arrest and $600,000. He tricked his Brazilian lover into traveling to Miami to sell her condominium to a buyer he had found. He told her it would be a cash deal because the buyer wanted to keep the transaction secret. The "buyer" was a DEA agent, and Groebe's lover went to prison for money laundering. Groebe also approached a businessman, Wolfgang von Schlieffen, claiming to have buyers for his cars and condominiums. Again the buyers were DEA agents, who entrapped von Schlieffen by offering cash.

The FBI used to have high standards that required that they only investigate crimes after they had been committed. They were prohibited from engaging in undercover sting operations designed to incite people to commit crimes. But that has changed now. During the Carter administration, FBI undercover agents entrapped some US representatives by poising as Arab sheiks offering bribes. Later, the FBI entrapped District of Columbia Mayor Marion Barry by hiring a woman to lure the mayor with sex and cocaine while the FBI filmed. Today, it is routine for federal agents to create criminal enterprises, which are often used to entrap unsuspecting, innocent people.

Faustino Rico Toro was an official of the Bolivian government in charge of anti-drug efforts. Informed that he had been indicted in the United States on the basis of charges by a person unknown to him, Toto voluntarily came to the United States to resolve the issue. Unknown to Toto, federal agents had purchased testimony from four "co-conspirators" who had been coached to testify that he protected drug lords. Toto lost five years of his life to the plot fabricated against him. But he hired a good investigator who finally managed to unearth the details of the plot, and, faced with exposure in court of their criminal behavior, prosecutors then dropped the charges.

John Pree was facing a life sentence for armed robbery, but he was offered a deal. Federal agents briefed Pree on several crimes to which he would plead guilty. He would testify that he was acting on the orders of their real target, Detroit crime boss Vito Giacalone. Pree did not know Giacalone, but federal agents fabricated his testimony to meet their needs. Pree's false testimony got seventeen suspected mobsters indicted. In place of a life sentence for his real crime, Pree served less than ten years for the invented crimes. He also received cash and a new identity.

Dr. George Pararas-Carayannis was set up by a sexy, young woman who, unknown to him, was an illegal alien who had agreed to entrap victims in exchange for permission to remain in the United States. The woman tricked Carayannis into running through his credit card account some credit card charges that she said were from customers of her business. He was then arrested for laundering money from prostitution. Apparently there was no prostitution, but he was convicted and sent to prison because the woman testified that she had told him her business was an "escort business." This allegation was the sole "proof" against Carayannis.

A paid government informant lured Loren Pogue under false pretenses into a trap. Thinking he was going to sell a land parcel to a legitimate buyer, he was confronted by DEA agents posing as a drug gang, who claimed they wanted the land for an airstrip to be used for smuggling cocaine. Because he listened to the agents describe their plot, he was charged with being part of a drug conspiracy, and was sentenced to twenty-two years in federal prison.

All the money flowing into the "War on Drugs" has produced the inducement to set up victims to get convictions. Many parts of the criminal justice system have been totally corrupted. Federal law enforcement officers know that they will not suffer for their misconduct. No matter what their transgression, it is almost impossible for a criminal defendant to sue a federal officer or prosecutor for damages, and they are rarely disciplined by the Justice Department.[2]

As one example, federal prosecutors charged Candisha Robinson with "using" a gun during a drug offense. Actually during the alleged drug sale, the gun was unloaded, and was inside a locked trunk in the bedroom closet. With such an unbelievable distortion of the English language, the federal government was able to convict Robinson of this offense.[3] This makes one wonder if there are any limits to the abuses of prosecutorial power.

One way to reduce some of this abuse is for jurors to recognize and use the power they have. First, they need to know that a grand jury indictment is almost meaningless. Prosecutors have total control over the grand jury, so there is no fairness involved in the process. Jurors also need to know that when they see an obvious unjust indictment, they have the right to acquit regardless of what the judge says. The judge will instruct the jury that, if the defendant did commit the act, then the jury is required to find him guilty. But that is not true. If the juror believes, for whatever reason, that the accused does not deserve to be punished, the juror has the right, and even the duty, to vote "not guilty." Juries have the right to acquit "against the evidence," even in the face of a judge who believes the defendant to be guilty. And a juror might decide that he thinks a law is unconstitutional, or just being applied unfairly, and vote not guilty for that reason.[4] "The jury was originally understood as having not only the power to judge the facts of a case," explains Law Professor Michael Paulsen, "but an independent right to interpret the *law* as well." This gives juries just as much right as the judge to interpret the Constitution.[5] Jurors must also bring a healthy dose of skepticism into the courtroom. It is natural for them to want to believe that prosecutors are telling the truth, not knowing that many of them are merely ambitious people pursuing careers without regard for justice and truth.

TRIAL BY JURY

The right to "an impartial jury," as guaranteed by the Sixth Amendment, occupies a revered place in the Western legacy of justice. It was used in Athens and the Roman Empire. Then the Magna Carta provided that "no freeman is to be taken or imprisoned . . . save by lawful judgment of his peers or by the law of the land." When Britain imposed unjust laws in the American Colonies, the jury stood as a bastion of defiance, nullifying the hated laws and freeing those accused. The Right to a Fair Trial is recognized internationally as a fundamental human right. It is guaranteed by the Sixth Amendment to the US Constitution, and as part of international law by the Universal Declaration of Human Rights and the International Covenant on Civil and Political Rights. The requirement that the trial be open to the public has always been recognized as a safeguard against any attempt to employ our courts as instruments of persecution, and to assure the criminal defendant a fair and accurate adjudication of guilt or innocence.

The framers of the Constitution wanted to protect the jury, because they understood that that was one of the only ways that an ordinary citizen could exercise power, as a check against any unjust or corrupt actor in the justice system. The jury remains the obstacle between the vast power of the state and the individual at risk of losing his liberty. Unfortunately, the jury trial in America is now close to extinction.[6]

In the federal justice system, the legal procedures and rules of evidence all seem to favor the prosecutor. Prosecutors use this power to put enormous pressure on a defendant to accept a plea bargain, with a guilty plea to a lesser offense. At one time, it was understood that the primary function of the justice system is to establish the truth or falsity of the charges levied against the accused. This emphasis on truth protected the innocent, even if conviction was made more difficult. But now, the focus has changed. Today, the convenience of the prosecutor is paramount, and we see defendants confessing to crimes they did not commit to avoid the risk of greater punishment for more serious crimes which they may or may not have committed. The prosecutor has many ways to pressure a defendant:

- He might offer leniency through a charge reduction, or a reduced sentence.
- He could harass the defendant's family and friends, and produce all kinds of bad publicity
- He can threaten to seize the defendant's assets.
- The prosecutor can add ten years to the sentence by filing information that the defendant has a previous drug conviction, for example. He will say, "If you don't accept the plea, and insist on going to trial, I will file the prior conviction, and you'll get ten more years in prison."
- A person who wants a jury trial on a federal charge automatically receives a longer sentence, if found guilty, than he would receive if he pled guilty to the charge.
- The police may have evidence that points to the defendant's innocence, or that might impeach a witness's credibility. But the prosecutor is not required to give that evidence to the defendant when she is deciding whether to take a plea bargain.[7]
- For the same action, the prosecutor can frequently pile on many different charges, which have the effect of greatly increasing the potential length of the prison sentence which the defendant is facing.
- The sentences prescribed by statute in the United States are generally much more severe than for comparable offenses in Europe.

This makes the risk of a trial unacceptably dangerous. Even an innocent defendant has to balance the risk of going to trial and getting a possible very lengthy prison sentence, against accepting the deal of a guilty plea and cooperation. The defendant is almost forced to accept a plea bargain.

Many of the statutes are so vague that they are subject to all manner of creative interpretation. And the plea bargain resolution allows the prosecutor to avoid the adversarial testing of his creative interpretations. Many judges are themselves former prosecutors, and they are more willing to accept the amorphous definitions of federal crimes favored by prosecutors.

The prosecutor has the power to offer many different types of bribes to witnesses, including money, reduced sentencing, new identities, immunity for loved ones, and other goodies.[8] There is a law that makes it illegal to bribe a witness, and a three judge panel of the Tenth Circuit Court of Appeals actually did rule one time that prosecutors were not allowed to threaten and then reward government witnesses for their testimony. The opinion, written by Judge Paul Kelly Jr. stated that "The judicial process is tainted and justice cheapened when factual testimony is purchased, whether with leniency or money. Because prosecutors bear a weighty responsibility to do justice and observe the law in the course of a prosecution, it is particularly appropriate to apply the [anti-bribery statute] to their activities."

Judge Kelly's groundbreaking ruling shocked and outraged the government. The full membership of the court panicked, and immediately reviewed the case. They somehow decided that when Congress wrote the law prohibiting bribery, they didn't really mean to say what it looked like they said, and so prosecutors could continue bribing witnesses.[9] The anti-bribery statute says that it applies to "whoever . . . gives, offers, or promises anything of value . . . " The court astonishingly managed to decide that the meaning of the word "whoever" in the statute is not clear. Then it invented a brand new idea that a law did not apply to the government unless the government is specifically mentioned in the law. As Judge Kelly noted in his ruling, "one of the oldest principles of our legal heritage is that the king is subject to the law."[10] But now the courts have found a way to get around this, even though it is one of our most cherished and fundamental doctrines.

When a corporation is the defendant, it frequently has a strong incentive to settle, even if it has some evidence to support its position, rather than go to trial. It is often cheaper to make a deal than it is to risk the enormous legal fees, publicity, and distraction that fighting entails. And the government has yet another weapon: if it gets a criminal conviction, it could follow that with a "debarment" proceeding that would disqualify a company from doing business with any government funded program. For many companies, this would be a death sentence.[11]

There is another tactic the government sometimes uses to try to deprive a defendant of the funds to hire a capable attorney. Congress has enacted corporate sentencing guidelines, and judges are under great pressure to follow these guidelines. This law took much of the discretion away from judges as far as sentencing, but it gave more power to the prosecutor, because he is now able to increase or decrease the sentence based on various factors. The prosecutor, for example, is able to reduce the sentence if he certifies that the company is "cooperating" with the government.[12] Many companies have a policy that they will pay for an attorney for one of their executives on a matter relating to her employment. But one thing a company can do to earn this "cooperative" status is to refuse to pay for their employee's attorney.[13] Of course, this is another way to force the defendant to accept a plea bargain.

According to Justice Department statistics, 90 to 95 percent of all federal, state, and local criminal cases are settled by plea bargains.[14] So in effect, we have all but lost one of the rights that used to be cherished so highly, the right to a trial by jury. The defendant's fate is dependent on his lawyer's negotiating skills, rather than a jury of his peers, as was guaranteed by our Constitution.

With so many cases settled by plea bargains, this means that most of the criminal cases are never tested in federal appeals courts. Normally, the appeals process would be an opportunity for an independent review of the case to see if the defendant was treated unfairly. But now most defendants have lost this opportunity. Our valuable Fifth Amendment right against self-incrimination has been almost totally eliminated in the plea bargain process. Transparency suffers as well, because the high number of plea bargains has the functional result of hiding these prosecutions from the public, and avoiding scrutiny by the press. That is because cases in which defendants take plea bargains receive much less attention in the media than those which have a lengthy trial with lots of exciting testimony and suspense.

In the plea bargain system, finding the truth is no longer important. A deal is negotiated to create a false narrative about false crimes. All the parties involved—prosecutors, judges, defense lawyers—are complicit in this fiction. The systematized falsehoods corrupt and destroy the public's respect for the entire criminal justice process. It also makes our crime statistics much less reliable, since crimes committed frequently have no relation to the actual convictions.

When the prosecutor brings the full, awesome power of the government to bear against a defendant, this is intimidating and coercive. The parallels between our plea bargaining system and the ancient system of judicial torture are many and chilling. In medieval Europe, an accused person could be tortured until he confessed. Similarly, a modern prosecutor puts more and more intense pressure on the defendant until he is forced to confess.[15]

How did we get to this point? Gradually, over the years, our system of jury trials has gotten more and more complex and procedural, with convoluted rules of evidence, jury selection, and adversarial practices. The system has become so awkward and complicated and time-consuming that it is unworkable as a routine procedure for adjudication. Even though most people will not say that they really like the plea bargain system, all the players in the justice system have accepted that it is a necessary expedient. Even the Supreme Court has acknowledged that it would not be practical to have a full scale jury trial for all criminal cases with our current intricate system.[16]

But our plea bargain system is not the inevitable solution—there are other methods of determining guilt and innocence that preserve the rights that we hold dear. For example, Germany has an efficient criminal justice system that includes laymen on the jury, the right of appeal, the right against self-incrimination, a requirement to investigate exculpatory evidence, and full adjudication in every case of serious crime. Their standard of proof is comparable to our "beyond reasonable doubt" requirement. They have a rapid, streamlined trial procedure, and they do not use plea bargaining. In fact, the German Supreme Court has expressly prohibited courts from pressuring defendants to confess. The Germans view our plea bargain system with amazement and disgust.[17]

THE ASSISTANCE OF COUNSEL

The Sixth Amendment's right to the assistance of counsel was an empty promise for poor people for most of this country's first two centuries. Except in cases carrying the death penalty, lawyers were not provided for indigents until 1938, and then it was only in federal courts.[18] In 1963, the Supreme Court extended this right to state courts.[19]

The right to counsel is important, not only for the trial, but even during interrogation. The police know that extended interrogation without counsel can break the will of a suspect, and get him to say things out of confusion or exhaustion. So this is an important right for suspects, and some law enforcement officials will use various ruses to try to question a person without having a lawyer present.

While the Supreme Court ruling upholding the right of counsel was certainly a welcome advance for poor defendants, something was still missing. Neither the Constitution nor the courts have said much about the quality of counsel. There have been cases where a defendant lost his case and his freedom because his lawyer did a poor job of representing him. Some lawyers may just be new and inexperienced. Some are incompetent or unethical. But in many cases, the problem of ineffective counsel is a result of inadequate funding in the indigent defense system. Proving innocence is expensive. A conscientious defense lawyer works many hours outside the courtroom in addition to the actual trial time. It may be necessary to hire costly experts to expose sloppy police lab work. He might need to pay investigators to find out the true facts to counter the police's theories. The amount of money authorized by states for indigent defense is frequently inadequate to do a first class job.

There have been rare convictions overturned due to "ineffective assistance of counsel," but this is very difficult to prove. Of course, quality of representation is a subjective appraisal, and leaves much to the discretion of the judge. It is almost impossible for a judge to evaluate how good a job the lawyer did investigating the case outside of court. When an appellate court is trying to decide whether to hear a case where effectiveness of counsel is being challenged, they do not have the entire trial record to review. They only have a summary of the case, which makes it difficult for them to evaluate the lawyer's performance. The defense attorney himself is not eager to admit his own failures, so he is likely to resist this type of appeal. And courts have ruled that the government is obligated to pay for a lawyer only through the first level of appeal, so the ability of a poor defendant to move his case to higher courts is very limited.

Chapter Eight

Fourteenth Amendment

All persons born or naturalized in the United States, and subject to the jurisdiction thereof, are citizens of the United States and of the State wherein they reside. No State shall make or enforce any law which shall abridge the privileges or immunities of citizens of the United States; nor shall any State deprive any person of life, liberty, or property, without due process of law; nor deny to any person within its jurisdiction the equal protection of the laws.

Section 1 of the Fourteenth Amendment

The Civil Rights Act of 1866 was intended to protect the rights of the newly freed slaves to make contracts, to sue, to hold and sell property, and to enjoy the full benefits of laws "for the security of person and property, as is enjoyed by white citizens," and no more than that. These protections were specifically tailored to counteract the discriminatory laws passed by some of the Southern states, known as the "Black Codes." The rights intended to be protected were spelled our explicitly in the Civil Rights Act.[1] The Fourteenth Amendment was originally intended to put those same rights into a constitutional amendment, in order to make them more permanent and less subject to revision by a future Congress.

The Fourteenth Amendment created one very important change to the original federal system that our Founders had created. It allowed Congress to intrude into the actions of the states. And it was done using terms like "due process" and "equal protection," which could be twisted to mean almost anything. One of the fundamental principles of the Constitution was the division of power between the federal and state governments. "Such a loose, flexible, uncontrolled standard . . . will amount to a great unconstitutional shift of power to the courts," said Supreme Court

Justice Hugo Black, "which . . . will . . . jeopardize the separation of powers the Framers set up and . . . take away much of the power of States to govern themselves which the Constitution plainly intended them to have."[2]

The Framers originally intended for the Bill of Rights to be restrictions on the federal government, not the states. But the Supreme Court has used the Due Process Clause of the Fourteenth Amendment as an excuse to say that the Bill of Rights is now applicable to the states, giving the federal government enormous new powers over the states. The authors of the Fourteenth Amendment never intended for this amendment to produce such a colossal transfer of power from the states to the federal government. The Due Process Clause was originally intended only to guarantee that the proper judicial procedures were followed. But the Court has read incredible new meanings into it which have no basis in the historical meaning of the phrase.

AMENDMENT IS LIMITED

In order to get the amendment passed in Congress, its proponents told everyone that their intention was to incorporate exactly the identical provisions that were covered in the Civil Rights Law of 1866, for the protection of the newly freed slaves. They did not propose to go at all beyond that limited objective. Senator Lyman Trumbull, a primary author of the Amendment, said that he "clearly and unhesitatingly declared [Section 1 of the Amendment] to be a reiteration of the rights as set forth in the Civil Rights Bill."[3] He said that "the bill is applicable exclusively to civil rights. It does not propose to regulate political rights of individuals; it has nothing to do with the right of suffrage, or any other political right."[4] Senator Trumbull also stated, "The great fundamental rights set forth" in the Bill are "the right to acquire property, the right to come and go at pleasure, the rights to enforce rights in the courts, to make contracts and to inherit and dispose of property." These were carried into the Act, and Act and Amendment were viewed as "identical."[5]

Representative George R. Latham of West Virginia emphasized that "the civil rights bill which is now a law. . . covers exactly the same ground as this amendment."[6] Future president James Garfield was in the House of Representatives at the time, and he said that "this section [1] of the Amendment was considered as equivalent to the first section of the Civil Rights

Bill."[7] Representative Martin Thayer of Pennsylvania stated that "it is but incorporating in the Constitution . . . the principle of the Civil Rights Bill which has lately become a law" in order that it "shall be forever incorporated in the Constitution"[8] He also explained that "to avoid any misapprehension" as to what the "fundamental rights of citizenship" are, "they are stated in the bill. The same section goes on to define with great particularity the civil rights and immunities which are to be protected by the bill,"[9] Congressman Henry Van Aernam of New York said that the Amendment gives "constitutional sanctions and protection to the substantial guarantees of the Civil Rights Bill."[10]

Other scholars recognized the same purpose. Howard Jay Graham wrote that "virtually every speaker in the debates on the Fourteenth Amendment—Republican and Democrat alike—said or agreed that the Amendment was designed to embody or incorporate the Civil Rights Act."[11] Horace Flack stated that "The general opinion held in the North . . . was that the amendment embodied the Civil Rights Bill."[12] Supreme Court Justice Joseph Bradley said that "The first section of the bill covers the same ground as the fourteenth amendment."[13] Justice Hugo Black wrote that "The declarations and statements of newspapers, writers, and speakers, . . . show very clearly, . . . the general opinion held in the North. That opinion, briefly stated, was that the Amendment embodied the Civil Rights Bill.[14] The "privileges or immunities" clause was borrowed from Article Four of the Constitution, which had been construed to allow a visitor from one state to engage in trade or commerce in another.[15] A Report of the House Committee on the Judiciary, submitted in 1871 by Representative John Bingham of Ohio, recited that the Fourteenth Amendment "did not add to the privileges or immunities" of Article Four.[16]

The rights included in the Civil Rights Law and the Fourteenth Amendment were intended to be strictly limited to those listed. James F. Wilson, chairman of the House Judiciary Committee, stated that the rights enumerated in the Civil Rights Bill were no "greater than the rights which are included in the general terms 'life, liberty, and property.'"[17] James W. Patterson, Representative from New Hampshire, said that he was opposed "to any law discriminating against [blacks] in the security of life, liberty, person, property and the proceeds of their labor. These civil rights all should enjoy. Beyond this I am not prepared to go, and those pretended friends who urge political and social equality . . . are . . . the worst enemies of the colored race."[18]

However, when the amendment passed out of Congress, the language actually used was much more vague and broad. This left it open to all the expansive interpretations given it by the twentieth century Supreme Court. The modern Court has assumed for itself an awesome array of powers which have no foundation in the Constitution. Brand new previously unknown powers of the federal government expanded to cover reapportionment, abortion, school desegregation, and many other issues.

REAPPORTIONMENT

In the case of *Baker v. Carr* (1962), the Supreme Court ruled that it had the authority to control a state's reapportionment procedure under the Fourteenth Amendment.[19] But actually, it was widely recognized at the time that the Fourteenth Amendment was adopted that it was never designed to take the power to control apportionment away from the states. In 1868, during the debate on readmission of the rebel states, Representative Farnsworth of Illinois pointed out that the Florida apportionment provision gave "to the sparsely populated portions of the State the control of the Legislature." But Massachusetts Congressman Ben Butler responded that the Senate Judiciary Committee "have found the [Florida] constitution republican and proper," as did the Senate, the House Committee on Reconstruction, and the House itself, thus reaffirming that such malapportionment did not violate the guarantee of a "republican form of government," nor the equal protection clause, which was the work of Butler and others.[20] Legal Scholar and US Solicitor General Archibald Cox said that the reapportionment cases are a "dramatic" example of "reading into the generalities of the Due Process and Equal Protection Clauses notions of wise and fundamental policy which are not even faintly suggested by the words of the Constitution, and which lack substantial support in other conventional sources of law."[21] William W. Van Alstyne, an American law professor and constitutional law scholar, gave his understanding that "there is no evidence that paragraph two [of the Fourteenth Amendment] was applicable to abridgment of the right to vote resulting from malapportionment of state legislatures."[22] At one time, it was suggested that Congress might want "to regulate the State elections of members of State legislatures." In response, former Supreme Court Justice Joseph Story stated, "It would be deemed a most unwarrantable transfer of power, indicating a premeditated design to destroy the State governments."[23] When the Supreme Court decided in *Baker* that it would intervene in matters of state reapportionment, Justice Harlan issued a dissenting opinion in which he stated:

> I can find nothing in the Equal Protection Clause or elsewhere in the Federal Constitution which expressly or impliedly supports the view that state legislatures must be so structured as to reflect with approximate equality the voice of every voter. Not only is that proposition refuted by history, as shown by my Brother Frankfurter, but it strikes deep into the heart of our federal system. Its acceptance would require us to turn our backs on the regard which this Court has always shown for the judgment of state legislatures and courts on matters of basically local concern. . . . It is surely beyond argument that those who have the responsibility for devising a system of representation may permissibly consider that factors other than bare numbers should be taken into account. The existence of the United States Senate is proof enough of that. . . . No intention to fix immutably the means of selecting representatives for state governments could have been in the minds of either the Founders or the draftsmen of the Fourteenth Amendment. . . . What the Court is doing reflects more an adventure in judicial experimentation than a solid piece of constitutional adjudication.[24]

Justice Frankfurter also issued a dissenting opinion in the same case, in which he further reacted to the actions of the Court:

> From its earliest opinions, this Court has consistently recognized a class of controversies which do not lend themselves to judicial standards and judicial remedies. To classify the various instances as "political questions" is, rather, a form of stating this conclusion than revealing of analysis. . . . The Court has been particularly unwilling to intervene in matters concerning the structure and organization of the political institutions of the States. The abstention from judicial entry into such areas has been greater even than that which marks the Court's ordinary approach to issues of state power challenged under

broad federal guarantees. . . . We should be very reluctant to decide that we had jurisdiction in such a case, and thus in an action of this nature to supervise and review the political administration of a state government by its own officials and through its own courts. . . . In effect, today's decision empowers the courts of the country to devise what should constitute the proper composition of the legislatures of the fifty States. . . . There is not under our Constitution a judicial remedy for every political mischief, for every undesirable exercise of legislative power. The Framers, carefully and with deliberate forethought, refused so to enthrone the judiciary. In this situation, as in others of like nature, appeal for relief does not belong here. Appeal must be to an informed, civically militant electorate.[25]

Justice Frankfurter also pointed out that the states which ratified the Fourteenth Amendment had "a wide variety of apportionment methods which recognized the element of population in differing ways and degrees." It would be unthinkable, he said, to assume that "by voting for the Equal Protection Clause, they . . . struck down *sub silentio* not a few of their own state constitutional provisions."[26] He recognized the many variables that have to be considered in the complex job of apportionment when he called it "a subject of extraordinary complexity, involving . . . considerations of geography, demography, electoral convenience, economic and social cohesions or divergences among particular local groups, communications, the practical effects of political institutions like the lobby and the city machine, ancient traditions and ties of settled usage, respect for proven incumbents of long experience and senior status, mathematical mechanics, censuses compiling relevant data, and a host of others."[27] Equality of representation has to be only one of many factors to be considered in the complicated task of apportionment. For example, large cities sometimes have inordinate political influence in their state government. City leaders are frequently strong political forces in the state and even federal legislative process. The concentration of wealth and of the means of communication can exert powerful influence, and these are generally found in the cities. States should be allowed to take these imbalances into consideration in the apportionment process.

DESEGREGATION

Another area where the Court has illegally assumed control is desegregation of schools. Most of us would agree that school segregation required by law has no place in America today. But that issue should be addressed by legislation in the states. The federal government has no constitutional authority to control such matters. It was understood at the time it was ratified that the Fourteenth Amendment did not require integration of schools. In fact, the same Congress that passed the Fourteenth Amendment also voted to segregate schools in the District of Columbia.[28] James Wilson, chairman of the House Judiciary Committee, told the House that the words "civil rights . . . do not mean that all citizens shall sit on juries, or that their children shall attend the same schools. These are not civil rights." Wilson was the House manager of the bill, therefore his statement could be taken as proof that segregation was not included in the scope of the Civil Rights Act. Senator Charles Sumner, in 1867, after the Fourteenth Amendment had been passed out of Congress, proposed a bill that would require desegregation of schools. This is more evidence that Congress recognized that the Fourteenth Amendment did not accomplish this. In fact, Senator Morrill of Maine opposed Senator Sumner's bill because he said the "Federal Government had no right to take cognizance of matters of education, amusement . . . it is without warrant in the Constitution."[29] Actually, most of the Northern states were opposed to the integration of schools. Eight Northern states either provided for separate schools or left it up to local communities to adopt that practice if they wished. Five Northern states either directly or by implication excluded colored children entirely from their public schools.[30] Senator James Harlan of Iowa said: "It would be impossible to carry a proposition in Iowa to educate the few colored children that now live in the State in the same school houses with white children. It would be impossible, I think, in any one of the States in the Northwest." The acceptance of segregated schools in the North is further shown by the history of the Civil Rights Act of 1875. Although the Act prohibited discrimination in some places, Congress debated and specifically rejected a ban against segregated schools.[31]

In preparation for the Supreme Court case of *Brown v. Board of Education*, Justice Frankfurter researched the legislative history of the Fourteenth Amendment. He concluded that "in all likelihood, the framers of the amendment had not intended to outlaw segregation."[32] An Ohio court ruled in 1871 that "Equality of rights does not involve the necessity of educating white and colored persons in the same school."[33] A Nevada court held in 1872 that separate schools do not offend the Fourteenth Amendment.[34] In 1874, a California court made a similar ruling.[35] Also in 1874, an Indiana court held that the Constitution does not empower Congress "to exercise a general or special supervision over the states on the subject of education."[36] A Federal Circuit Court ruled in 1887 that separate schools for blacks did not constitute a denial of "equal protection."[37] Even the Supreme Court acknowledged that the Fourteenth Amendment did not outlaw segregation. In 1896, the Court ruled that the Fourteenth Amendment has allowed "the establishment of separate schools for white and colored children, which has been held to be a valid exercise of the legislative power even by courts of States where the political rights of the colored race have been longest and most earnestly enforced."[38]

Law professor Lino Graglia said that the effect of *Brown v. Board of Education* is "that it changed the view of the proper role of the Supreme Court . . . The result has been a perversion of the system of government created by the Constitution, the basic principles of which are self-government through elected representatives, decentralized power (federalism), and separation of powers." Instead, we now have "government by majority vote of a committee of nine unelected, life-tenured lawyers making the most basic policy decisions for the nation as a whole from Washington, DC" In January 1958, Learned Hand, one of the most respected Federal Circuit Judges in the United States, blasted the Supreme Court for overstepping its constitutional bounds, acting like a "third legislative chamber," and jeopardizing America's democratic system of government. In his talk, Hand referenced a series of decisions that invalidated popularly enacted law, including the segregation cases. According to Hand, "nothing" in the Constitution explicitly granted the Court the power to invalidate Jim Crow laws in the South. To Hand, issues like public school segregation were little more than choices between "relative values" that the Court had no business deciding.[39]

In an amazing display of arrogance, courts took over control of entire school districts, in some cases forcing children to be bused for many miles across town in order to balance the ratios of different races at various schools. The result in many places was chaos and massive disruption. Many families were angry about having to send their children miles away to an unfamiliar school. There was an increase in discipline problems, and studies showed that black academic performance did not improve. In many cases, race relations suffered due to busing, and schools are becoming more segregated because of changes in demographic residential patterns. In one case, the Supreme Court acknowledged that "the educational progress of all the students, white and colored, of that school has suffered" but it still refused to consider modifying the desegregation plan.[40]

INCORPORATION

The First Amendment to the Constitution says "Congress shall make no law . . . ." This is clearly a restriction on the power of Congress, not the states. The first ten amendments, the Bill of Rights, are intended to limit the power of the federal government, not the states. This was clearly understood by everyone at the time. In fact, James Madison tried to introduce another amendment that would limit the states, but it was defeated.

That was one of the fundamental principles of the Constitution—the division of power between the federal and state governments. For example, the First Amendment doesn't say much about freedom of religion and freedom of speech, other than to make it clear that this is a state, rather than a federal, area of concern. The reason the First Amendment doesn't say much about those things is that it was to be left up to the states to work out the details and enact statutes related to freedom of religion and freedom of speech. The federal government was not expected to have any involvement. "Congress shall make no law . . ." made it pretty clear what was contemplated.

When Congress wrote the Fourteenth Amendment (and the Civil Rights Act of 1866, which was identical in effect), it repeatedly took pains to reassure the states that this would not affect the rights of the states. Senator Lyman Trumbull said: "The States were, and are now, the depositaries of the rights of the individual against encroachment. The Fourteenth Amendment has not changed an iota of the Constitution as it was originally framed."[41] He also stated, "This bill in no manner interferes with the municipal regulations of any State which protects all alike in their rights of person and property. It would have no operation in Massachusetts, New York, Illinois, or most of the States of the Union."[42] Representative Samuel S. Marshall of Illinois emphasized that "it is a fundamental principle of American law that the regulation of the local police of all the domestic affairs of a State belong to the State itself, and not to the Federal Government."[43] Representative John Bingham of Ohio said, "Under no possible interpretation can [the Fourteenth

Amendment] ever be made to operate in the State of New York while she occupies her present proud position."[44] And George R. Latham, Representative from West Va., repeated that Congress "has no right to interfere with the internal policy of the several states."[45]

The Supreme Court repeatedly recognized this obvious truth—that the Fourteenth Amendment was not intended to make the Bill of Rights effective against the states. Five years after the ratification of the Fourteenth Amendment, this question came before the Supreme Court. In the Slaughterhouse cases, the Supreme Court ruled that the Fourteenth Amendment was intended to protect former slaves, and did not give the federal government broad power over the states. The Court explained it this way:

> Was it the purpose of the fourteenth amendment . . . to transfer the security and protection of all the civil rights which we have mentioned, from the States to the Federal government? And where it is declared that Congress Shall have the power to enforce that article, was it intended to bring within the power of Congress the entire domain of civil rights heretofore belonging exclusively to the States? We are convinced that no such results were intended by the Congress which proposed these amendments, nor by the legislatures of the States which ratified them.[46]

The main purposes of the Thirteenth, Fourteenth, and Fifteenth Amendments, according to the Court, "was the freedom of the African race, the security and perpetuation of that freedom, and their protection from the oppressions of the white men who had formerly held them in slavery."[47]

The Court could not assume such power over the states, it said, because this "would constitute this court a perpetual censor upon all legislation of the States, on the civil rights of their own citizens." These consequences would be

> so serious, so far-reaching and pervading, so great a departure from the structure and spirit of our institutions; when the effect is to fetter and degrade the State governments by subjecting them to the control of Congress in the exercise of powers heretofore universally conceded to them of the most ordinary and fundamental character; when, in fact, it

radically changes the whole theory of the relations of the State and Federal governments to each other and of both these governments to the people.[48]

In another decision, Justice Frankfurter said:

Between the incorporation of the Fourteenth Amendment into the Constitution and the beginning of the present membership of the Court—a period of seventy years—the scope of that Amendment was passed upon by forty-three judges. Of all these judges, only one, who may respectfully be called an eccentric exception, ever indicated the belief that the Fourteenth Amendment was a shorthand summary of the first eight Amendments theretofore limiting only the Federal Government, and that due process incorporated those eight Amendments as restrictions upon the powers of the States. . . . Those conversant with the political and legal history of the concept of due process . . . would hardly recognize the Fourteenth Amendment as a cover for the various explicit provisions of the first eight Amendments.[49]

Another opinion held that "We have held from the beginning and uniformly that the Due Process Clause of the Fourteenth Amendment does not apply to the States any of the provisions of the first eight amendments as such. The relevant historical materials have been canvassed by this Court and by legal scholars. These materials demonstrate conclusively that Congress and the members of the legislatures of the ratifying States did not contemplate that the Fourteenth Amendment was a shorthand incorporation of the first eight amendments, making them applicable as explicit restrictions upon the States."[50] In 1875, the Court explained that for protection of the First Amendment right to assemble, "the people must look to the States. The power for that purpose was originally placed there, and it has never been surrendered to the United States."[51] In 1900, the US Supreme Court ruled in the case of *Maxwell v. Dow* that the first ten amendments to the Constitution "were intended as restraints and limitations upon the powers of the General Government, and were not intended to, and did not, have any effect upon the powers of the respective States. This has been many times decided."[52] However, beginning in the 1920s, a series of United States Supreme Court decisions made the amazing claim that the

Fourteenth Amendment could be interpreted to "incorporate" most portions of the Bill of Rights, making these portions, for the first time, enforceable against the state governments. This was a major distortion of the Fourteenth Amendment, which was never intended to accomplish such a thing. This turns that whole system upside down, giving the federal courts almost infinite power to oversee and control everything the states do in these areas. A fundamental aspect of the Constitution was the division of powers between the federal and state governments. But now we no longer have a system of federalism, as designed by the Framers, where the states would delegate a small amount of their power to the federal government. The federal government now has complete control over everything the states do, all in the name of "rights." The entire political structure of the United States has been changed into a centralized, authoritarian government.

The esteemed Supreme Court Justice Oliver Wendell Holmes was disturbed by this trend, when he wrote: "I have not yet adequately expressed the more than anxiety that I feel at the ever increasing scope given to the Fourteenth Amendment in cutting down what I believe to be the constitutional rights of the states. As the decisions now stand, I see hardly any limit but the sky to the invalidating of those rights if they happen to strike a majority of this Court as for any reason undesirable."[53] Chief Justice Thomas Cooley said that the Fourteenth Amendment had "not been agreed upon for the purpose of enlarging the sphere of powers of the general government, or of taking from the States any of those just powers of government which . . . were reserved to the States respectively."[54] When speaking of the First Amendment, Justice Potter Stewart observed that

> As a matter of history, the First Amendment was adopted solely as a limitation upon the newly created National Government. The events leading to its adoption strongly suggest that the Establishment Clause was primarily an attempt to insure that Congress not only would be powerless to establish a national church, but would also be unable to interfere with existing state establishments. . . . Each State was left free to go its own way and pursue its own policy with respect to religion. . . . It is not without irony that a constitutional provision evidently designed to leave the States free to go their own way should now have become a restriction upon their autonomy.[55]

Law Professor Stanley Morrison made a good point when he said "If it was one of the chief objects of the Fourteenth Amendment to incorporate the Bill of Rights, it is certainly surprising that it should have taken so long to find this out. Whatever obscurity may clothe the question today, the major purposes of a major constitutional amendment should not have been obscure to its contemporaries."[56] Incorporation was not discussed in the Joint Committee on Reconstruction that drafted the Amendment, and it was not debated on the floors of Congress, an extraordinary omission given the vast incursion on State sovereignty by incorporation of the Bill of Rights.[57]

Without this "incorporation" doctrine, the federal government would have far less power to interfere with actions by the states. And that is as it should be. That is what was intended by the Framers. If a state wants to restrict pornography, pass more gun control laws, or have prayer at football games, the federal government should have absolutely no control over these matters. These are not among the enumerated powers given to the federal government in the Constitution, so the federal government should have no power in these areas. These issues would be left to the states, and would be controlled by the state constitutions.

All the available evidence from the congressional debates, the state ratifying proceedings, and other original sources make it obvious that the authors of the Fourteenth Amendment did not intend for it to make the Bill of Rights specifically applicable to the states.[58] If they intended to do that, they would have said so explicitly. They would not have used such vague language for such a radical action. We have to understand, this was right after the Civil War, and it was a time of high emotion. Many people were angry at the Southern States for their "rebellion." People did not like to see the freed slaves deprived of their rights, and they wanted to fix that. So the Fourteenth Amendment was written with broad general language that said give the freedmen their rights. But the authors were careless with their construction, and did not thoroughly think through exactly how it was going to be litigated. And they did not think (or did not care) about the damage they were doing to the federal system of government. Their attitude was that the states could not be trusted to do the right thing, and so the federal government had to take control. That's what usually happens when you lose a war—you lose some of your freedoms. In this case, it was not just the losing Southern

States that paid the price. The loss of our federal system would prove to be a curse to the entire country.

DUE PROCESS

The Supreme Court has taken the phrase "due process" and stretched it far beyond its original meaning to use it as an excuse for an astounding expansion of federal powers. The phrase "due process" was copied from the Fifth Amendment. Naturally, it had the same meaning in both places. If there was any doubt about that, it was clearly stated by the Supreme Court when it said "The same words are contained in the Fifth Amendment. . . . When the same phrase was employed in the Fourteenth Amendment . . . it was used in the same sense and with no greater extent."[59] The meaning of this phrase was well established through many years of usage, and was well understood by the drafters of the Fourteenth Amendment to mean the use of the proper legal procedures. Alexander Hamilton made it clear that the words "due process" have a precise technical import, and are only applicable to the process and proceedings of the courts of justice; they can never be referred to an act of the legislature.[60] When Representative John Bingham of Ohio was asked by Representative Rogers "what do you mean by 'due process of law,'" he curtly replied, "the courts have settled that long ago, and the gentleman can go and read their decisions"—a reply that showed he deemed the question frivolous. He gave it the customary meaning recognized by the courts, and that was procedural.[61] Supreme Court Justice John Harlan also recognized its procedural nature when he said, "The Due Process Clause of the Fourteenth Amendment requires that those [State] procedures be fundamentally fair in all respects."[62] John Hart Ely, dean of Stanford Law School, said that he found no references in the legislative history that gave the Due Process Clause of the Fourteenth Amendment "more than a procedural connotation."[63] The remarks of Representative John Baker of Illinois confirm that they were making no changes to the meaning, but it was still viewed in existing procedural terms: "The Constitution already declares generally that no person shall be deprived of life, liberty, or property without due process of law. This declares particularly that no State shall do it."[64] Lawyer and author Charles P. Curtis explained that when the framers put due process "into the Fifth Amendment, its meaning was as fixed and definite as the common law could make a phrase. It had been chiseled into the law so incisively that any lawyer, and a few others, could read and understand. It meant a procedural process, which could be easily ascertained from almost any law book."[65] The Supreme Court ruled that due process "refers to that law of the land in each State. . . . Each State prescribe its own mode of judicial proceeding."[66]

The Supreme Court has, with no constitutional authority, stretched and expanded the phrase "Due Process" from its original meaning of proper legal procedure, to a new almost unlimited scope to give the federal government power over many traditional state functions. The first eight amendments to the Constitution were originally limitations on the federal government only—not the states. But the Supreme Court has magically discovered that Due Process now allows it to apply these to the states. Based on this assertion, the federal government now can control what the states do in fields such as pornography, assembly, trials, abortion, voting, reapportionment, marriage, child rearing, education, police operations, gun control, religion, property rights, etc., where the states should have primary control.

Justice Hugo Black understood that due process was a procedural protection, which would not allow the government to "deprive any person of those great fundamental rights . . . of life, liberty, and property, except by due process of law; that is, by an impartial trial according to the laws of the land."[67] But he expressed his dismay at the path taken by the Supreme Court by saying, "There is no constitutional support whatever for this Court to use the Due Process Clause as though it provided a blank check to alter the meaning of the Constitution as written, so as to add to it substantive constitutional changes, which a majority of the Court at any given time believes are needed to meet present-day problems."[68] Justice Black saw "a new and hitherto undiscovered scope for the Court's use of the due process clause."[69] Justice Felix Frankfurter was also concerned about the abuse, and said, "Through its steady expansion of the meaningless meaning of the 'Due Process' Clause of the Fourteenth Amendment, the Supreme Court is putting constitutional compulsion behind the private judgment of its members upon disputed and difficult questions of social policy."[70] Justice Byron White accused the Court of "imposing its own philosophical predilections upon state legislatures or Congress."[71] Supreme Court Justice William O Douglas put it another way when he said: "Due Process, to use the vernacular, is the wild card that can be put to such use as the judges choose."[72]

EQUAL PROTECTION

After the Civil War, the Southern States had passed laws which discriminated against blacks, and the Fourteenth Amendment was intended to guarantee that blacks would receive "equal protection of the laws," without discrimination based on race. Everyone at that time understood that that was its purpose and that was its meaning. But it was not intended to give blacks total equality in all aspects of life. For example, it did not give blacks the right to vote; that was done later by the Fifteenth Amendment. It clearly did not cover additional items like desegregation, reapportionment, and others.

The choice of language used in the Amendment—"nor deny to any person within its jurisdiction the *equal protection* of the laws"—was unfortunate, however, because, strictly speaking, it is impossible for all laws to always treat all people equally. There are many legitimate reasons for classifying people in different categories where the laws will treat them unequally. We have different laws for married and single people; for juveniles, adults and the elderly; for military, veterans and civilians; for indigents and millionaires; for residents of different states; for different types of businesses; and the list goes on. Since the Amendment contained an unenforceable and impossible phrase, that left the door open for future judges to "interpret" the words creatively to favor some particular group or cause that the judge wanted to help. Over the years, whenever a majority of Supreme Court Justices felt like they saw a possible injustice they wanted to address, they could use "equal protection" as an excuse, in total disregard for the original meaning of that phrase. We have reached the preposterous situation now where we have to give special legal rights to people based on the way they like to have sex.[73]

Chapter Nine

Clauses

THE GENERAL WELFARE CLAUSE

Article 1, Section 8, Paragraph 1 of the Constitution begins with the statement that the Congress "shall have power to lay and collect taxes, duties, imposts and excises, to pay the debts and provide for the common defence and general welfare of the United States." This is called the "General Welfare Clause." This is then followed with a list of specific enumerated powers given to Congress. Those who wanted to expand the power of the federal government tried to claim that the General Welfare Clause meant that Congress could do anything it wanted as long as it was said to be for the "general welfare" of the country. Others pointed out that our federal government was supposed to be one of limited powers, and so it could do nothing that was not included or implied in the specific enumerated powers listed. This meant that the phrase "general welfare" was not a grant of any additional powers, but was limited to actions within the powers specifically enumerated. If this phrase had been intended as a grant of unlimited authority, then there would have been no need to accompany it with a list of specific powers.

The General Welfare Clause can never be used, by itself, as the authority for any act of Congress. In The Federalist No. 41, James Madison says:

> It has been urged and echoed, that the power "to lay and collect taxes, duties, imposts, and excises, to pay the debts, and provide for the common defense and general welfare of the United States," amounts to an unlimited commission to exercise every power which

may be alleged to be necessary for the common defense or general welfare.... Had no other enumeration or definition of the powers of the Congress been found in the Constitution, than the general expressions just cited, the authors of the objection might have had some color for it.... But what color can the objection have, when a specification of the objects alluded to by these general terms immediately follows, and is not even separated by a longer pause than a semicolon.... For what purpose could the enumeration of particular powers be inserted, if these and all others were meant to be included in the preceding general power? Nothing is more natural nor common than first to use a general phrase, and then to explain and qualify it by a recital of particulars.

He went on to point out that the phrase appears to be copied from the Articles of Confederation, in which context there is universal agreement that a general grant of power was not intended.[1]

Madison expressed it well in a letter where he wrote, "If Congress can do whatever in their discretion can be done by money, and will promote the general welfare, the government is no longer a limited one possessing enumerated powers, but an indefinite one subject to particular exceptions."[2]

Thomas Jefferson said in a letter to Albert Gallatin in 1817 that "Congress had not unlimited powers to provide for the general welfare, but were restrained to those specifically enumerated."

In other words, it is absurd to claim that the phrase "general welfare" amounts to an unlimited authority for Congress to do anything it might claim is for the general welfare, because this phrase is immediately followed by a specific listing of the powers which are granted to Congress. However, in its desire to give the federal government almost unlimited power to do whatever it wanted, the Supreme Court has yielded to the temptation to give such an interpretation to that phrase. The Court stated in the case of *United States v. Butler* that the General Welfare Clause allows Congress to tax and spend in pursuit of the general welfare. The opinion stated that "public funds may be appropriated to provide for the general welfare of the United States.... The power of Congress to authorize expenditure of public moneys for public purposes is not limited by the direct grants of legislative power found in the Constitution."[3] In the 1937 case of *Helvering v. Davis*, the Court ruled that the General Welfare Clause was a separate source of congressional authority in that "Congress may spend money in aid of the general welfare."[4] *Helvering* also affirmed that the Court would defer to Congress in determining what legislative acts met the requirement of serving the general welfare. In other words, the Court would no longer be much of a check on Congress.

COMMERCE CLAUSE

Article I, Section 8, Paragraph 3 of the Constitution gives Congress authority "to regulate commerce with foreign nations, and among the several states, and with the Indian tribes." Under the Articles of Confederation, the original thirteen sovereign states had sometimes erected protectionist trade barriers for each individual state, such as tariffs, quotas, and taxes. The authors of the Constitution wanted to eliminate restrictions that would interfere with trade between states. They attempted to do this by giving Congress authority over trade between the states, in an effort to create a national free-trade zone.

The twentieth century Supreme Court wanted us to believe that they have discovered a new truth, that manufacturing and agriculture are now closely interrelated to interstate commerce, and that should allow the federal government broad discretion to regulate them. But this interdependence is not a recent development. This close relationship was a reality in 1787, and the Framers were well aware of it. Alexander Hamilton, in The Federalist No. 12, observed that the interests of agriculture and commerce are "intimately blended and interwoven."[5] Charles Pinkney discussed the interdependence of commerce and agriculture at the Constitutional Convention in Philadelphia. Thomas Dawes and James Bowdoin, both delegates at the Massachusetts ratifying convention, provided detailed discussions of this fact. James Wilson mentioned the same thing at the Pennsylvania ratifying convention, as did William Davie at the North Carolina convention. And yet the Founders gave repeated reassurances that manufacturing and agriculture and other local functions would remain under state control.[6]

There has been some debate in the past about the meaning of the word "commerce." Some have tried to claim that this meant "all gainful activity" in general, which would give the government much greater power. But Supreme Court Justice Clarence Thomas did extensive research to determine the meaning of this word at the time our Constitution was written.[7] He found conclusive evidence from multiple sources that "commerce among the states" meant marketing, trade and transportation between different states, and did not include activities internal to a single state, such as manufacturing, agriculture, or local trade. Eighteenth century dictionaries universally defined "commerce" to mean exchange, trade, or traffick. Justice Thomas found that the documents and exchanges during the debates when the states were ratifying the Constitution reveal the relatively limited reach of the Commerce Clause, and of federal power generally. The Founding Fathers confirmed that most areas of life (even many matters that would have substantial effects on commerce) would remain outside the reach of the Federal Government. Such affairs would continue to be under the exclusive control of the states.

In The Federalist No. 36, Alexander Hamilton treated commerce, agriculture, and manufacturing as three separate endeavors.[8] In The Federalist No. 17, Hamilton acknowledged that the federal government could not regulate agriculture:

> The administration of private justice between the citizens of the same state, the supervision of agriculture and of other concerns of a similar nature, all those things in short which are proper to be provided for by local legislation, can never be desirable cares of a general jurisdiction.[9]

Again, in The Federalist No. 34, he stated that the "internal encouragement of agriculture and manufactures" was an object of state expenditure. In fact, the Constitutional Convention had rejected a resolution that would have empowered the federal government directly to regulate manufacturing.[10] The Constitutional Convention also rejected a proposal to create a Secretary of Domestic Affairs, who would have authority to regulate agriculture.[11] So the control of manufacturing and agriculture was very deliberately excluded from the authority of the federal government.

We know how the people understood the states' authority because, during the debates at the time the Constitution was being ratified in the state conventions, advocates of the Constitution publicly listed examples of activities over which the federal government would have no authority. They did this to reassure everyone about the limited scope of federal power. Among the activities listed as being under the exclusive control of the states were marriage, divorce, manufacturing, agriculture, other business enterprises, property outside of interstate trade, commerce wholly within state lines, most crimes, social services, religion, education,[12] real property, firearms, domestic and family affairs, the press, and fisheries.[13] Obviously, many of these fields "substantially affect" interstate commerce, yet they were intended to be under state control.

Even early Supreme Court decisions recognized the limited reach of the Commerce Clause. In the case of *United States v. Dewitt* (1869), the Court said that the Commerce Clause "has always been understood as limited by its terms; and as a virtual denial of any power to interfere with the internal trade and business of the separate States."[14] In another case, in 1923, the Court clarified that "mining is not interstate commerce, but, like manufacturing, is a local business subject to local regulation."[15] The Court also found in 1936, "That commodities produced or manufactured within a state are intended to be sold or transported outside the state does not render their production or manufacture subject to federal regulation under the commerce clause."[16]

Some people have tried to question the meaning of the phrase "among the several states," claiming that this did not mean "between people of different states" (interstate), but rather had a broader connotation meaning "among the people of the states." If this were so, this broader interpretation might allow the federal government to regulate activity internal to a state. However, an analysis of the documentation relating to the drafting of the Constitution makes it clear that the more narrow interpretation is the correct one. It is obvious that this clause was intended to exclude intrastate commerce; otherwise it would simply say the "power to regulate commerce." So this power was not intended to extend to that commerce which is completely internal to a state.

In The Federalist No. 23, Alexander Hamilton explained that "the principal purposes to be answered by Union are these—the common defense of the members . . . the regulation of commerce with other nations and between the States."[17] Later, as Secretary of State, Hamilton repeatedly referred to Congress's power under the Commerce Clause as the power to regulate the "trade between the States."[18]

Unfortunately, the Supreme Court has moved away from this very logical interpretation, and allowed even the most fanciful relationship with interstate commerce to bring almost every conceivable activity under the Commerce Clause. Congress has used this as an excuse to commit all manner of intrusions upon our lives. The pinnacle of this arrogance came when the government told a farmer that he could not grow wheat on his own land for use by his own family, and the Supreme Court agreed.[19] The reasoning was that if he had not grown the wheat he would have had to purchase the wheat, therefore he was affecting interstate commerce. Of course, the Commerce Clause gives Congress authority to regulate "commerce," not "matters affecting commerce." But the Supreme Court continues to ignore the clear language, and sweeps up more and more activities under its authority:

- In 1937, the Supreme Court agreed that the federal government could apply labor regulations to an intrastate manufacturing company.[20]
- The federal government is allowed to fix prices for milk produced and sold within a single state because it is in competition with interstate milk.[21]
- The government is permitted to regulate wages and hours for local businesses, even though this has absolutely nothing to do with interstate commerce.[22]
- In 1975, the Supreme Court ruled that the federal government could control wages for state employees.[23]
- Restaurants, medical marijuana and loan sharking are now legitimate targets of federal control.[24]
- Why does the US Congress have any authority to rule that a felon cannot possess a gun? Because the gun has previously traveled in interstate commerce.[25]
- Even local mining operations are now under the control of the federal government because they are "impairing natural beauty" and might affect the environment,[26] and for the purpose of restoring mining sites to agricultural uses.[27] These purposes have nothing to do with facilitating interstate commerce, but the statute was written with the pretext that it affects interstate commerce because the coal from the mine will travel in interstate commerce.

Supreme Court Justice Sandra Day O'Connor recognized that there are no "meaningful limits on the Commerce Clause . . . Congress can regulate intrastate activity without check."[28] She also observed that

The Court's definition of economic activity is breathtaking . . . the Court's definition of economic activity for purposes of Commerce Clause jurisprudence threatens to sweep all of productive human activity into federal regulatory reach . . . It

will not do to say that Congress may regulate
noncommercial activity simply because it may have
an effect on the demand for commercial goods, or
because the noncommercial endeavor can, in some
sense, substitute for commercial activity. Most
commercial goods or services have some sort of
privately producible analogue. Home care substitutes
for daycare. Charades games substitute for movie
tickets. Backyard or windowsill gardening
substitutes for going to the supermarket. To draw the
line wherever private activity affects the demand for
market goods is to draw no line at all . . . We have
already rejected the result that would follow—a
federal police power.[29]

Through a series of similar Supreme Court decisions over
the years, the Court has effectively destroyed any distinction
between interstate and intrastate commerce. The effect of this has
been to give the federal government almost unlimited power to
regulate every facet of our lives. Supreme Court Justice Clarence
Thomas described this abuse:

By holding that Congress may regulate activity that
is neither interstate nor commerce under the
Interstate Commerce Clause, the Court abandons any
attempt to enforce the Constitution's limits on federal
power . . . . It can regulate virtually anything—and
the Federal Government is no longer one of limited
and enumerated powers . . . . The Government's
rationale—that it may regulate the production or
possession of any commodity for which there is an
interstate market—threatens to remove the
remaining vestiges of States' traditional police
powers . . . . This carves out a vast swath of activities
that are subject to federal regulation . . . . If the
majority is to be taken seriously, the Federal
Government may now regulate quilting bees, clothes
drives, and potluck suppers throughout the 50 States.
This makes a mockery of Madison's assurance to the
people of New York that the "powers delegated" to the
Federal Government are "few and defined," while
those of the States are "numerous and
indefinite." . . . One searches the Court's opinion in

vain for any hint of what aspect of American life is reserved to the States.[30]

How did the Supreme Court manage to so distort the meaning of this clause? As we have seen, the answer is not in any vagueness in the language. No rational person who is trying to give an honest interpretation could say that the consumption of homegrown wheat is "commerce among the several states." The Justices who perpetrated this travesty apparently hold to a strong belief that the government should do everything it can do to further the public good. Basically, they reject the idea of limited federal government. The only reason to restrict the power of the government is if there is some danger that the government might abuse that power. But, in their view, the government generally acts in the public interest, so any limitation on government power is just reducing the amount of good that the government can do. With this logic, they can rationalize the abuse of their authority to give the government almost unlimited power over the people.

NECESSARY AND PROPER CLAUSE

Article I, Section 8 of the Constitution is a list of the specific powers which are given to the Congress. Following this listing of its enumerated powers, the last paragraph in the section says that Congress has the power "to make all laws which shall be necessary and proper for carrying into Execution the foregoing Powers, and all other Powers vested by this Constitution in the Government of the United States, or in any Department or Officer thereof."

Alexander Hamilton pointed out that the phrase "necessary and proper" was not intended to create any new powers in addition to the enumerated ones. In The Federalist No. 33 he stated:

It may be affirmed with perfect confidence, that the constitutional operation of the intended government would be precisely the same, if these clauses were entirely obliterated, as if they were repeated in every article. They are only declaratory of a truth, which would have resulted by necessary and unavoidable implication from the very act of constituting a Federal Government, and vesting it with certain specified powers.[31]

During the debates over ratification, attorney and Congressman Archibald Maclaine explained to his fellow North Carolinians that "this clause gives no new power, but declares that those already given are to be executed by proper laws."[32]

Thomas Jefferson argued that "necessary" means include only "those means without which the grant or power would be nugatory," and not those that are merely "convenient." Otherwise, he said, any non-enumerated power may be allowed by such latitude of construction.[33]

Unfortunately, the phrase "necessary and proper" has been interpreted very broadly by the Supreme Court to allow a wide variety of actions by Congress. This phrase should be understood to allow only those laws that are *necessary* to accomplish the specific enumerated powers spelled out in the Constitution. But the Court has lowered the standard, so that instead of a law having to be *necessary*, it is adequate now if a law just makes it more *convenient* for Congress to execute their powers. This was spelled out in the 1805 case of *United States v. Fisher*, where the Court said Congress "must be empowered to use any means which are in fact conducive to the exercise of a power granted by the Constitution."[34] In the 1819 case of *McCulloch v. Maryland*, the Court took it further, and actually said that Congress would be allowed to use any measures that are "convenient or useful," and which are not specifically prohibited by the Constitution.[35] If Congress can do anything that is not prohibited by the Constitution, that gives it a blank check to write virtually any laws it wants. This is a dramatic shift from the original concept of a government of limited powers.

What is the solution? Interpreting "necessary" to be the same as "convenient" is clearly inappropriate, giving Congress virtually unlimited power. But going to the other extreme, and saying that something has to be absolutely and indispensably necessary would be too restrictive, and would not allow for reasonable implied powers. The correct approach must obviously be somewhere between these extremes. Experience has shown that we need to move far away from the "convenient" interpretation toward something similar to the legal concept of "strict scrutiny," requiring the government to prove a "compelling purpose" to justify the legislation, and that the law is the "least restrictive" alternative from the standpoint of protecting individual liberty.

CONTRACTS CLAUSE

Another example of the courts moving away from the Constitution is the Contracts Clause. Paragraph 1 of Section 10 of Article 1 of the Constitution contains the requirement that "No State shall . . . pass any . . . Law impairing the Obligation of Contracts." That sounds like a perfectly reasonable rule. After two parties have entered into a contract, it would not be fair for the state to do something to change the terms of that contract to cause one of the parties to suffer some loss. But over the years, we have seen a great expansion of the intrusive role of government.

Before our constitution was written in 1787, there had been a proliferation of special interest laws to give relief to some debtors. This was always justified by a claim of some economic emergency. A primary purpose of the Contracts Clause in the Constitution was to stop these types of laws, which penalized creditors for every economic downturn.[36]

In 1933, in response to a large number of home foreclosures, Minnesota passed a law which altered the terms of the contracts of mortgages, reducing the creditors' rights to foreclose on their mortgages. The Supreme Court upheld this law in the case of *Home Building & Loan Association v. Blaisdell,* saying that the state has the "authority to safeguard the vital interests of its people," and also that "the economic interests of the State may justify the exercise of its continuing and dominant protective power notwithstanding interference with contracts."[37] In his dissent to this ruling, Justice Sutherland wrote that the "effect of the Minnesota legislation, though serious enough in itself, is of trivial significance compared with the far more serious and dangerous inroads upon the limitations of the Constitution." The Court also stated that the law "was not for the mere advantage of particular individuals, but for the protection of a basic interest in society." This is a very incorrect and dangerous philosophy. The Constitution was intended to protect individuals and minorities from the tyranny of a more powerful majority. This is one of the central foundations of our unique form of government.

This seems like an almost unlimited power if the State can disregard the Constitution based on this vague idea of helping the "interests of its people," or the "interests of the State." And doesn't this violate the most fundamental concepts of "due process?" Of course it does, but the Court pretends to get around that by simply redefining the term. This new definition shows up in another case, where the Supreme Court said that "regulation which is reasonable in relation to its subject, and is adopted in the interests of the community is due process."[38] Here we see another vague notion of "the interests of the community," which supposedly gives the government a blank check to ignore the Constitution.

Esteemed law professor Richard A. Epstein said it very well when he wrote:

> The passage contains some of the most misguided thinking on constitutional interpretation imaginable. The operative assumption seems to be that questions of constitutional law are to be answered according to whether or not we like the Constitution as it was originally drafted. If we do not, we are then free to introduce into the document those provisions that we think more congenial to our time.[39]

In the 1937 case of *West Coast Hotel v. Parrish*, the Supreme Court upheld a law establishing a minimum wage for women.[40] No longer would the freedom of contract be safeguarded as a fundamental right, and given the highest degree of constitutional protection by the Supreme Court. According to the Court, the protection of the "health, safety, morals, and welfare of the people" is more important than "freedom of contract." This is a remarkable shift from the 1923 case of *Adkins v. Children's Hospital*, where the Supreme Court ruled that a federal law guaranteeing a minimum wage to women was unconstitutional because it interfered with the ability of companies and their workers to contract with each other.[41] The Court said:

> That the right to contract about one's affairs is a part of the liberty of the individual protected by this clause, is settled by the decisions of this Court and is no longer open to question. . . . Within this liberty are contracts of employment of labor. In making such contracts, generally speaking, the parties have an equal right to obtain from each other the best terms they can as the result of private bargaining.

In a Supreme Court case in 1978, Justice Potter Stewart wrote the opinion saying that, even if a law substantially impaired a contract, it might still be valid if it claimed to "protect a broad societal interest," or "to deal with a broad generalized economic or social problem."[42] Of course, we know that a legislature could probably make those kinds of claims for almost any law. In another case, in 1983, Supreme Court Justice Harry Blackmun made the amazing statement that impairment of a contract could be justified by the state interest in protecting "consumers from the escalation of natural gas prices."[43] In the case of *Exxon Corp. v. Eagerton*, Exxon had a contract which allowed them to pass through the cost of a tax increase to their customers. The state passed a law prohibiting them from passing through this tax increase, and the Supreme Court upheld this law because of the state's interest in protecting consumers from higher prices.[44] In *Blaisdell*, the excuse for allowing the state to impair a contract was a temporary emergency—a high rate of foreclosures. Over time, the Court created more relaxed standards that gave more deference to state legislatures. The problem now no longer had to be called an *emergency*, but need only be a mere economic hardship. It is obvious that the Court has assumed the authority to do whatever seems right to them, regardless of the text of the Constitution. The right of contract is one that is no longer going to be diligently protected by the Supreme Court.

EX POST FACTO

For centuries, men have instinctively known that it was unjust to enact a law that would be applied retroactively. If an act was legal when it was done, then the person could not have intentionally engaged in illegal conduct, and it would be terribly unfair to punish him for that act. Individuals must be given fair notice of what is prohibited by the law, so that they can comply with the laws. This was such an important principle to the authors of our Constitution, that they put it in the Constitution twice. In Section 9 of Article 1, the national Congress is forbidden to enact ex post facto laws. In Section 10 of Article 1, the states are also prohibited from enacting ex post facto laws. The Supreme Court has outlined two essential elements needed for a law to violate the ex post facto prohibition: a law cannot retroactively alter the definition of the crime, or increase the punishment for the crime.[45]

The desecration of this constitutional requirement began early. In 1798, the Supreme Court ruled that the ex post facto clause applied only to criminal, not civil, statutes.[46] Many people saw a problem with this interpretation, including Supreme Court Justice William Johnson, who, in 1829 complained about "that unhappy idea that the phrase '*ex post facto*' in the Constitution of the United States was confined to criminal cases exclusively." He opined that the prohibition against ex post facto laws "does extend to civil as well as criminal cases," and he gave historical evidence for that position.[47] Other scholars, law professors, and even some Supreme Court Justices have echoed his concerns, but without success.[48]

The exception for civil law does not make sense for several reasons. In both civil and criminal matters, people should be able to rely on existing law when ordering their affairs. But this may be especially important in the civil law because firms research and rely on existing law in making deals regarding investments and businesses. It has been said that investment currently lags in Russia, in part, because of individuals' inability to rely on ever-changing administrative rules and regulations.[49] The possibility for abuse of retroactive law is also present more in civil law than in criminal law, because legislatures can enact retroactive laws to reward contributors and constituent groups, or to punish political opponents.

One of the worst pieces of retroactive legislation in our history is the so-called "Superfund" law, enacted in 1980. The purpose of this law was to finance cleanup of toxic waste dumps, but there are many problems with this statute. Judges trying to interpret it have labeled it a hastily and inadequately drafted piece of compromise legislation, marred by vague terminology. The bill was the product of private and off-the-record discussions between senators representing different interests and with varying understandings of what was being accomplished. The bill was passed so quickly that it lacked the very basic and valuable legislative history, such as committee reports, bill markups, and hearing transcripts. The reason for this near panic to pass this legislation was the discovery of noxious materials leaking out of the ground at the Love Canal housing development. The resulting media hysteria convinced the public of a national toxic waste crisis. The alleged health risks at Love Canal were actually greatly exaggerated. The dire warnings generated by early speculation captured headlines, but later more responsible research yielded different results. A June 19, 1981, *Science* article, "Cancer Incidence in the Love Canal Area," stated that "data from the New York Cancer Registry show no evidence for higher cancer rates associated with residence near the Love Canal toxic waste burial site in comparison with the entire state outside of New York City."

The biggest problem with this law was the assignment of retroactive liability for cleanup costs. The idea was that the EPA would somehow identify hazardous toxic waste dumps for cleanup across the country. The EPA would then recover the costs of the cleanup from so-called responsible parties. However, the statute never defined exactly who these liable parties might be. The way it has been interpreted is that a company that deposited a small amount of waste in the site many, many years ago might be held liable for a large share of the cleanup costs. This could easily amount to millions of dollars. George Clemon Freeman Jr., chairman of the business law section of the American Bar Association, said Superfund's retroactive liability is "without any precedent in the civilized or uncivilized world." The actual cleaning up of sites has been limited, but Superfund has enriched lawyers, and ruined many small businesses that could be connected, however remotely, with waste disposal practices that were legal at the time they occurred. One sign painter had to pay because wood scrap from his signs found its way to a site. The same thing happened to a pizzeria, identified by its discarded cardboard boxes.

Banks that foreclosed on businesses linked to waste sites have been held liable, as have insurance companies that insured truck fleets. Landlords have been held liable for not preventing acts of tenants before the actions became illegal. One iron and metal works in Milwaukee, Wisconsin, had occasionally purchased scrap metals from a landfill but did not deposit waste there. Nevertheless, one former employee of the landfill said he thought that the iron and metal works was a hauler of waste, so the EPA lawyers forced the firm to pay a $15,000 settlement.[50]

Another retroactive law had a particularly cruel effect. In 1982, Humberto Fernandez-Vargas, an alien who had previously been deported, reentered the United States illegally. Over the next 20 years, he remained here. He worked as a truck driver, owned a trucking business, fathered a child, and eventually married the child's mother, a United States citizen. The laws in place at the time of his entry, and for the first 15 years of his residence in this country, would have rewarded this behavior, allowing him to seek discretionary relief from deportation on the basis of his continued presence in, and strong ties to, the United States.

In 1996, however, Congress passed a new version of the applicable provision, eliminating almost entirely the possibility of relief from deportation for aliens who reenter the country illegally having previously been deported.[51] Based on this new law, the immigration authorities in 2003 reinstated his deportation order based on his actions fourteen years before the law was passed. This is an obviously harsh and unfair retroactive effect.

Chapter Ten

Overcriminalization

We have seen a virtual explosion of federal criminal laws in recent years which stems from several factors. One source of new criminal laws is the knee-jerk reaction of congressmen to want to rush to pass a law to pretend that they are trying to solve whatever the hot-button problem of the month is. It might be a financial scandal, a child kidnapping, or an environmental mess, but the politicians will rush to introduce a new bill to show that they are "doing something." Dramatic news stories about violent crime are especially effective in arousing fear in the public. Legislators realize that their reelection may depend on the public's perception of their toughness against crime.

In the last century, Congress has also increasingly used the criminal law to enforce complex regulatory systems. The Constitution says that "All legislative Powers herein granted shall be vested in a Congress of the United States."[1] Nevertheless, in spite of this very clear directive, Congress has delegated much of its lawmaking authority to unelected bureaucrats. Congress writes laws very broadly, and then relies on unelected government agencies to write thousands of regulations to implement these laws. Even though Congress is given legislative power by the Constitution, rules carrying the force of law are routinely written today entirely within executive branch agencies. Many of these regulations are detailed and complex and have criminal penalties for violations. Actually, only about 1 percent of the rules we must live by are enacted by the most accountable branch of government—Congress.[2]

Some scholars have likened this making of administrative edicts outside of Congress to the proclivity of pre-modern kings to rule through proclamations or decrees.[3] This practice was gradually resisted through the Magna Carta and by acts of British Parliament. The Framers of our Constitution tried to preclude this by the division of powers, to prevent the concentration of all power in a single entity. However, it has now returned in the actions of the unelected agencies that control many aspects of American life.

When this question of delegation came before the Supreme Court, the Court ruled in 1928 that Congressional delegation of legislative authority is constitutional so long as Congress provides an "intelligible principle" to guide the executive branch.[4] The agencies cannot be left to create laws at their discretion, but must be given detailed instructions and criteria in the law passed by Congress. Of course, as in many other areas, the Court has watered down these restrictions until they are almost meaningless. For example, in 1943, the Supreme Court upheld a delegation to the Federal Communications Commission to regulate radio broadcasting. The so-called "intelligible principle" was that the regulation had to be consistent with the "public interest, convenience, or necessity."[5] In the 1989 case *Mistretta v. United States*, the Court stated that "this Court has deemed it constitutionally sufficient if Congress clearly delineates the *general policy*, the public agency which is to apply it, and the boundaries of this delegated authority."[6]

When Congress wrote the Clean Air Act, it delegated legislative authority to the Environmental Protection Agency (EPA) to set air quality standards. The EPA was directed to apply criteria "requisite to protect the public health" with "an adequate margin for safety." When this was challenged in the case of *Whitman v. American Trucking Associations*, the federal Court of Appeals agreed that such nebulous and ambiguous guidelines were an unconstitutional delegation of legislative power.[7] Congress had not given the EPA adequate criteria for just how much is too much pollution. Air pollution controls are expensive, costing Americans many billions of dollars each year. These significant matters must be debated in Congress so the voters can see what their congressmen are doing to them. Unfortunately, the Supreme Court disagreed with the Court of Appeals, and upheld the delegation.[8] These nebulous guidelines from Congress are the same as no guidelines, so the bureaucrats are essentially free to do whatever they want to do with no accountability to Congress or to the American people.

Nobel Prize winning economist Milton Friedman described the problem well:

> As the scope and role of government expands . . . the bureaucracy that is needed to administer government grows and increasingly interposes itself between the citizenry and the representatives they choose. . . . The unelected congressional bureaucracy almost surely has far more influence today in shaping the detailed laws that are passed than do our elected representatives. The situation is even more extreme in the administration of government programs. The vast federal bureaucracy spread through the many government departments and independent agencies is literally out of control of the elected representatives of the public. Elected Presidents and senators and representatives come and go but the civil service remains. . . . The high-level bureaucrats who have been assigned these functions cannot imagine that . . . the rules and regulations they issue . . . are the problem rather than the solution. They inevitably become persuaded that they are indispensable, that they know more about what should be done than uninformed voters or self-interested businessmen.[9]

Small businesses are the economic engine of America, providing over half of our gross domestic product, and creating the majority of net new jobs. Most of these numerous regulations are applicable to small businesses just the same as they are to large businesses. The problem is that this imposes disproportionate burdens on smaller companies. The cost of compliance with federal regulations is significantly higher per employee for small businesses than for larger corporations. So large companies and their armies of lobbyists sometimes say they support certain regulations, knowing that these regulations will impose sizable penalties on their smaller competitors. For example, shoemaker Nike got considerable favorable publicity for its support of severe restrictions on carbon emissions. This doesn't bother Nike because its factories are in Asia, and these rules only cover the United States. On the other hand, it will impose major costs on smaller competitors, like New Balance, which produces shoes in the United States.[10]

If the people cannot vote for these bureaucrats, then at the very least these regulation writers should be accountable to someone who the people do elect such as the President. However, many of the regulatory agencies have an astounding level of independence. They are not accountable to anyone. The Supreme Court has ruled that the President does not have the power to dismiss some of these officials at will. They are not even accountable to the courts—it is nearly impossible to get a federal regulation overturned by a court because the Supreme Court has decreed that lower courts must defer to an agency's interpretation of the law unless it is completely irrational.[11] What is even worse is that this massive bureaucracy is now a permanent form of government. Presidents come and go, but the nonelected bureaucrats remain.

One reason why politicians like this system is that it helps the politicians avoid accountability. The elected members of Congress are not punished by the voters for this overreach, because no one knows who the unelected bureaucrats who generated these regulations are. This defeats one of the basic features of our system which is the accountability of lawmakers at the ballot box. The result is that the general public is largely locked out of the decision-making process. The individual voter generally has no influence at all with the regulatory agencies. In fact, politically powerful special interests and corporations, with their hordes of lawyers and lobbyists, often control the regulatory process, and write rules which benefit them financially.

It is an absolute fantasy to expect the average person to be able to find, much less understand, these hundreds of thousands of laws and regulations. The Congressional Research Service tried to identify and count all of the federal criminal laws, and it could not do it. With all of these vague and unfathomable laws, everyone is unknowingly violating laws all the time, and is vulnerable to possible criminal prosecution for doing what no one could have known was illegal. The devastating result of this situation is that it gives the government prosecutors tremendous discretion to decide who to prosecute. The government then has the potential to use the justice system as a weapon against its political opponents. US Attorney General Robert Jackson recognized that a prosecutor could pick a person and then look for an offense. "With the law books filled with a great assortment of crimes," he said, "a prosecutor stands a fair chance of finding at least a technical violation of some act on the part of almost anyone."[12]

The proper role of the government in a criminal case should be to search for truth and justice. To this end, the government should not only be the plaintiff, but also represent the defendant to ensure that he is treated fairly, and that his rights are respected. For many an ambitious prosecutor, however, the principles of fairness and justice are expendable in his quest to get a conviction at any cost. Ideally, the most important function of the law should not be merely to punish wrongdoers, but to prevent the government from using the legal system as an instrument of oppression. That concept has sadly been lost today as prosecutors take advantage of the law's vagueness, complexity, vastness, and frequent inequity to advance their careers by sometimes persecuting perfectly innocent persons.

The situation is totally out of control. The federal criminal code needs to be streamlined. Duplicate laws should be consolidated. Obsolete and unnecessary laws should be removed. Federal criminal laws are now scattered throughout the various titles of the US Code. All criminal laws need to be consolidated into Title 18. They should be well organized and indexed, and made available free of charge on the internet for anyone to read them. A sunset provision should be included in all new and revised regulations and criminal laws. Congress should enact a general blanket requirement that all executive agency regulations would be void unless, within a certain time, Congress enacted them into law. This would allow constituents to see how their congressman voted on a particular onerous regulation. Violations of regulations issued by government agencies should also be changed from criminal penalties to civil penalties.

STATE CRIMES

One of the major problems with the recent huge increase in federal criminal laws is that much of this legislation significantly overlaps crimes traditionally prosecuted by the states. Especially in the late twentieth century, concern with organized crime, drugs, street violence, and other problems precipitated a huge rise in federal legislation tending to criminalize activity involving local conduct, conduct previously left to state regulation. For example, there is a federal criminal law against carjacking. Logically, that is a very local matter which should be handled by local police and local courts. But this is just one example among many where the feds have imprudently stepped in.

Many of these new laws are driven by political popularity and not federal need. Laws are often enacted in a patchwork response to sensational events, rather than as part of a cohesive plan. Lawmakers have found that criminal legislation is popular among their constituents. Lay people can easily be fooled into believing that this means a tougher stance against crime. So this greater federalization of crime is creating the illusion of more effective crime control. Much of this legislation results from the Supreme Court twisting the meaning of the Constitution to allow laws to be justified under the Commerce Clause, even though these laws have nothing to do with interstate commerce.

We now have the situation where a person could be tried and acquitted of a crime in a state court, and then that person could be tried again based on the same act in a federal court. This obviously violates the Fifth Amendment's prohibition against double jeopardy. However, the Supreme Court has allowed this based on the technicality that the state and federal governments are separate, so a federal prosecution is not exactly a repeat of the state prosecution. But to a rational person, this argument is not credible. From the point of view of the defendant, it seems like he is being tried again for the same action, so his protection against double jeopardy has been stolen from him (see Chapter 6).

Many state laws have provisions designed to give greater protection to the rights of the defendant than the federal laws covering the same crime. Sometimes the prosecutor will decide to charge a person under federal law, rather than state law, just for the purpose of avoiding these state laws which are more favorable to the accused. The penalties under federal law are frequently much more severe than the state laws for the same offense, so the seemingly arbitrary decision of whether to go federal or state can have a significant effect on the time served in prison. All this contributes to the image of a justice system that is subjective, unfair, arbitrary, and capricious.

This over-federalization is inconsistent with the traditional notion that law enforcement and prevention of crime in this country are basically state functions. For much of our national history, we recognized a deeply rooted principle that the general police power resides in the states, and that federal law enforcement should be narrowly limited. This was even acknowledged by the Supreme Court, when it said "Preventing and dealing with crime is much more the business of the States than it is of the Federal Government."[13] Several years ago, the Judicial Conference of the United States adopted the *Long Range Plan for the Federal Courts*. The first recommendation of the plan says: "Congress should commit itself to conserving the federal courts as a distinctive judicial forum of limited jurisdiction in our system of federalism. Civil and criminal jurisdiction should be assigned to the federal courts only to further clearly defined and justified national interests, leaving to the state courts the responsibility for adjudicating all other matters." The Chief

Justice of the Supreme Court, William Rehnquist, in his address to the meeting of the American Law Institute in 1998, said that he was concerned "that our system will look more and more like the French government, where even the most minor details are ordained by the national government in Paris."

The American Bar Association (ABA) created a Task Force on Federalization of Criminal Law to study this issue. This task force identified several adverse consequences of inappropriately federalized crime, including these:

- This process can undermine the strength of the states, which are an independent intrinsic component of the American governmental system. The disruption of the delicate balance between the state and federal governments can cause serious problems.
- We have always had a healthy distrust of the centralization of criminal law enforcement power in the federal government. Creation of a powerful national police force has always been considered a potentially dangerous proposition.
- Where there is both a state and federal law covering the same or similar acts, there is frequently a large difference in the penalty associated with the two laws. This seems fundamentally unfair because two people convicted of the same act might spend greatly different times in prison depending on the unpredictable decision of the federal prosecutor as to whether he wanted to prosecute in federal court or leave it to the state to prosecute.
- It can have a detrimental impact on the state courts, state prosecutors, attorneys, and state investigating agents who bear the overwhelming share of responsibility for criminal law enforcement.
- It has the potential to diminish citizen confidence in both state and local law enforcement mechanisms.
- It increases unreviewable federal prosecutorial discretion.[14]

Congress and the courts both need to resist the enactment of federal laws for criminal activity that is essentially local in character. To create a federal crime, a strong federal interest in the matter should be clearly shown. The ABA Task Force found that "there is no persuasive evidence that federalization of local crime makes the streets safer for American citizens." Supreme Court Justice Potter Stewart expressed his concern that, if this trend continues, Congress could nationalize nearly all crime and, in the process, take over a core function of the states. He said, "The definition and prosecution of local, intrastate crime are reserved to the States under the Ninth and Tenth Amendments."[15] The basic foundation of our constitution is federalism—the idea that some powers are reserved to the states. This concept is being destroyed in our inexorable move toward a powerful, centralized government.

MILITARIZATION OF POLICE

The Founders of this country had a fear of a standing army in peacetime. They knew that despotic governments have used standing armies to control the people and impose tyranny. The current police state shows that their fears were justified. We are seeing an increasing militarization of the police. This has not occurred suddenly, but rather so subtly that most American citizens are hardly even aware of it. Little by little, police authority has expanded, more and more military style weapons have been acquired by the police, and one exception after another has been made to the constitutional standards that have historically restrained police authority. In a recent year, there were 1,575 law enforcement officers involved in excessive force reports.[16]

In some cities, the police have adopted the routine practice of stopping and frisking people who are merely walking down the street, where there is no evidence of wrongdoing. This is the mark of a police state, where everyone is a suspect.[17] Roadside strip searches in plain view of passing traffic are becoming a more common police tactic. The police now have more authority to break down the door of a person's home or apartment without a warrant (see Chapter 5).

Police Special Weapons and Tactics (SWAT) teams are heavily armed and specially trained units, which were originally established for the purpose of handling unique, high-risk operations. They typically have advanced, specialized firearms and equipment intended for challenging and dangerous tasks. Now, however, these paramilitary units are frequently being used for routine matters that could have been satisfactorily performed by traditional civilian officers. For example, 75–80 percent of SWAT team actions are now for mere warrant service. One study indicated that SWAT teams are deployed an average of 4.5 times per day in Maryland, with 94 percent of these deployments being for something as minor as serving search or arrest warrants. In one county, more than 50 percent of SWAT operations were for misdemeanors or non-serious felonies.[18]

The military mindset adopted by many SWAT team members encourages a tendency to employ lethal force. The mere presence of SWAT units during routine police actions has actually injected a level of danger and violence into police-citizen interactions that was not present when these interactions were handled by traditional civilian officers. In one drug raid, for example, an unarmed pregnant woman was shot as she attempted to flee the police by climbing out a window. In another, an 88-year-old African American woman was shot and killed when police barged unannounced into her home. There are many documented instances of police who have broken down doors, entered the wrong houses, and killed innocent people. In many cases, nonviolent offenders, such as recreational pot smokers, were needlessly killed. Many times, innocent families, sometimes with children, were roused from their beds at gunpoint, and subjected to the terror of being apprehended and searched. Excessive collateral damage to both people and property tends to go hand in hand with an overuse of paramilitary forces.

At least 50,000 no-knock police raids are carried out each year, usually by heavily armed paramilitary units. At first, no-knock raids were generally employed only in situations where innocent lives were determined to be at imminent risk. That has changed with the unsettling rise in the use of paramilitary units in routine police work.[19]

- An undercover detective observed optometrist Sal Culosi wagering on college football games at a bar. The police department sent a heavily armed SWAT team to Mr. Culosi's home even though he had no prior criminal record or any history of violence. Mr. Culosi was alone and unarmed, and made no threatening movements or gestures, but a SWAT team officer shot him in the chest with a .45 caliber handgun, killing him.[20]
- A group of Tibetan monks were in the United States on a church-sponsored mission of world peace, hoping to share the plight of the Tibetan people. Through a mix-up, the group did not realize that their visas had expired. The next thing they knew, immigration officials showed up at their door with a SWAT team in full riot gear, and arrested them.

- Ray Schulze was working in the barn of the Society of St. Francis animal shelter in Wisconsin, when a swarm of squad cars arrived with a search warrant for a baby fawn. A family who thought the animal had been abandoned had brought the fawn to the shelter. The agents told the staff they had come to seize the deer because the law forbids possession of wildlife. Schulze explained that the deer was scheduled to go to the wildlife rehabilitation reserve the following day. He believed the officers were going to take the deer to the shelter, but instead the officers killed the fawn. When Schulze asked why the fawn was killed, an officer said, "That's our policy."
- Kathryn Johnston was a 92-year-old woman who lived in a crime-ridden neighborhood in Atlanta. Police lied about seeing drug activity at her house in order to get a search warrant. The officers cut off burglar bars and broke down her door. A terrified Johnston, thinking she was being victimized by a home invasion, fired a warning shot through the door. Narcotics officers responded with a hail of gunfire, killing her. After the shooting, the police planted marijuana in Johnston's home to make it look like a drug house.
- On May 7, 1998, police broke down the door and threw a flashbang grenade into the home of Jeanine Jean. Frightened, Jean ran into a closet with her six-year-old son and called 911. Police pulled Jean from the closet, handcuffed her, and then questioned her at gunpoint in front of her son. Jean, who had had surgery the day before, began bleeding when her surgical wound ruptured during the raid. After 90 minutes, police realized they had the wrong apartment and left without explanation. They left Jean's door hanging from its hinges.[21]
- A heavily armed team from the Department of Education broke down the door at the home of Kenneth Wright at 6 a.m. on June 7, 2011. They handcuffed Mr. Wright, and put him and his three young children in a police car for six hours while they searched his house. The children, ages 3 through 11, were terrified and crying. The federal agents were looking for evidence related to fraud in connection with student financial aid.[22]

The police have tried to claim that the increased armament and hardware is needed because of the more powerful military weapons used by criminals. But actual data does not back up such claims. Multiple research studies over a period of many years have confirmed that only a very small percentage of crimes in the United States were committed with military-style weapons.[23]

The use of SWAT was originally for the purpose of diffusing already violent situations, such as hostage situations, or engaging heavily armed suspects. We have now seen many instances where heavily armed men with badges were sent into an otherwise non-violent situation, and created violence where none existed before. Sending adrenaline pumped men with military weapons into someone's home in the middle of the night creates a volatile environment that not only puts suspects and bystanders at risk, but the officers themselves. The inevitable result is that people are needlessly killed.

SCHOOL

Whereas in the past minor behavioral infractions at school such as shooting spit wads may have warranted a trip to the principal's office, today they are sometimes elevated to the level of criminal charges with all that implies. Consequently, young people are now being forcibly removed by police officers from the classroom, arrested, handcuffed, transported in the back of police squad cars, and placed in police holding cells until their frantic parents can get them out. Not only is everyone unnecessarily traumatized, but the experience will follow the child for the rest of his life in, not only fear of the police, but a suspension on his school record, and in some cases a criminal arrest record.

Several years ago, it became fashionable for schools to adopt what was called "zero tolerance" policies. This means to punish all offences severely, no matter how minor the misbehavior. These rules primary apply to drugs and weapons, but are frequently applied to other minor transgressions such as disrespect and over-the-counter medications. The result is that innocent childish behavior is punished the same as a person who acts with criminal willful intent to commit harm. This apparently helps schools and parents feel like "something is being done" in response to the school shootings and gang violence. Of course, this is absurd because the people who shot up schools and killed students would not have been deterred from their shooting sprees by the existence of a zero tolerance police.

- At Pensacola High School in Florida, a 15-year-old girl was expelled for a year for bringing nail clippers to class. She had a strong academic record and no record of disciplinary problems, but the 2-inch nail file attached to the clippers was considered by the school to be a weapon.

- A five-year-old Pennsylvania girl had a pink Hello Kitty toy gun that blew soapy bubbles. As she was waiting for the school bus one day, she told another girl that she was going to shoot her with the toy gun. For that, she was suspended from kindergarten for 10 days for making a "terroristic threat."

- Three teenagers, all students at Cypress Lake High School in Fort Myers, Florida, were on a school bus when two other students got into a heated argument. One of them pulled a loaded revolver on the other, and aimed it at his head. The three didn't hesitate— they tackled and disarmed the suspect, who was later arrested. The three students who prevented a possible murder did not receive a hero's welcome when they returned to school. Instead, the school suspended them for the remainder of the week because they were involved in a gun "incident."

- An honor student in the ninth grade at Spotsylvania High School in Virginia was playing with a plastic tube, shooting small plastic pellets at fellow students. The school responded by expelling him for the rest of the school year, and reporting him to the police which initiated juvenile proceedings for criminal assault against him. He had hoped to attend the US Naval Academy, but now his criminal record will make that impossible.

- Three 13-year-olds were suspended from school for a year because they were caught playing with a small laser pointer in class. The laser pointer was shaped to resemble a gun, so the school considers it a "firearm facsimile," and a violation of their zero tolerance rules.

- Ten-year-old James was dealing with severe emotional and behavioral disturbances. Over a two-month period, other students harassed him repeatedly. James reported the harassment to school officials, but to no avail. A week after being choked by a student, James was knocked to the ground by the same student while others watched and laughed. Frustrated, angry and frightened, James jumped to his feet shouting, "I could kill you!" When school officials called the police, James was removed from the school in handcuffs, placed alone in the back of a police van, and charged with making "terroristic threats."

- A freshman at Poston Butte High School in Arizona was given a three day suspension because he used a photo of an AK-47 as the desktop background on his school-issued laptop computer.

- At Mary Blair Elementary School in Loveland, Colorado, a second grader was playing a make believe game where he was trying to save the world. He threw an imaginary grenade into a box with pretend evil forces inside. But the school says that he broke their rule against all weapons, both real and imaginary, and they suspended him from school.

- Angelina Branham's family has two small antique knives, which they use as letter openers. The 13-year-old says she was opening a letter, and absentmindedly pocketed the knives when she jumped on the school bus. When she got to school and realized she had the knives in her pocket, she immediately turned them in to her teacher at Ola Middle School in McDonough, GA. Angelina ended up in the principal's office and then in handcuffs in the back of a patrol car. She eventually spent two days in a youth detention facility for her honesty.

- The grandmother of a third-grade girl sent a birthday cake, and a knife for cutting the cake, to school. How did the teacher show her gratitude? The teacher used the knife to cut the cake, and then reported the girl to the authorities as having a dangerous weapon. The girl was expelled from school for a year.

- A ten year old student at Sunrise Elementary School in Ocala, Florida, brought her lunch to school, and in that lunch was a knife for her to cut her meat. When teachers saw the knife, they called the police. The girl was arrested and taken to the juvenile center. Not only was she suspended from school, but she faced a felony charge for the possession of a weapon on school property. The school admitted that "She did not use it inappropriately. She did not threaten anyone with it."

- When students at a Texas school were assigned to write a "scary" Halloween story, one 13-year-old chose to write about shooting up a school. Although he received a passing grade on the story, school officials reported him to the police, resulting in his spending *six days in jail* before it was determined that no crime had been committed.

- Four kindergarten students at Wilson Elementary School in Sayreville, N.J., played a make-believe game of "cops and robbers" during recess. In their game of pretend, the boys used their fingers as guns. Without notice to their parents, the boys were suspended from school for three days.

- A second grade student at Park Elementary School in Baltimore was enjoying his Pop Tart at school one day. He was playfully nibbling pieces out of it to form different shapes. His teacher saw it and thought it was in a shape that looked like a gun. The 7-year-old was certainly surprised when he was told that he was being suspended for two days for this act.

- Nine year old Michael Parson was suspended from school for a day and ordered to undergo a psychological evaluation after mentioning to a classmate his intent to "shoot" a fellow classmate with a wad of paper. Despite the fact that the "weapon" consisted of a wadded-up piece of moistened paper and a rubber band with which to launch it, district officials notified local police. Incredibly, the police went to Michael's home after midnight in order to question the fourth grader about the so-called "shooting" incident.

- A Louisiana tenth grade girl was expelled from high school for possessing Advil, a common over-the-counter pain reliever. An Alabama student was sent to an alternative school after being caught taking Motrin, another over-the-counter pain reliever.

- Kaitlin Nootbaar was a straight A student in high school, and had been selected as valedictorian of her class. She was getting ready to go to college on a full scholarship. But she gave a graduation speech before the school body, and in that speech she accidently said the word "hell" instead of "heck." The school principal refused to give her her diploma because of that word in her speech.

These school policies are not only stupid and ineffective, but they are cruel, sadistic and downright mean to the students. The American Psychological Association (APA) formed a task force to study the effects of zero tolerance policies in schools. They found that the widespread adoption of zero tolerance policies has not been shown to improve school climate or school safety. Proponents of zero tolerance would like to think that these policies would deter future misbehavior. However, the APA found that students who have been suspended are actually more likely to cause problems.[24] Another study found that schools with higher suspension rates also tended to have lower graduation rates.[25]

The American Bar Association has formally come out in opposition to zero tolerance policies. The National Education Association, the nation's largest teachers' union, opposes zero tolerance, saying that these policies may have an adverse effect on student academic and behavioral outcomes. The American Federation of Teachers, the nation's other major teachers' union, says that zero tolerance policies should be used only in rare circumstances such as lethal weapons or violent assaults. The National Association of School Psychologists (NASP) maintains that zero tolerance policies are ineffective, and cause negative consequences. NASP says there is no evidence that removing students from school makes a positive contribution to school safety. Even the US Department of Education makes the point that research has consistently demonstrated the negative impact of punitive and exclusionary school discipline practices.

Steps must be taken immediately to move schools away from these policies, which are actually harmful to the students. Suspensions and expulsions should be reserved only for offenses that place someone in actual immediate physical danger. One-size-fits-all disciplinary strategies should be replaced with graduated systems of discipline, wherein consequences are geared to the seriousness of the infraction. Any punishment must take into account the intentions of the student. School personnel should be given more discretion to exercise greater flexibility. Most experienced teachers realize that many minor issues are best dealt with in the classroom.

THE LAW SAYS WHAT?

Over the years, it seems like Congress is becoming less and less inclined to write laws that are clear and easy to understand. One of the basic requirements of good legislation is that ordinary citizens should be able to understand the law so they will know what is required and what is prohibited. Frequently, however, the language of a law is so vague that nobody, not even lawyers, can totally comprehend exactly what it means until it gets into court and a judge can give his opinion. And even then, different judges might disagree.

This continues despite the fact that the Supreme Court has repeatedly emphasized the need for clarity in the statutes. The Court said that a statute must "define the criminal offense with sufficient definiteness that ordinary people can understand what conduct is prohibited and in a manner that does not encourage arbitrary and discriminatory enforcement."[26] In another case, the opinion insisted "that laws give the person of ordinary intelligence a reasonable opportunity to know what is prohibited, so that he may act accordingly."[27] Even though the Supreme Court says it wants clarity, the courts still do not take this seriously enough. If they did, many convictions would be overturned under the "Void for Vagueness" Doctrine.

There used to be a general attitude that the justice system should not only punish wrongdoers, but should also attempt to protect the rights of the accused. Instead, the laws now seem more concerned with giving more advantages to the prosecutors rather than protecting the citizens from injustice. And the vague language in a law is a benefit to the government, since the law can be twisted to mean whatever the prosecutors and judges want it to mean in a particular situation. This gives government officials unbelievable arbitrary and unpredictable power to choose when and how to enforce their own interpretations of the law against people who could not know at the time that their conduct would someday be called illegal.

For example, there is a federal law that makes it a crime to "deprive another of the intangible right of honest services." Even lawyers and judges cannot agree on what that means. Supreme Court Justice Antonin Scalia pointed out that, if taken literally, the honest services law would make it a federal crime to call in sick to work and go to a ball game instead.

Georgia Thompson, a Wisconsin civil servant, was charged with federal "honest services" fraud after she awarded a state contract for travel services to the low bidder. The prosecutors did not claim that she had any conflict of interest. Instead they said that the contract award technically violated Wisconsin state procurement rules because, they claimed, the contract made her supervisors look good. Of course, there is no reason why a state issue like this should have any federal jurisdiction. But a jury convicted her under this preposterous theory, and a federal judge sentenced her to four years in federal prison. By the time a federal court of appeals reversed her conviction, Ms. Thompson had lost her job, career, and reputation; had fallen into bankruptcy; and had spent four months in a federal prison.

You might hope that a person could avoid violating the honest services law by faithfully following all the rules and regulations enacted by her employer. Unfortunately, that would not protect her, because the Ninth US Circuit Court of Appeals has ruled that this statute imposed duties in addition to those articulated by the state or the employer.[28] So the employee or official is forced to guess what additional requirements the prosecutors and courts might impose after the fact.

Most people have heard again and again that it is a felony to lie when under oath. So if a person were required to testify in court, she would be very careful to have her facts straight, and would probably talk to her attorney to make sure that she didn't inadvertently make some mistake. But many people don't know that it is a felony to lie even when not under oath. This frequently gives the government a weapon that it can use against the unwary citizen. In fact, crafty investigators will often give a subject multiple temptations to lie, sometimes when the underlying conduct being investigated is not even criminal. Of course the double standard is alive and well, for it is not illegal for the government officials to lie to citizens.[29]

The Sarbanes-Oxley Act of 2002 has a provision that prohibits the destruction of documents in contemplation of a future investigation, even if no formal investigation had begun. So a person could get in trouble for destroying a document that might someday be used in some future investigation, even if there was no investigation in progress, and the person had not been notified that an investigation was contemplated. Connecticut US Attorney Kevin O'Connor said that the statute "does not require corrupt intent." Most companies have policies dictating a schedule for routine document retention and destruction. So the perfectly innocent routine destruction of old documents, in accordance with standard company policy, could later be called a criminal act.[30]

The wiretapping statute prohibits the interception and recording of transmitted messages. But in one case, the owner of an Internet service provider was prosecuted under this law because he made routine backup copies of e-mails stored on his company's server. This dragged on for nearly a decade before he was finally acquitted.

Another area ripe with innovative interpretations is securities laws. These laws are intentionally kept vague in order to make prosecutions easier. For the crime of "insider trading," for example, there is no lucid definition. The law is basically made up as it is being enforced, with prosecutors and a court deciding in each case just what is prohibited.[31]

Some of the most flagrant examples of vagueness are found in the environmental regulations. Many offenses which used to be civil matters, with punishments of fines and monetary damages, have been elevated to criminal matters in which the offender is subject to jail time. The regulations have become incredibly complex to the point where no one understands them. The lawyers, prosecutors, and even the technical experts frequently disagree about their interpretation. Many statutes are written so broadly as to give limitless delegation to EPA and other agencies to interpret the requirements.

The Clean Water Act (CWA) is written to control the "discharge of pollutants into the navigable waters [of the United States]." That sounds like it should be pretty easy to understand what this means. But the EPA has stretched this mandate absolutely beyond belief. First, they decided that "navigable waters" also includes any waters that connect to navigable waters. Then they ruled that their scope also includes waters that do not connect to navigable waters. Next, without any change in the language by Congress, the EPA decided that the CWA also allows them to control what they call "wetlands." What exactly are wetlands, you might ask? There is no concise definition, but the EPA has created hundreds of pages of regulations, notices, guidance documents, letters, memos and opinions that describe places that are included in this unwritten (in legislation) mandate. Originally wetlands meant swamps, marshes, bogs, and similar locations that were actually wet. But the scope has grown and grown until it now can include locations that are dry most of the time, but contain certain types of vegetation. The EPA has now assumed jurisdiction over millions of acres, which affects an almost unlimited number of industries, businesses and individuals.

And what is meant by "discharge of pollutants?" You can imagine that this ambiguous phrase could allow for some creative interpretation. For example, putting clean fill dirt on a site is considered a "discharge of pollutants." In fact, a "discharge" may include a "redeposit" of soil onto the same site from which it had been removed.[32]

In 1989, Ocie Mills and Carey C. Mills, father and son, were found guilty of "discharging pollutants into the waters of the United States." What they actually did was to place clean dirt on a plot of dry land. They were each sentenced to twenty-one months in prison.[33] The judge assigned to the case, Roger Vinson, sympathized with the Millses. He admitted that a "layman" would not expect "waters" to include "land that appears to be dry, but which may have some saturated–soil vegetation, as is the situation here." But he had to follow the regulations as written.[34]

Another example is the Resource Conservation and Recovery Act (RCRA), which governs hazardous waste. The statute is extremely detailed, complex, and obscure. The law's definition of hazardous waste is confusing, and great power is delegated to the

EPA to write regulations. As you might imagine, their regulations are also confusing and complicated. A federal judge called RCRA's provisions "mind-numbing."[35]

On the label of a can of bathroom cleaner, this statement appears: "It is a violation of Federal law to use this product in a manner inconsistent with its labeling."[36] So if you hold the can 5 inches from the surface being cleaned, instead of the 6 inches required by the instructions, then you have violated federal law. You are a criminal. This idiotic EPA labeling requirement is just one more example of why people have completely lost all respect for our dysfunctional government. It also reinforces the fear that many people have of any contact with the police, no matter how innocent. Who knows what might happen if a policeman saw you holding that can too close to the surface.

We have seen laws and regulations which contain hundreds or even thousands of pages of incomprehensible legal jargon and vague mandates. Not only is this impossible for people to understand, but it gives the government almost unlimited power to intimidate and blackmail citizens and businesses, or to punish practically anyone they choose. James Madison anticipated this problem when, in The Federalist No. 62, he stated: "It will be of little avail to the people that the laws are made by men of their own choice, if the laws be so voluminous that they cannot be read, or so incoherent that they cannot be understood."[37] Much needs to be done in this area, but one useful law would be a general requirement that ambiguities in a criminal statute are to be resolved in favor of the defendant. This would give a person some protection against the multitude of vague laws which can be twisted by the prosecutor to mean whatever he wants them to mean.

RICO

The Racketeer Influenced and Corrupt Organizations Act (RICO) was enacted in 1970. This act was originally sold as a tool to fight organized crime. However, because of the vague language in the law, prosecutors have discovered that it can be a powerful weapon against almost anyone that they choose to target. Even the Supreme Court has recognized the abuses of RICO, when it said:

> Underlying the Court of Appeals' holding was its distress at the "extraordinary, if not outrageous," uses to which civil RICO has been put. Instead of

being used against mobsters and organized criminals, it has become a tool for everyday fraud cases brought against "respected and legitimate enterprises."[38]

What this statute does is create new artificial federal crimes based on a "pattern of racketeering activity." Racketeering activity includes a variety of "predicate" crimes, which are already defined under state laws and some federal laws. The RICO law criminalizes being part of an enterprise that is somehow related to some of these other crimes. The term "enterprise" can mean not only a business, but any informal group of individuals, or even an illegal operation. And the prosecutors do not have to actually prove that the defendants committed the basic crimes. They must show only that it appears the defendants carried on those activities. Also, a lower standard of proof is required instead of "guilt beyond a reasonable doubt" that is traditional for criminal prosecutions. So even an innocent person who has not been convicted of the underlying crimes could still fall victim to a RICO prosecution under this vague and ill-defined law.

These predicate crimes were already illegal under state law. The RICO statute did not add anything by making it a new and separate crime to associate with others (in an "enterprise") through commission of these crimes. What it did was to give federal prosecutors a potent weapon with which to persecute their victims. The much more severe penalties for federal crimes give prosecutors a strong bargaining tool to force defendants to accept a plea bargain. There is no requirement for intent or even knowledge of the illegality. This, along with the weak requirements for evidence, makes it easy to get convictions, and is a strong incentive for prosecutors to pile on RICO charges along with any other charges.

Astonishingly, the RICO statute has even been used against political activists to try to cripple their freedom of speech. For example, the National Organization for Women (NOW) tried to use RICO to obtain a ruinous money judgment against national anti-abortion groups in order to stop their pro-life protests. Amazingly, the US Justice Department actually filed a brief supporting NOW's right to bring RICO charges. That particular case had to go all the way to the Supreme Court before the conviction was reversed.[39]

This is just one more way that a citizen has lost the protection of due process. Giving such immense arbitrary power to federal prosecutors is a huge mistake. This Act must be repealed or drastically modified.

RESPONSIBLE CORPORATE OFFICERS

Under the Responsible Corporate Officers theory, if a low level employee of a company violates some regulation, then the company's CEO or other official can be held responsible and even sent to jail, even though

- The CEO did not know about the violation
- The CEO did not have any intent to violate the law
- The company explicitly instructed the employee not to do the illegal act

This is obviously a tremendous injustice, to criminally prosecute a company official who is perfectly innocent. The courts have been inconsistent in their rulings on this issue, but in some cases it seems like they would be willing to sentence an innocent company officer to jail just because he was an official of the company. In fact, both the Clean Water Act and the Clean Air Act include language holding responsible corporate officers individually liable in order to encourage this kind of prosecution.[40]

In the 1991 case of *United States v. Brittain*, the Tenth Circuit Court said: "We think that Congress perceived this objective [to restore and maintain the integrity of the nation's waters] to outweigh hardships suffered by responsible corporate officers who are held criminally liable in spite of their lack of consciousness of wrong-doing. . . . Under this interpretation a responsible corporate officer, to be held criminally liable, would not have to willfully or negligently cause a permit violation. Instead, the willfulness or negligence of the actor would be imputed to him by virtue of his position of responsibility."[41]

John Park was the president of Acme Markets, a large national food chain. The Food and Drug Administration sent Park a letter telling him that they had found unsanitary conditions at one of his company's warehouses. Park referred the matter to one of his vice presidents, who said he would fix the problem. But when a subsequent inspection found the conditions still existed, Park was indicted for violations of the Federal Food, Drug and Cosmetic Act. The appellate court overturned Park's conviction because he did not do anything wrong, and he had tried to correct the problem. But the Supreme Court reinstated his conviction.[42] The result of this ruling is that an honest executive can be branded a criminal if an employee in a different city disobeys instructions and violates a regulation.

Congress should act decisively to abolish the Responsible Corporate Officer doctrine. This has absolutely no place in a free society.

PUNISHING THE INNOCENT

We used to have a relatively small number of laws, and they generally prohibited things that were obviously wrong, such as robbery, murder and rape. It was easy for ordinary people to instinctively know that these types of things were wrong. So "ignorance of the law" was no defense for criminal punishment. But things are much different now. Congress and the states have enacted thousands of criminal laws, and government bureaucrats have written hundreds of thousands of regulations that can involve criminal penalties. Many of these cover acts which no one would intuitively know was "wrong." The only reason they are prohibited is because they are simply violations of some arbitrary regulation enacted by Congress or some bureaucrat. For example, you can go to prison for unauthorized use of the Smokey Bear image. Likewise, unauthorized use of the slogan "Give a Hoot, Don't Pollute" is a crime. One man got lost in a snowstorm and accidentally drove a snowmobile onto federal land, which is illegal. When he went to authorities for help in finding his abandoned snowmobile, he was arrested and now has a criminal record. A man had a gun which he owned legally. His estranged wife took out a state restraining order against him. Unknown to him, a federal law makes it illegal for a person under a restraining order to have guns, and he was sentenced to three years in prison.

Now no one, not even lawyers, can hope to know and understand even a small portion of these laws and regulations. So it happens all the time that people are convicted and sent to prison for violating one of these rules when they did not have any idea that what they were doing was illegal. Criminal prosecution involves the single most powerful action that any government can take against its citizens: the deprivation of human liberty or even life itself. So we should be extremely careful to insure that this is done with the utmost fairness and respect for the individual.

A core principle of American justice is that no one should be subjected to criminal punishment for conduct that he did not know was illegal. An important aspect of this is the doctrine of fair notice. In order for a person to be punished criminally, the offense with which she is charged must provide adequate notice that the conduct was prohibited. The Supreme Court at one time recognized this in stating: "No one may be required at peril of life, liberty or property to speculate as to the meaning of penal statutes. All are entitled to be informed as to what the State commands or forbids."[43] The Court also said that "a fair warning should be given to the world in language that the common world will understand."[44] But today, with so many laws and regulations that no one could possible know about, much less understand, this principle is being abandoned. In 2010, the Supreme Court repeated the warning that we are all in danger from these unknowable laws, when it said, "We have long recognized the common maxim, familiar to all minds, that ignorance of the law will not excuse any person, either civilly or criminally."[45]

Another fundamental component of our justice system is the presumption of innocence. A person must be presumed innocent until proven guilty. In the case of *Estelle v. Williams*, the Supreme Court stated, "The presumption of innocence, although not articulated in the Constitution, is a basic component of a fair trial under our system of criminal justice."[46] In another case, the Court emphasized it even more strongly, "The principle that there is a presumption of innocence in favor of the accused is the undoubted law, axiomatic and elementary, and its enforcement lies at the foundation of the administration of our criminal law."[47] But now a person is no longer presumed innocent until conviction. The authorities are sometimes allowed to freeze a person's assets when she is indicted, without waiting until she is convicted. This could make her unable to get a first class defense council by taking away the assets that she would use to pay for her attorney. This takes away her right to defend herself vigorously, and thereby takes away her right to a fair trial. Using this power, the government has actually forced some businesses into bankruptcy, without them being convicted of anything.

There is also a worrisome tendency to criminalize (with severe penalties) acts of simple negligence, which should be handled through a civil suit, with punishments consisting of fines and damages. It should be absolutely unthinkable that a person could be sent to prison for an act of simple negligence, but it happens here in the United States.

In the past, people understood our legal system to require that a prosecutor prove beyond a reasonable doubt that the defendant intentionally committed a wrong act. There are two separate elements to a crime, which are expressed in legal language as "actus reus," which is Latin for "bad act," and "mens rea," which is Latin for "guilty mind." People have always known instinctively that intent matters, and in fact that often makes the difference between a mistake, an accident, and a crime. Supreme Court Justice Robert Jackson wrote:

> The contention that an injury can amount to a crime only when inflicted by intention is no provincial or transient notion. It is as universal and persistent in mature systems of law as belief in freedom of the human will and a consequent ability and duty of the normal individual to choose between good and evil. A relation between some mental element and punishment for a harmful act is almost as instinctive as the child's familiar exculpatory "But I didn't mean to," and has afforded the rational basis for a tardy and unfinished substitution of deterrence and reformation in place of retaliation and vengeance as the motivation for public prosecution. Unqualified acceptance of this doctrine by English common law in the Eighteenth Century was indicated by Blackstone's sweeping statement that to constitute any crime there must first be a "vicious will."[48]

The Utah Supreme Court put it this way: "To prevent the punishment of the innocent, there has been engrafted into our system of jurisprudence, as presumably in every other, the principle that the wrongful or criminal intent is the essence of crime, without which it cannot exist."[49]

But now the legal system frequently fails to recognize this reality, and there are many situations where a person can be convicted without any proof that he had any intention to do wrong. Much of the blame can be placed on Congress and the state legislatures. When they wrote laws, it used to be common practice to include in appropriate statutes a requirement that a person knowingly intended to commit a crime.[50] Accidents and mistakes were not considered crimes. That has been a fundamental principle of criminal law. Now that requirement is frequently omitted from the law, and courts have instructed juries that, if the law does not include the element of intent, then it is not necessary for the prosecutor to prove intent. A recent study found that 64 percent of the laws enacted in one session of Congress contained inadequate requirement of intent.[51] But the courts also have to take a large part of the blame for this situation. The courts have not been consistent in their opinions.[52] Sometimes the courts will express some concern that intent was not proven, but other times it is not required. In the 1957 Supreme Court case of

Lambert v. California, Justice William Douglas cavalierly stated "We do not go with Blackstone in saying that 'a vicious will' is necessary to constitute a crime."[53]

John Thorpe had a criminal record. When he was confronted by a thief with a gun, a scuffle ensued, and Thorpe took the gun away from the thief. When the police arrived on the scene, Thorpe was arrested and prosecuted under a law that made it illegal for any felon to possess a firearm. Thorpe tried to explain the situation, and the appellate court acknowledged the "harsh result," but noted that the law did not require criminal intent.[54]

Hunters and farmers are routinely ensnared by the Migratory Bird Treaty Act for inadvertent violations. This is a strict liability law, which allows conviction without the need to show that the accused had any intent to violate the law. Ronald Rollins, an Idaho farmer, applied a mixture of registered pesticides to 50 acres of alfalfa on his farm. A flock of geese came to the field, ate the alfalfa, and died from ingesting the pesticides. Rollins was found guilty of killing the birds, even though he had applied the chemicals "in the recommended quantities [and] at the appropriate time." In fact, the local farming community had used the pesticides "for a number of years without major incident."[55] There is absolutely no possible reason that Rollins deserved to be punished for his actions, and there is no excuse for the poor judgment of the prosecutor in bringing these charges. Unfortunately, these injustices are not uncommon.

An oil supertanker, the Exxon Valdez, ran aground in Alaska and spilled 11 million gallons of oil. Of course, Exxon was responsible for enormous cleanup costs, as well as civil tort damages. But the US Justice Department decided to go beyond reasonable liability penalties, and brought preposterous criminal charges against the oil company. It is illegal under the Clean Water Act and the Refuse Act to discharge refuse into a waterway without a permit. This is intended to stop towns and businesses from using waterways as garbage dumps. But the Justice Department claimed that the oil that accidently spilled into Prince William Sound was "refuse matter," discharged by Exxon without a permit. Another count charged Exxon with violating the Migratory Bird Treaty Act, which prohibits the hunting and killing of migratory birds without a permit. The idea that Exxon deliberately dumped the oil as a way of getting rid of some refuse, and also in an effort to kill migratory birds, was so absurd that it almost sounds like some kind of joke. The Attorney General, Richard Thornburgh, acknowledged that the felony charges against Exxon required "some innovative legal approaches," but still said that Exxon should pay hundreds of millions of dollars in criminal liability. Despite the ridiculousness of the charges, Exxon lacked sufficient confidence in our crumbling justice system to go to trial. They settled out of court.[56]

The idea that one person can be held criminally responsible for the acts of another has generally been limited to the situation where they both conspired or acted together to commit a crime. If A and B both decide to rob a bank, but all A does is drive the getaway car, A can still be held criminally liable for the robbery and for whatever violence B perpetrates inside the bank. But should a supervisor be *criminally* liable for the illegal actions of an employee, if those actions were not authorized by the supervisor, and the supervisor had no knowledge of the actions? The answer to that used to be no. In fact, an early English case, *Rex v. Huggins* (1730), was a good example of that principle, when the court said, "So that if an act be done by an under-officer, unless it is done by the command or direction, or with the consent of the principal, the principal is not criminally punishable for it." But the modern trend in American criminal law is to expose innocent supervisors to possible jail time for unauthorized acts of others. Supreme Court Justice Clarence Thomas recognized the problem with criminalizing commercial accidents, when he said, "I think we should be hesitant to expose countless numbers of construction workers and contractors to heightened criminal liability for using ordinary devices to engage in normal industrial operations."[57]

Some lawmakers have tried to remedy this problem by adding the term "knowingly" to a statute. However, this is inadequate because the understanding of that term in the legal system only relates to knowing the facts of the activity. It does not protect the innocent person who did not know he was breaking the law. The Supreme Court has ruled that "the term 'knowingly' does not necessarily have any reference to a culpable state of mind or to knowledge of the law."[58]

To stop these injustices, Congress and the states should pass laws that instruct the courts that, even if some laws were written without a strong requirement for intent, all criminal laws should automatically be assumed to have a requirement that the defendant acted with "knowledge" that he was committing a crime. Ohio and Michigan have passed laws addressing this issue. This intent requirement must apply to all elements of the crime. Many regulations make it a criminal offense to enter erroneous data on a form, even if it was just an honest mistake. The law must make it clear that there is no crime unless the government can prove that the error was material to the purpose of the form, and that the person did this with intent to defraud.

Congress could, where it wished in special situations, include a statement in a law explicitly saying that intent is not required. But where the law is silent, then a default mens rea rule would be assumed.[59] This would go a long way toward preventing the destruction of the lives of morally innocent people, and restoring the public's respect for the integrity and fairness of our criminal justice system.

Legislatures should do away with the "ignorance of the law is no excuse" maxim by enacting a blanket requirement that prosecutors have to prove that a defendant knew his conduct was illegal. There is another move that Congress could make to greatly improve the fairness of our justice system. That would be a statute requiring the federal government to give a party notice that he or she has violated a regulation, and an opportunity to remedy the matter, before criminal charges could be brought. It is true that society has a strong interest in enforcing the law, but it has an even more powerful interest in not punishing morally blameless people.

Chapter Eleven

Informed Voter

If a nation expects to be ignorant and free in a state of civilization,
it expects what never was and never will be.

Thomas Jefferson

Our system of government gives the people the responsibility of electing the officials who will actually lead this country. But in order to make responsible decisions about who to vote for, the people need to be informed. A voter needs to know the major issues of the day, or at least the ones which most concern him. He needs to know who the candidates are, and their positions on the issues. And he needs at least a basic understanding of how our government is structured, and the responsibility of each branch of government.

In the early days of this country's history, there was a very high literacy rate in the American colonies. Americans loved to read, and they were skillful readers. They could understand intricate philosophical and political arguments. They had a great respect for education and reading, and took very seriously the education of the young. The men who founded this country and who wrote our Constitution were generally very intelligent men, widely read in science, history, politics and law. This knowledge gave them the perspective to try to avoid the mistakes made by other countries.

Contrast that with the situation today. Many people are now woefully ignorant about American history and government. They do not read as much. They have great difficulty in understanding complex philosophical and political discussions compared to our eighteenth century ancestors. Their attention span is very short. Much of the power in our government has been transferred from our representatives in Congress, who are responsive to the electorate, to unelected bureaucrats who write thousands of regulations that are never put to a vote. Most Americans do not understand this because they do not know how the system was intended to work. We maintain a naïve assumption that the system operates as the Framers originally intended it to operate. The government makes a big show of trying to protect our right to vote because that provides the illusion that the people are participating in their government.

It is obvious that an educated and informed citizenry is an absolute necessity for a representative form of government such as ours to be successful. A voter has to understand the alternative policies being considered, and be able to predict the effects of each of those policies. Then he can decide which of the available policy options he would prefer, and which candidate that leads him to support. If voters do not have at least this minimum level of knowledge about politics, they are woefully unprepared to make rational decisions to exercise control over government policy. And there has been considerable research over a period of many years showing that most individual voters are extremely ignorant of even the most basic political information. Just before the 2012 presidential election, a Pew Research survey found that only 40 percent of registered voters knew which party controlled the House of Representatives, and only 54 percent knew that Mitt Romney was the pro-life candidate.[1] The USA PATRIOT Act was enacted in 2001, and was followed by an enormous amount of controversy, publicity, and press coverage. Yet a survey taken in 2004 found that 58 percent of people had heard very little or nothing about this law.[2]

TELEVISION

A person with such limited knowledge is forced to find alternate ways of making decisions about voting. This person is more likely to form an opinion based on emotions and feelings, unpolluted by facts. He may hear one speech by a candidate with something that sounds appealing, and he may decide to vote for that candidate. There is no thoughtful comparison of alternative policies or candidates. Many people are influenced by the charisma and charm of a candidate, and say they have a "good feeling" about that person. In general, voters tend to remember personal information about candidates rather than hard facts about issues. Also, the ignorant voter can be more easily manipulated by a persuasive individual or group who is trying to promote its own agenda.

Study after study shows that the political spots on television are one of the voters' chief sources of information—and often the only source. These attack ads filled with character assassinations, name calling, insults, and downright lies, are very effective in influencing voters' opinions. Image is much more important than substance. That is why television is such a powerful medium for manipulation of people. If a politician makes a single misstatement or odd gesture in a televised debate, that can be more devastating to his campaign than a statement about a serious issue. People say they have confidence that, because they can see a candidate on television, they "know" who he is. That is ridiculous.

Television has become so pervasive and so much a part of our life, that it has largely replaced books as our chief source of information, and the way we think about life. Of course, television is very attractive. The industry does an amazing job of producing excellent entertainment about a wide variety of subjects. However, the problem is that all subject matter is presented as entertaining. Even the so called "news" programs are evolving into just another entertainment program. Think about a typical evening news program. It consists of a series of fragmented segments, each only a few seconds long. When one item is finished, there is no discussion or analysis, and you are not given any time to reflect on it yourself, for it is immediately followed by another unrelated item which commands your attention. Not only is there no continuity, but the items are presented without context, and almost all of them are totally irrelevant to your own personal life or activities.

In this modern age, our freedom to read has definitely been impaired. This has not been done by censorship, as has happened in some totalitarian countries. Television does not ban books, it simply displaces them. The television culture does not try to limit our access to information, but in fact widens it. It does everything possible to encourage us to watch continuously. But what we watch is a medium which presents information in a form that renders it simplistic, non-substantive, non-historical and non-contextual.[3] It is pure entertainment. And it is dragging down the intellectual level of our society.

When politics and television inevitably get together, the result is something that we are all too familiar with (especially during campaign season)—the political advertisement. In order to be most effective, the political advertisement has adapted to the medium of television. This means brevity, eye catching visual images, avoidance of lengthy intellectual discussions, and appeal to the emotional and psychological needs of the viewer. The candidate who is most attractive on television, is a good public speaker, and can deliver witty one-liners, has a big advantage in the world where the visual image is king. Where the TV image is everything, it makes it more difficult for the voter to actually find out what a candidate really believes.

CIVICS EDUCATION

We depend primarily on the public schools to prepare our children for life in the modern world. An important part of this preparation is teaching them about our history and our government. This is a complex world, and everyone needs to have at least a certain minimum level of political knowledge in order to participate as a responsible citizen. Under our system of government, the people are supposed to have the ultimate authority. But that carries with it a certain responsibility to make informed and thoughtful decisions when electing government officials. Unfortunately, the public schools are doing a poor job of teaching about our history and our political system. As detailed above, Americans in general have a shamefully low level of knowledge about our government. We urgently need a renewed commitment in the schools to teach our children about their government.

American Bar Association president Stephen N. Zack wrote this about our public schools in the September 2010 issue of the ABA Journal: "Today there is significantly less understanding and appreciation of our Constitution and its role in preserving freedom. . . . We are producing a generation of citizens who are ill-equipped to govern themselves as participants in our democracy."[4]

We need a citizenry knowledgeable about our government and our political system. One important part of that effort would be a renewed emphasis on teaching civics in our schools. Each generation must be taught these lessons in schools, and that is not being done. Colleges also should increase their teaching of civics, as unpopular as that might be.

A variety of different approaches to teaching civics can be effective, but there are some general guidelines which most experts can support. First, students should learn about the great and eternal ideals, such as those in the Declaration of Independence and the Constitution. These important concepts must be connected to practical, current real-world issues. Discussions of current public issues are sometimes avoided for fear of inviting controversy, but that is a mistake, because these discussions are essential for a well-rounded education. Of course, the teacher has to create a climate where students feel like their opinions are respected, and they are free to disagree with the teacher. When the teacher raises an issue for discussion, she should fairly present the different viewpoints. And students should feel like they can make their own suggestions about current events for discussion in class. On the other hand, if a school adopts "zero tolerance" policies, or other arbitrary or unfair procedures, the school climate will deteriorate, and students will have less confidence in the democratic political processes in general.[5]

Civics courses should be made enjoyable for the students, instead of being dull and boring as many are today. Research has shown that enjoyable courses will increase students' interest and knowledge about the subject. To achieve this, lectures could be supplemented with the opportunity for students to do things like debate, conduct research, experiment, take field trips, and create art projects. Another factor often neglected is teaching students that conflict is an important and normal part of American politics. Students have sometimes come to view disagreement and conflict as negative, and something to be avoided. To be prepared to participate in contemporary politics, students must acknowledge that conflict is unavoidable, and learn to resolve disagreements without demonizing opponents.

One reason for the decline in civics instruction in high schools is that parents don't give it a high priority. If the question is asked in a poll, most people will agree that it is important to prepare students to be responsible citizens who participate in our democratic society. But when parents make the difficult choices about where and how to educate their own children, they have a different priority. Parents want their own kids to get an education that will help them to get ahead, which means marketable skills. This means math, science and reading skills, and preparation for college and the workplace. In many cases, civics and history have been pushed aside.

One of the major advantages of our form of government is the concept of federalism, which is the division of power between federal and state governments. This complex subject can be difficult to understand for the citizen who lacks even the most basic knowledge of our political system. Public attention rarely focuses on federalism as a general subject. Federalism is an abstract and complicated system compared to many underlying public policy issues like drugs and education, which are more concrete and more likely to engage the passions of citizens. Thus, when a federalism issue becomes a matter of public controversy, it almost always focuses on the specific policy question at hand, rather than on federalism in general. Federalism is a very important issue, however, and its erosion in recent decades makes it even more necessary that citizens not only understand it, but also give it a high importance in their evaluation of competing policies.

Only people who are knowledgeable and informed will be able to fulfill their responsibilities as citizens. A well-informed citizenry will help to improve the public discourse about important issues, demand more accountability from elected officials, promote improved knowledge and better decisions about current problems and policies, and be more engaged in the political process. They will have an appreciation of American history, and a respect for our Constitution, and the Declaration of Independence. We will have no chance at all of retaining our freedoms if we continue down the path of ignorance, disinformation, and apathy.

Former congressman Tom Tancredo had an interesting suggestion. He said, "Naturalized citizens must prove they understand some fundamental facts about the US Constitution, the Bill of Rights, separation of powers, federalism and so forth. But every man-on-the-street interview of voters documents the abysmal ignorance of too many Americans about the fundamental pillars of American freedom. Why not require that every American take and pass the same civics test as new citizens must pass before they indulge in that most sacred civic duty, voting for the representatives who will deliberate and decide on the next public debacle?"

A report entitled "Guardian of Democracy: The Civic Mission of Schools"[6] explains the situation this way:

> At a time when the nation is confronting some of the more difficult decisions it has faced in a long time, a lack of high quality civic education in America's schools leaves millions of citizens without the wherewithal to make sense of our system of government. Reasons for concern are reflected in the answers our Annenberg Public Policy Center surveys elicited from national samples of the US population in the past decade. These were among our findings:

- Only one-third of Americans could name all three branches of government; one-third couldn't name any.
- Just over a third thought that it was the intention of the Founding Fathers to have each branch hold a lot of power, but the president has the final say.
- Just under half of Americans (47%) knew that a 5–4 decision by the Supreme Court carries the same legal weight as a 9–0 ruling.
- Almost a third mistakenly believed that a US Supreme Court ruling could be appealed.
- When the Supreme Court divides 5-4, roughly one in four (23%) believed the decision was referred to Congress for resolution; 16% thought it needed to be sent back to the lower courts.

Self-government requires far more than voting in elections every four years. It requires citizens who are informed and thoughtful, participate in their communities, are involved in the political process, and possess moral and civic virtues. Generations of leaders, from America's founders to the inventors of public education to elected leaders in the twentieth century, have understood that these qualities are not automatically transmitted to the next generation— they must be passed down through schools. Ultimately, schools are the guardians of democracy.

Improved civic learning can address many of our democratic shortfalls. It increases the democratic accountability of elected officials, since only informed and engaged citizens will ask tough questions of their leaders. It improves public discourse, since knowledgeable and interested citizens will demand more from the media. It fulfills our ideal of civic equality by giving every citizen, regardless of background, the tools to be a full participant. Despite these obvious benefits, a majority of America's schools either neglect civic learning, or teach it in a minimal or superficial way (too often as an elective). The consequences of this neglect are staggering, but unsurprising. On a recent national assessment in civics, two-thirds of all American students scored below proficient. On the same test, less than one-third of eighth graders could identify the historical purpose of the Declaration of Independence, and fewer than one in five high school seniors were able to explain how citizen participation benefits democracy. . . .

A large body of research demonstrates the tangible benefits of civic learning. First and foremost, civic learning promotes civic knowledge, skills, and dispositions—research makes clear that students who received high-quality civic learning are more likely than their counterparts to understand public issues, view political engagement as a means of addressing communal challenges, and participate in civic activities. Civic learning has similarly been shown to promote civic equality. Poor, minority, urban, or rural students who do receive high-quality civic learning perform considerably higher than their counterparts, demonstrating the possibility of civic learning to fulfill the ideal of civic equality.

Research also demonstrates the non-civic benefits of civic learning. Civic learning has been shown to instill young people with the "twenty-first century competencies" that employers value in the new economy. Schools that implement high-quality civic learning are more likely to have a better school climate and are more likely to have lower dropout rates. . . .

America as a new nation was not created out of devotion to a motherland, a royal family, or a national religion. Americans are instead defined by our fidelity to certain ideals, expressed in the Declaration of Independence, Constitution, and Bill of Rights and subsequent amendments. While citizenship is formally acquired through either birth or naturalization, all of us must learn to become Americans. Peoples from diverse cultural, religious, and racial backgrounds can fully join the American community by sharing its defining commitments. If Americans are not bound together by common values, we will become fragmented and turn on one another.

Knowledge of our history, ideals, and system are not innate, but acquired through education. As former Associate Justice Sandra Day O'Connor has written: "The better educated our citizens are, the better equipped they will be to preserve the system of government we have. And we have to start with the education of our nation's young people. Knowledge about our government is not handed down through the gene pool. Every generation has to learn it, and we have some work to do."

The Founders understood this. Many state constitutions, including several that predated our national constitution, put the diffusion of knowledge and the civic mission of schools at the center of public education. George Washington and James Madison both went so far as to envision a national university to educate generations of good citizens. It was well understood that an educated citizenry was basic to a functioning society.

This education should include the important facts of our history. Americans should be familiar with the miracle at Philadelphia, the bravery at Valley Forge, the sacrifices at Gettysburg and Iwo Jima, and the courage displayed in Selma and Little Rock. But civic learning does not consist of facts or stories alone, as dramatic and inspiring as they may be. It must also be an education in the duties that we owe to one another and to the future of our country. . . .

From the earliest days of the republic, the civic mission of school enjoyed broad support: Federalist John Adams wrote that "liberty cannot be preserved" without civic education, and his Democratic-Republican counterpart Thomas Jefferson argued that since the citizenry is "the only safe depository of government power . . . if we think them not enlightened enough . . . the remedy is not to take it from them, but inform their discretion by education." As public schools began to proliferate in the early nineteenth century, advocates for universal education held the shared view that the only guarantor of democracy resided with those schools. This vision of public education as serving civic ends animated both the establishment of the American public school system and the development of its curricula. Many state constitutions explicitly set out civic education as a basis for the newly established systems of public schools. Alexis de Tocqueville noted that the primary difference between European-style schooling and American schooling was that, in America, "[t]he general thrust of education is directed toward political life."

By 1890, nearly every American child between the ages of five and 13 attended school regularly, with the vast majority in schools funded and administered by newly emergent school districts. Civic education was integral to curricula nationwide. . . .

We are reminded, again, of the wisdom of the founders, who knew that an educated citizenry is essential to the practice of representative government that is accountable to its citizens. There is simply no other way to ensure that elected leaders represent the values, needs, and wishes of their constituents.

Research shows that Americans who are not properly educated about their roles as citizens are less likely to be civically engaged by nearly any metric. They are less likely to vote, less likely to engage in political discourse, and less likely to participate in community improvement projects than their counterparts who receive civic education.

Our system requires democratic accountability as a check on government officials—accountability that becomes nearly impossible if citizens do not understand how to make it happen and how to demand better when it doesn't. Because disengaged citizens fail to ask hard questions of their leaders, it is no wonder that problems become crises and power is so easily abused.

Complaints about the influence of "special interests" abound, yet it is axiomatic that such interests will have disproportionate influence over public policy if the citizenry is uninformed, disengaged or both. Citizens who do not receive civic education are likely to either disengage, or, if they want to engage, often do not know how to do so. Either way, when citizens are unwilling or unable to advocate for their interests or the public good, those with narrower interests are pushing against an open door. Resultant policies can lead to further cynicism and disengagement, trapping us in a cycle that provides little opportunity for citizens to engage. . . .

The late and influential public education champion, Al Shanker, himself a child of immigrants, once noted that the purpose of American public education is for immigrant children to "learn what it means to be an American with the hope that they would then go home and teach their parents."

For generations, new immigrants from across the world have come to America from nondemocratic nations in search of liberty and a new life. Once in American public schools, they learned about our history, our government, and the role of citizens in a democratic society. As America continues to welcome immigrants to our shores, civic learning remains vital to inculcating civic values in the newest Americans.

Unlike in other nations, Americans are not united by race or religion, but rather by a shared commitment to a set of core civic ideals. Our vision of pluralism, of E Pluribus Unum, is only possible with civic learning to imbue all citizens with shared knowledge of, and commitment to, American democratic ideals. Given that studies show many native-born Americans would fail to pass the citizenship test, the aim of civic learning must be not only to teach immigrants the tools of citizenship, but also to teach them to every American. . . .

More recently, civic learning has continued to face challenges. The competitiveness movement in education shifted the national focus to math and science, often at the expense of other disciplines, including civics. Concerns about introducing controversial issues into the classroom, the very issues most important for students to discuss, has led some teachers and districts to shy away from current events. And the omission of civics from many assessment regimes provided yet another excuse for ignoring civic learning altogether. The absence of civic content from assessments signals its status as a second-class subject, a conclusion held by too many superintendents, principals, teachers, and students nationwide.

Jefferson's warning is just as applicable today as it was over two centuries ago: "If a nation expects to be ignorant and free, it expects what never was and never will be." Statistics about the state of civic learning and civic engagement in the United States confirm the urgency of this crisis. Upon examining the data, it becomes impossible to ignore the individual disempowerment, lack of participation, and civic achievement gap that threaten the fairness and democratic nature of our system of government.

A LACK OF CIVIC KNOWLEDGE

- On the most recent National Assessment of Educational Progress (NAEP) Civics Assessment, more than two-thirds of all American students scored below proficient.
- On the same test, less than one-third of eighth graders could identify the historical purpose of the Declaration of Independence, and less than a fifth of high school seniors could explain how citizen participation benefits democracy.
- In a nationwide study of basic civic knowledge, researchers defined competency as the ability to correctly answer three-quarters of questions on subject based tests. The results were staggering: only 5% of Americans were competent in economics, only 11% in domestic issues, only 14% in foreign affairs, only 10% in geography, and only 25% in history.
- In 2006, in the midst of both midterm elections and the Iraq war, fewer than half of Americans could name the three branches of government, and only four in ten young people (aged 18 to 24) could find Iraq on the map.
- Only one in five Americans between the ages of 18 and 34 read a newspaper, and only one in ten regularly click on news web pages. . . .

Civic learning is, at its heart, necessary to preserving our system of self-government. In a representative democracy, government is only as good as the citizens who elect its leaders, demand action on pressing issues, hold public officials accountable, and take action to help solve problems in their communities. Our founding fathers, the founders of American public education, and generations of leaders have all recognized the centrality of civic learning to American democracy and to an active civil society upon which it depends.

To neglect civic learning is to neglect a core pillar of American democracy. Our commitments to civic equality, democratic accountability, public deliberation, and a political culture based on shared values, all depend on widespread civic knowledge, skills, and dispositions. We face dramatic challenges as a nation, and overcoming them requires revitalizing our government "of the people, by the people, and for the people."

The Founders of America were uniquely concerned that in creating a nation expressly founded on rights—life, liberty, and the pursuit of happiness and those many rights guaranteed in amendments to the US Constitution—future generations that were distant from the struggles of the Revolution and its aftermath would need to be reminded of their duties of active citizenship. They made civic education central to that realization.

Civic learning is the tool by which individuals living here become Americans, equipped with the knowledge, skills, and dispositions to participate in the life of their nation. Without civic learning, we cannot hope to preserve the republic born over two centuries ago. With it, we can unleash generations of Americans who are prepared to address our greatest challenges and leave future generations with the true blessings of liberty to continue to create a more perfect union. . . .

CIVIC KNOWLEDGE

Civic knowledge begins with a fundamental understanding of the structure of government and the processes by which government passes laws and makes policy. Democratic citizenship is all but impossible if citizens fail to understand basic concepts such as separation of powers, federalism, individual rights, and the role of government. But responsible citizenship requires even more knowledge—it demands that students understand the history that continues to shape the present, aspects of geography that are vital to understanding America and the world, and the economics that is necessary to assess public policy options.

Recent research suggests that students who have taken civics courses score better on civic knowledge tests than students who have not had such classes, even once researchers adjust for demographics, type of school and community, and many other factors that might affect knowledge. Focusing on specific topics produces more striking results. For example, students who specifically recall studying the First Amendment know more about the First Amendment than other students do, even after many factors are controlled. The original Civic Mission of Schools report perhaps put it best in summarizing the potential of civic learning: "If you teach them, they will learn."

Program evaluations of high-quality civic learning programs find positive impacts on students' knowledge. For example, "Kids Voting USA" enhances students' knowledge of politics (measured by current factual questions, such as "Who is the governor of Texas?"), reduces gaps in knowledge between the most and least knowledgeable students, and increases the consistency between students' opinions on issues and their own potential voting behavior. A study of civics courses in which students were required to read and discuss the newspaper similarly found gains in knowledge and smaller knowledge gaps.

Overall, the research suggests that taking civics courses boosts civic knowledge. Studying a particular topic can strongly enhance knowledge of that topic when the curriculum and teaching conform to best practices. Some programs have positive effects not only on the children who participate, but also on their parents, who demonstrate increased discussion and media use at home when their students have higher civic knowledge.

In turn, civic knowledge encourages civic action. Young people who know more about government are more likely to vote, discuss politics, contact the government, and take part in other civic activities than their less knowledgeable counterparts. This holds even when the researchers controlled for income and race, showing that as powerful as socioeconomic factors are, civic learning can increase the knowledge of all students.

HISTORY EDUCATION

High school students are also being shortchanged in instruction about US history. Only about 12 percent of high school seniors demonstrated proficiency in history in a recent test called the National Assessment of Educational Progress (NAEP), also known as the "Nation's Report Card." A major federal initiative, the *No Child Left Behind Act*, required schools to raise scores in math and reading but in no other subject. This gave schools and teachers an incentive to spend less time on history and other subjects in order to meet the requirements for math and reading. In the NAEP test, most fourth graders were unable to say why Abraham Lincoln was an important figure, and few high school seniors were able to identify China as the North Korean ally that fought American troops during the Korean War.[7] A survey of public high school social studies teachers done for the American Enterprise Institute found that only about six in ten teachers thought it imperative for their students to understand such concepts as federalism, separation of powers, and checks and balances.

A new evaluation made by the American Council of Trustees and Alumni discovered that most elite colleges no longer require students to study American history. Colleges often allow students to take worthless classes to satisfy core curriculum requirements. For example, at California State University, Monterey Bay, students can count the *History of Rock and Roll* as their required course in US History. Emory University allows students to choose among 600 courses to fulfill the History, Society and Culture requirement, including one called *Gynecology in the Ancient World*.[8]

Schools were once thought of as places where a society's knowledge and experience were passed on to the next generation. But in the twentieth century, the Progressive movement injected into the teachers' colleges the idea that teachers should be change agents. They should use their positions to condition students to want a different kind of society. All kinds of politically correct ideas were implanted into students' minds, and they grew up believing that America is bad, we have treated other countries badly, we have treated our own people unjustly, and this country cannot be trusted to do the right thing. The Supreme Court even endorsed the need for the state to sometimes "awaken in the child's mind" views "contrary to those implanted by the parent."[9]

Other countries have tried this experiment. In France, between the two World Wars, schools decided to replace patriotism with internationalism and pacifism. Books that told the story of the suffering of heroic French soldiers were replaced by books that spoke impartially about the suffering of all soldiers, both French and German. Germany invaded France again in 1940, and this time the world was shocked when the French surrendered after just six weeks of fighting, even though military experts had expected France to win. But two decades of undermining French patriotism and morale had done their work. American schools are now similarly undermining American society as one unworthy of defending. If we were attacked by a foreign power, how long would we fight before begging for some kind of "accommodation" (surrender)?[10]

HISTORY TEXTBOOKS

A widely used history textbook in US public schools is *A People's History of the United States* by Howard Zinn. It is required reading in many high schools and colleges, but it is a very left-wing history book, full of multicultural and class-war propaganda. It is based on the thesis that America is not a republic, but an empire controlled by a few white men. Its heroes are anti-establishment protestors. The book debunks traditional heroes, such as Christopher Columbus and Andrew Jackson, and doesn't mention great Americans such as Thomas Edison.

Zinn's textbook deprives young readers of the opportunity to learn that they are part of the great story of American exceptionalism. His book inspires guilt and the belief that success comes only through exploitation. He belittles patriotism, never allowing pride in America. Zinn himself was an active member of the Communist Party.[11]

This is what Michael Kazin, professor of history at Georgetown University and editor of the leftist *Dissent* magazine, says about the book:

History for Zinn is thus a painful narrative about ordinary folks who keep struggling to achieve equality, democracy, and a tolerant society, yet somehow are always defeated by a tiny band of rulers whose wiles match their greed. . . . Nothing of consequence, in his view, changed during the industrial era, notwithstanding the growth of cities, railroads, and mass communications. Zinn views the tens of millions of Europeans and Asians who crossed oceans at the turn of the past century as little more than a mass of surplus labor. He details their miserable jobs in factories and mines and their desperate, often violent strikes at the end of the nineteenth century—most of which failed. The doleful narrative makes one wonder why anyone but the wealthy came to the United States at all and, after working for a spell, why anyone wished to stay.

Numerous historians may regard George Washington, Thomas Jefferson, James Madison, and Alexander Hamilton as astute, if seriously flawed, men who erected a structure for the new nation that has endured for over two centuries. But Zinn curtly dismisses them as "leaders of the new aristocracy" and regards the nation-state itself as a cunning device to lull ordinary folks with "the fanfare of patriotism and unity."

The fact that his text barely mentions either conservatism or Christianity is telling. The former is nothing but an excuse to grind the poor ("conservatism" itself doesn't even appear in the index), while religion gets a brief mention during Anne Hutchinson's rebellion against the Puritan fathers and then vanishes from the next 370 years of history. . . . Of course, as an imperial bully, the United States had no right, in World War II, "to step forward as a defender of helpless countries." Zinn thins the meaning of the biggest war in history down to its meanest components: profits for military industries, racism toward the Japanese, and the senseless destruction of enemy cities-from Dresden to Hiroshima.[12]

In 1995 a federally tax-funded book called *National Standards for United States History* was released to the public. This was intended to be a national guideline for history curriculum, but it was widely criticized for attempting to omit or debunk our country's heroes, while teaching about obscure individuals deemed more politically correct. Entirely omitted from the *National Standards* were such outstanding Americans as Paul Revere, Thomas Edison, Daniel Webster, the Wright brothers, and General Robert E. Lee. When John D. Rockefeller is mentioned, students are instructed to conduct a trial in which he is accused of participating in unethical and amoral business practices. America's achievements in science and technology are downplayed in favor of giving emphasis to unflattering aspects of American society. For example, McCarthyism is mentioned 19 times, and the Ku Klux Klan is mentioned 17 times. The founding of the National Organization for Women is considered a noteworthy event, but the first gathering of the US Congress is not. The politically correct bias of the *Standards* was so blatant that it was denounced in the United States Senate in a vote of 99 to 1.[13] This is just one more reason for our hostility to the idea of a federal curriculum for our schools.

ISLAM

In their eagerness to show respect to all religions, many of the textbooks will seldom discuss the role of religious belief as a source of conflict. The treatment of Islam, for example, rarely gives any clue to the conflicts between Islamic fundamentalism and Western liberalism. Most textbook publishers employ advisors from the Islamic community who try to ensure that nothing uncomplimentary about Islam gets into the books. The texts try to emphasize that the status of women has improved some under Islamic rule. But they do not honestly portray the differences between the still restricted rights of women in the Muslim world and the Western views of gender equality. Most textbooks will not explain to students the difference between a society such as ours that protects diverse religious expressions, and a theocracy that is ruled by religious authorities.

Some history books relate that in 1979, the repressive Shah of Iran was replaced by the Ayatollah Khomeini, who formed a government based on Islamic law. But most don't acknowledge that the new theocratic system has turned out to be just as oppressive as the Shah's regime. Most of the books will not tell students that many nations today are undemocratic societies ruled by dictators, where ordinary people have few rights or freedoms. Students reading these books will not have a good understanding that there are serious and difficult political, social, and economic problems in the world.

Some textbooks show their bias in other ways. The Jews had rebelled several times against their oppressive Roman rulers. After another rebellion in AD 135, the Romans finally had had enough, and decided to get rid of those troublemakers. They sent a large part of the Jewish population into exile, and changed the name of the area to Palestine. The old names of Judaea and Samaria were abolished in an attempt to destroy the Jewish memory. Under the influence of some Islam special interest groups, some textbooks are trying to promote the fiction that the name Palestine had been in common use for that area for thousands of years prior to that event. That is supposed to help make more legitimate modern Palestinians' claim to the land of Israel by pretending that they had ties to the land going back to ancient times. Some history textbooks, such as *Harcourt Horizons World History*, describe the circumstances accurately. But other books, in an attempt to damage the creditability of America's strong ally Israel, give a variety of erroneous accounts. The textbook *World History: The Human Journey, Modern World*, has a map labeled "Egypt: The New Kingdom, c. 1450 BC," in which it uses the inaccurate label "Palestine" for the western Mediterranean coastal plain. *World History: Continuity & Change* says that Abraham "migrated with his family to Palestine." According to the Bible, his destination was Canaan; it was not called Palestine. The book *Glencoe World History*, overlays "Palestine" onto the labels Judah and Israel in a map entitled "Ancient Israel."[14]

The world history textbook called *History Alive! The Medieval World and Beyond*, contains foreign propaganda masquerading as American history. This book, which is authorized for seventh-grade students by the state of California, contains at least five chapters promoting Islam. This book gives the history and beliefs of Islam lengthy and favorable treatment, far above and beyond what is given to every other religion, according to scholar Stephen Schwartz in the *Weekly Standard* (August 9, 2010). The textbook uses what he calls a "sanitized vocabulary" to conceal Muslim practices that would be criminal in the United States. These include forced marriage, forced divorce, marriage to children, polygamy, and punishments imposed by Sharia law such as public beheadings, amputations, cruel floggings, and stonings.

Muhammad is the only person in this world history textbook who rates an entire chapter. Jesus gets only one sentence, and the contrast between the treatment of Islam and Christianity is shocking. The book gives an entirely positive account of

Muhammad's teachings, saying, for example, "He preached tolerance for Christians and Jews as fellow worshipers of the one true God." It says nothing about Jesus's teachings, but does describe examples of Christian persecution of non-Christians.

History Alive! was influenced by a Muslim pressure group, the Council on Islamic Education, which boasts of successfully "collaborating" with "K–12 publishers" to present a benign view of Islam to impressionable American schoolchildren. The Muslim lobby is particularly adept at influencing textbooks. The founder of the Council on Islamic Education calls this a "bloodless revolution . . . inside American junior high and high school classrooms." Islam is repeatedly described in textbooks as historical truth, whereas Christianity and Judaism are described as mere myths.[15]

Some of the textbooks used at the Islamic Saudi Academy (ISA) in Fairfax County, Virginia, contain passages promoting violent religious fanaticism. For example:

1. In a twelfth-grade *Tafsir* (Quranic interpretation) textbook, the authors state that it is permissible for a Muslim to kill an apostate (a convert from Islam to another religion), an adulterer, or someone who has murdered a believer intentionally: "He (praised is He) prohibits killing the soul that God has forbidden (to kill) unless for just cause." Just cause is defined as "unbelief after belief, adultery, and killing an inviolable believer intentionally."

2. A twelfth-grade *Tawhid* (monotheism) textbook states that "major polytheism [worship of any god besides Allah] makes blood and wealth permissible," which in Islamic legal terms means that a Muslim can, with impunity, take the life and property of someone believed to be guilty of this.

The ISA operates under the direct authority of the Royal Embassy of Saudi Arabia, and is funded by the government of Saudi Arabia. The US Commission on International Religious Freedom (USCIRF) investigated and found that the ISA is teaching violence and religious intolerance. The Saudi government claims to be revising its textbooks to eliminate extremist ideology, but it has not been completely transparent and cooperative in providing all the ISA teaching material for examination.[16]

The USCIRF has for many years expressed concern about the promotion of religious intolerance and religion-based violence in Saudi Arabia's official educational curriculum, and in government textbooks used both within Saudi Arabia, and at Saudi schools abroad, such as the ISA. The USCIRF actually visited Saudi Arabia in an effort to evaluate their educational materials, but the Saudi government would not allow inspection of much of the material requested. The US State Department, in its 2010 annual report on human rights, stated that Saudi textbooks "provided justification for violence against non-Muslims."

BIAS

The publishers of education textbooks and testing materials made an effort to eliminate from their published materials any negative racial bias. They developed guidelines that would alert writers to any words or images that could be problematic. Unfortunately, this grew and grew far beyond its original noble purpose into a monstrosity of political correctness. Under the influence of many special interest groups, all education publishers have become fearful of publishing anything that any group could label as racist, sexist or controversial. The publishers have all accepted an extreme language code that tries to eliminate anything that could possibly be considered the least bit offensive by any member of any group, even to the point of banning many common words and expressions far beyond the bounds of reasonableness and common sense.

For example, a story about the heroic achievement of a blind man who climbed a mountain was rejected because, in our new twisted meaning of bias, it is considered biased to acknowledge that lack of sight is a disability. The story suggested that people who are blind are somehow at a disadvantage and have a more difficult time than those who are not blind. A story about the creation of the monument at Mount Rushmore, located in the Black Hills of South Dakota, was not allowed in a test due to the fear that it might be offensive to some of the Lakota Indians, who consider the Black Hills to be a sacred place to pray. So American children should not be allowed to read about this acclaimed national monument because some Lakota Indians wish the sculpture were not there.

Another type of bias being attacked is "regional bias." This means that children should not be expected to read or comprehend stories set in unfamiliar terrain. A test including a story set in a desert would be "biased" against children who have never lived in a desert. Similarly, stories specifically describing a mountainous area or a seashore or a tropical jungle would be unfamiliar to some children. Just think of what we are doing to the imagination of children by limiting them in this way.

A charming story in a book by an African American author was about an African American girl who was good at jumping rope but was not very good at math. She met another African American girl who was good at math but poor at jumping rope. The two girls agreed to work together by teaching each other what they do best. This story was vetoed because showing an African American girl who was not good at math was considered offensive and stereotypical. One tale about owls described how their keen eyesight and hearing enabled them to hunt rodents at night. This was disallowed because owls are taboo for the Navajo Indians. So owls cannot ever be mentioned to our highly sensitive American schoolchildren. We will just pretend that they don't exist.

Men cannot be portrayed as strong and brave, for that would be stereotyping. It is all right, though, to show women as strong and brave, and to show men as weepy and emotional. Women may not be shown as nurses and secretaries, but they could appear as plumbers and lawyers. A forbidden stereotype would be to show men as athletic or working with tools, or women cooking or caring for children, or to have older people who are feeble or sedentary. In this pathetic effort to avoid stereotypes, older people cannot be described as mild-mannered, sweet, well-meaning, frail, white-haired, wrinkled, crabby, eccentric, grumpy, meek, stubborn, senior citizen, inactive, lonely, or weary.

A book cannot describe a culture as "primitive," because in this new fantasy world there are no primitive cultures. All cultures are equal and are equally advanced. The once traditional emphasis in history textbooks on the growth of democratic institutions has nearly vanished. Students will not understand why some civilizations flourished and others have been mired in poverty for generations. They will not be taught the strong connection between a nation's democratic institutions (based on the rule of law) and its prosperity. The great ideological struggles between democratic nations and their totalitarian adversaries will be a mystery to them. Most world history textbooks condemn slavery in the Western world but present slavery in Africa and the Middle East as benign. Many books imply that Europeans were primarily to blame for African slavery, even though slavery had existed in Africa for centuries before the Europeans arrived there. Some texts go to great lengths to try to present a "balanced" view of Communist China under Mao Tse-tung. Yes, he was responsible for the deaths of millions, but he built schools, bridges, and industry. Students who read these books will have no idea of the oppression and brutality of Communist tyranny.

A common theme in all this is denying reality. It is an effort to create a new society that will be completely inoffensive to everyone. Children can only read stories where everyone is happy almost all the time; stories that have no regional distinctiveness; stories in which men are fearful and women are brave and older people are never ill; stories in which blind people need no assistance from anyone because their handicaps are not handicaps. As one major publisher was working on its high school literature series and trying to comply with all these guidelines, some of its internal memos were leaked. One editor repeatedly conceded that a proposed story lacked literary quality but at least it had the right gender and ethnic representation.

This shameful dishonesty is reducing the curriculum in the schools to bland pablum. Do children really have to be shielded from anything challenging, controversial, or just plain interesting? Is it any surprise that so many children have decided that they just do not enjoy reading?[17] Could students be blamed for wondering how their lessons could in any way be relevant to the real world?

Chapter Twelve

Economic Freedom

Economic freedom is the condition in which individuals can act with autonomy while in the pursuit of their economic livelihood and greater prosperity. Economic freedom is an essential aspect of human liberty, without which a person's rights to life, liberty, and the pursuit of happiness may be fundamentally compromised.

In an economically free society, each person controls the fruits of his or her own labor and initiative. Individuals are empowered to pursue their dreams by means of their own free choice. In an economically free society, individuals succeed or fail based on their individual effort and ability.[1]

HOW DO YOU MEASURE ECONOMIC FREEDOM?

The cornerstones of economic freedom are (1) personal choice, (2) voluntary exchange coordinated by markets, (3) freedom to enter and compete in markets, and (4) protection of persons and their property from aggression by others. Economic freedom is present when individuals are permitted to choose for themselves and engage in voluntary transactions as long as they do not harm the person or property of others.

The US Chamber of Commerce has identified five factors which it believes are important:

- **Transparency**. Laws and regulations applied to business must be readily accessible and easily understood.
- Predictability. Laws and regulations must be applied in a logical and consistent manner regardless of time, place, or parties concerned.

- **Stability.** The state's rationale for the regulation of business—for example, promotion of negotiation and implementation of trade agreements and other vehicles that strengthen rule of law, sanctity of contracts, and compliance with international law—must be consistent and coherent over time, establishing an institutional consistency across administrations, and free from arbitrary or retrospective amendment.
- **Accountability.** Investors must be confident that the laws will be upheld and applied equally to government as well as the private sector and civil society: for example, anti-bribery and corruption issues.
- **Due Process.** When disputes inevitably arise, they must be resolved, not by ad hoc arrangements or special interventions, but in a fair, transparent, and predetermined process.

Where these factors are present, investment thrives, economies grow, jobs are created, and prosperity follows. Where they are absent, corruption thrives, ambiguity reigns, investment dollars flee, and tax revenues plummet.[2]

For over a quarter century, the Fraser Institute has studied and measured the level of economic freedom in different countries, and issued an annual report documenting the changes. Their measure of economic freedom judges how well a country provides secure protection of privately owned property, even-handed enforcement of contracts, and a stable monetary environment. A country with economic freedom also must keep taxes low, refrain from creating barriers to both domestic and international trade, and rely more fully on markets, rather than government spending and regulation, to allocate goods and resources. For these studies, countries are evaluated in the following five areas:

1. Size of government.
2. Legal system and property rights.
3. Sound money.
4. Freedom to trade internationally.
5. Regulation.

This book uses data for the year 2013, which is the most recent year for which comprehensive data is available.

SIZE OF GOVERNMENT

This category indicates the extent to which countries rely on the political process to allocate resources and goods and services. When government spending increases relative to spending by individuals, households, and businesses, government decision-making is substituted for personal choice, and economic freedom is reduced. Another factor is the extent to which countries use private investment and enterprises, rather than government investment and firms, to direct resources. Economic freedom is reduced as government enterprises produce a larger share of total output. Countries with high marginal tax rates are also rated lower.

LEGAL SYSTEM AND PROPERTY RIGHTS.

Protection of persons and their rightfully acquired property is a central element of economic freedom and a civil society. Indeed, it is the most important function of government. The key ingredients of a legal system consistent with economic freedom are rule of law, security of property rights, an independent and unbiased judiciary, and impartial and effective enforcement of the law. The independence, transparency, and effectiveness of the judicial system have proven to be critical to a country's economic success.

Security of property rights, protected by the rule of law, provides the foundation for both economic freedom and the efficient operation of markets. Freedom to exchange, for example, is meaningless if individuals do not have secure rights to property, including the fruits of their labor. When individuals and businesses lack confidence that contracts will be enforced and the fruits of their productive efforts protected, their incentive to engage in productive activity is eroded. Perhaps more than any other area, this area is essential for the efficient allocation of resources.

SOUND MONEY

Money oils the wheels of exchange. An absence of sound money undermines gains from trade. As Milton Friedman informed us long ago, inflation is a monetary phenomenon, caused by too much money chasing too few goods. High rates of monetary growth invariably lead to inflation. Similarly, when the rate of inflation increases, it also tends to become more volatile. High and volatile rates of inflation distort relative prices, alter the fundamental terms of long-term contracts, and make it virtually impossible for individuals and businesses to plan sensibly for the future. Sound money is essential to protect property rights and, thus, economic freedom. Inflation erodes the value of property held in monetary instruments. When governments finance their expenditures by creating money, in effect, they are expropriating the property and violating the economic freedom of their citizens.

The important thing is that individuals have access to sound money: who provides it makes little difference. Thus, in addition to data on a country's inflation and its government's monetary policy, it is important to consider how difficult it is to use alternative, more credible, currencies. If bankers can offer saving and checking accounts in other currencies, or if citizens can open foreign bank accounts, then access to sound money is increased and economic freedom expanded.

FREEDOM TO TRADE INTERNATIONALLY

In our modern world of high technology and low costs for communication and transportation, freedom of exchange across national boundaries is a key ingredient of economic freedom. Many goods and services are now either produced abroad or contain resources supplied from abroad. Voluntary exchange is a positive-sum activity: both trading partners gain, and the pursuit of the gain provides the motivation for the exchange. Thus, freedom to trade internationally also contributes substantially to our modern living standards. In order to get a high rating in this area, a country must have low tariffs, easy clearance and efficient administration of customs, a freely convertible currency, and few controls on the movement of physical and human capital. Trade restrictions also appear in more subtle ways, particularly in the form of regulatory barriers. The degree to which government hinders the free flow of foreign commerce has a direct bearing on the ability of individuals to pursue their economic goals and maximize their productivity and well-being.

REGULATION

When regulations restrict entry into markets, and interfere with the freedom to engage in voluntary exchange, they reduce economic freedom. Burdensome and redundant regulations are the most common barriers to the free conduct of entrepreneurial activity.

Many types of labor-market regulations infringe on the economic freedom of employees and employers. Among the more prominent are minimum wages, dismissal regulations, centralized wage setting, extension of union contracts to non-participating parties, and conscription.

Another factor is the extent to which regulations and bureaucratic procedures restrain entry and reduce competition. In order to score high in this portion of the index, countries and territories must allow markets to determine prices and refrain from regulatory activities that retard entry into business and increase the cost of producing products. They also must refrain from "playing favorites," that is, from using their power to extract financial payments and reward some businesses at the expense of others.[3] The proper role of government is to ensure transparency, disclosure of financial data, integrity of available information, and independent auditing.

WHY IS ECONOMIC FREEDOM IMPORTANT?

Numerous studies have found that countries with institutions and policies more consistent with economic freedom have higher investment rates, more rapid economic growth, higher income levels, and a more rapid reduction in poverty rates. In fact, there is a direct relationship between economic freedom in a country and the income earned by the poorest people in that country. One study found that the annual per capita income of the poorest 10% of the population was $1,629 in the countries having the lowest level of economic freedom, compared with an income of $9,881 in the countries having the highest level of economic freedom.[4]

Throughout history, governments have imposed a wide array of constraints on economic activity. Though sometimes imposed in the name of equality or some other noble societal purpose, such constraints are, in reality, most often imposed for the benefit of societal elites or special interests, and they come with a high cost to society as a whole. By substituting political judgments for those of the marketplace, government diverts entrepreneurial resources and energy from productive activities to the quest for economically unearned benefits. The result is lower productivity, economic stagnation, and declining prosperity.[5]

Government provision of goods and services beyond those that are clearly considered public goods imposes a separate constraint on economic activity as well, crowding out private-sector activity, and usurping resources that might otherwise have been available for private investment or consumption. Constraining economic choice distorts and diminishes the production, distribution, and consumption of goods and services (including, of course, labor services). The wealth of a nation declines as a result.[6]

There is a clear relation between economic freedom and the rate of unemployment. Dr. Horst Feldmann has done studies that show that a lower level of unemployment is correlated with a higher level of economic freedom, a stronger rule of law, and more flexible regulation. And the magnitude of the effect is substantial, especially among young people.[7]

The famous Nobel Prize winning economist Dr. Milton Friedman observed that "Economic freedom is an essential requisite for political freedom. . . . Restrictions on economic freedom inevitably affect freedom in general, even such areas as freedom of speech and press."[8]

The World Bank has done extensive research to find out what factors influence a country's economic success. According to Obiageli Ezekwesili, Vice President for the Africa Region at the World Bank, studies across many countries show that fundamental freedoms are paramount in explaining long-term economic growth and, by extension, job creation and poverty reduction. The expansion over time of the conditions of freedom positively influences long-run economic growth. It is clear that developed countries should prioritize economic freedom over social entitlements. "The greatest antidote to lack of freedom," he says, "is transparency."[9]

Dr. Matthew Mitchell, the Senior Research Fellow at the Mercatus Center at George Mason University, reports on other research which shows that "Economic freedom is indeed positively associated with economic prosperity." And he points out that one important reason why so many humans lack economic freedom is that some entrenched interests benefit from the current lack of economic freedom, and are prepared to go to great lengths to maintain the unfree status quo.

Many regulations allow some firms to profit at the expense of customers and competitors. Governments dispense privileges to particular firms and particular industries in both obvious and not-so-obvious ways:

- Direct subsidies, bailouts, protection from foreign competition, and grants of monopoly status are among the most conspicuous of privileges. What is less obvious is that even the *expectation* of a bailout can be a privilege if it allows the expectant firms to obtain credit at more-favorable terms.

- Loan guarantees are another form of privilege. These tend to escape taxpayer notice unless the loan falls through.
- Tax subsidies are quite common, in part because they are hard to trace. They offer politicians a tool to dispense privilege without having to take responsibility for a line-item in the budget.
- Private contracting presents another source of privilege if the contracting process is non-competitive.
- Finally, regulations can be a lucrative and inconspicuous source of privilege. While we tend to think of regulations as burdensome, it can be a privilege to be regulated if the regulations somehow limit competition, or disproportionately raise the costs of rival firms.

Whatever its guise, government-granted privilege is an extraordinarily destructive force. It undermines competition, misdirects resources, impedes genuine economic progress, breeds corruption, and undermines the legitimacy of both the government and the private sector. It raises prices, lowers quality, and discourages innovation.[10]

THE DECLINING ECONOMIC FREEDOM OF THE UNITED STATES

Throughout most of the period from 1970 to 2000, the United States ranked as the world's third-freest economy, behind Hong Kong and Singapore. The chain-linked[11] summary rating of the United States in 2000 was 8.65 (on a scale of 1 to 10), second only to Hong Kong. By 2005, however, the US rating had slipped to 8.22, and its ranking fallen to 8th. The slide has continued: the United States placed 16th in 2010 and 19th in 2011. The 7.73 rating of the United States in 2013 was nearly a full point less than the 2000 rating.

What accounts for the decline of economic freedom in the United States? While the US ratings and rankings have fallen in all five areas of the Fraser Institute index, the reductions have been largest in Legal System and Property Rights (Area 2), Freedom to Trade Internationally (Area 4), and Regulation (Area 5). The plunge in Area 2 has been huge. In 2000, the 9.23

rating of the United States was the ninth highest in the world. But by 2013, the Area 2 rating had slid to 6.95, placing the United States 38th worldwide. One factor in Area 2 looked at how independent the judiciary is from political influence. In 2011, the United States received a distressing rating of 6.84 for this component. Under Regulation (Area 5) one component evaluates how burdensome it is to comply with administrative requirements of the government, such as permits, regulations, and reporting. For this, the United States received a disturbing rating of 3.99.

While it is difficult to pinpoint the precise reason for this decline, the increased use of eminent domain to transfer property to powerful political interests, the ramifications of the wars on terrorism and drugs, and the violation of the property rights of bondholders in the auto-bailout case have all weakened the tradition of strong adherence to the rule of law in the United States, and have contributed to the sharp decline in the rating for Area 2.[12]

The explosive growth of the welfare state is a matter of grave concern. The major evil of these programs, according to economist Milton Friedman, "is their effect on the fabric of our society. They weaken the family; reduce the incentive to work, save, and innovate; reduce the accumulation of capital; and limit our freedom."[13]

Expanded use of regulation has been an important contributing factor to the declining ratings of the United States. During the past decade, non-tariff trade barriers, restrictions on foreign investment, and business regulation have all grown extensively. Dr. Michael Walker, founder of the Fraser Institute, and a key figure in the development of the economic freedom project, often stated, "Regulation is the raw material of corruption." Thus, he would not be surprised that the expanded use of regulation in the United States has resulted in sharp reductions in ratings for components such as independence of the judiciary, impartiality of the courts, and regulatory favoritism. To a large degree, the United States has experienced a significant move away from rule of law and toward a highly regulated, politicized state.

The approximate one-point decline in the summary rating between 2000 and 2010 on the 10-point scale of the index may not sound like much, but scholarly work on this topic indicates that a one-point decline is associated with a reduction in the long-term growth of GDP of between 1.0 and 1.5 percentage points annually.[14]

THE NEW DEAL

When Franklin D. Roosevelt became president in 1933, the Great Depression had devastated the country, with millions of people unemployed. Roosevelt and his liberal advisors were suspicious of big business, who they accused of "cutthroat competition." They thought the solution to the country's economic woes would be for the government to regulate business more closely. The people in government were so smart, the theory goes, that they could devise rules of fair competition that were much better than what the free market would do. In his inaugural address, Roosevelt said that he wanted to change the normal balance between Congress and the president, so that the executive branch would make and enforce rules for almost every aspect of our lives. And, sure enough, he was able to persuade Congress to delegate away much of its power.[15] The National Recovery Administration (NRA) was created in 1933, with the authority to set codes for different industries, which dictated minimum wages, minimum prices, and maximum working hours.

The businessman who was more efficient and innovative, and therefore could produce goods for lower prices, was criticized by the government. This efficiency was believed to contribute to lower wages and, therefore, diminishing purchasing power for the people. The NRA thought that it could eliminate this "problem" by rules that enabled all existing businesses to make fair profits and to pay high wages. Many large businesses were happy to participate in this scheme, which helped them by penalizing their competition. The minimum price rules hurt smaller businesses, which might compete with the larger businesses by charging lower prices.

What was the effect of all this central planning? The NRA itself collected statistics showing that in 1935 wages were up nationally, but retail prices were up even more. This means that real wages were actually lower than when the NRA became law. The National Recovery Review Board investigated the NRA, and found that it was having the effect of destroying many small businesses. Yale economist Irving Fisher told Roosevelt that the NRA has retarded recovery and has produced more unemployment.[16]

The NRA was declared unconstitutional by the Supreme Court in 1935, but many of its features survived in other forms, including the minimum wage and provisions designed to give more power to labor unions.

Another massive bureaucracy promoted by President Roosevelt was the Agricultural Adjustment Administration (AAA). This was supposed to help farmers by keeping prices that they received for their crops high. One factor that was keeping prices depressed was overproduction. The government tried to reduce production by paying certain farmers not to produce certain crops on part of their land. Some crops were being plowed under, and many pigs were killed at the same time that millions of people were unemployed and couldn't afford enough to eat. With all the land taken out of production, America was producing much less food than before, and for the first time we had to start importing massive amounts. For example, in 1935 the United States imported 34 million bushels of corn and almost 3 million pounds of pork.[17] Another unintended consequence was the massive eviction of tenant farmers. When farmers were being paid to remove much of their acreage from production, the farmers would often evict the tenant farmers who were working this land, forcing the tenants into unemployment.[18]

Another factor that was hurting farmers was the decline in export markets. The government caused this problem by passing the Smoot-Hawley tariff act in 1930. This established high protective tariffs for US imports, which inspired other countries to erect high retaliatory tariffs for US exports. The result was that Europeans greatly reduced their purchase of American farm products.

In 1936, the Supreme Court ruled that parts of the Agricultural Adjustment Act were unconstitutional. Many of the farm programs, however, continued under other legislation. In his inaugural address, President Roosevelt said that this emergency "may call for temporary departure from that normal balance of public procedure," meaning the division of power between the executive branch and Congress. The financial emergency of the Great Depression has long passed, but the "normal balance" never returned. Instead, the unaccountable administrative state is bigger than ever.[19]

Chapter Thirteen

War Fever

One of the favorite tactics of government officials is to use a crisis or emergency, either real or contrived, to create fear or anxiety in the population. When people are afraid, they are more willing to sacrifice some of their liberty in return for security. They in effect tell their government "Do whatever it takes to protect me." This gives the government the opportunity to enact policies that, in normal circumstances might have been questioned, but can now be justified for "national security" or the "protection of the people." In time of war, these emotions are amplified considerably. Our troops are in danger! Spies and terrorists are lurking everywhere! In such an atmosphere of fear, suspicion, and patriotism, we have seen many shameful examples of overreaction to the perceived dangers, where we have been willing to suppress dissent and punish the dissenters.

When we are trying to decide if our rights should be restricted in wartime, the Constitution actually does answer that question. Where the Framers thought such limitation was justified, they explicitly said that. In Section 9 of Article 1 of the Constitution, the writ of habeas corpus is allowed to be suspended "in cases of rebellion of invasion." Where this kind of exception is not stated, then the Constitution must apply equally in times of war as well as peace. Also, in wartime, many important life-and-death decisions have to be made, and it is important that the people be able to debate these issues and consider different opinions. Free and open access to ideas and information is essential for the proper functioning of a democracy.

Federal District Court Judge Marilyn Patel warned about the potential for war induced fear when she wrote: "In times of war or declared military necessity our institutions must be vigilant in protecting constitutional guarantees. . . . In times of distress, the shield of military necessity and national security must not be used to protect governmental actions from close scrutiny and accountability."[1] Supreme Court Justice David Davis was emphatic when he wrote: "The Constitution of the United States is a law for rulers and people, equally in war and in peace, and covers with the shield of its protection all classes of men, at all times and under all circumstances. No doctrine involving more pernicious consequences was ever invented by the wit of man than that any of its provisions can be suspended during any of the great exigencies of government. Such a doctrine leads directly to anarchy or despotism."[2] Supreme Court Justice Frank Murphy lamented the loss of our liberties when he said, "It does not follow, however, that the broad guaranties of the Bill of Rights and other provisions of the Constitution protecting essential liberties are suspended by the mere existence of a state of war."[3] But frequently wartime hysteria has led us to see dissent as disloyalty, and the First Amendment has been one of the biggest causalities.

SEDITION ACT OF 1798

In 1794 Europe was engulfed in war, and France was a powerful military force. America tried to stay neutral, but our close relations with Britain irritated France, who began a campaign against American shipping. Between June 1796 and June 1797, the French seized 316 American ships. The American people were afraid we might go to war, and at the same time were frightened of France's power. John Adams had been elected president of the United States in 1796. Adams sent a delegation to Paris to try to negotiate with France, but the French refused to meet with them. In what became known as the XYZ Affair, agents of the French Foreign Minister Talleyrand demanded bribes and a loan to France before negotiations could begin. Americans were outraged at this insult, and a wave of patriotism swept the nation. Congress allocated funds to expand the army and navy, and for fortification of harbors.

Rumors spread about French saboteurs and spies among us and a possible invasion. In this atmosphere of anxiety and patriotism, Congress passed the Sedition Act. It provided for punishment for anyone who "shall write, print, utter or publish . . . any false, scandalous, and malicious writing or writings against the government of the United States." Congressman Albert Gallatin of Pennsylvania argued against this law, reminding Congress that laws against political criticism had been used time and again by tyrants.

Representative Harrison Gray Otis of Massachusetts declared that the nation's very existence was endangered by that "crowd of spies and inflammatory agents" who had spread across the nation "fomenting hostilities" and "alienating the affections of our own citizens." Congressman John Allen said the act was necessary because a treasonable conspiracy of Republican congressmen and editors was attempting to ruin the government by publishing the most shameless falsehoods and by inciting the people to insurrection. To prove this conspiracy, Allen pointed to several items of "evidence," including a "false" accusation in the Aurora newspaper that the Adams administration had failed to exhaust all reasonable efforts to negotiate a peaceful settlement with France, and a "false" statement in the Aurora that it was no longer clear whether there was more "liberty to be enjoyed at Constantinople or Philadelphia." Albert Gallatin responded that the statements that Allen found objectionable contained "not only facts but opinions." How, he asked, could the truth of such opinions be proved?[4]

This law reminded many of the law of seditious libel in England. This law outlawed "any false news or tales whereby discord . . . may grow between the king and his people." Though the law originally covered only "false" statements, the English courts eventually held that even true statements could be punished.[5] The king used this statute relentlessly and cruelly to silence criticism. The authors of the First Amendment were certainly aware of this English law, and this was probably one reason they wrote in the First Amendment, "Congress shall make no law. . . abridging freedom of speech."

Even when England finally claimed to have given their subjects "freedom of speech and the press," this was interpreted to mean only that the government could not exercise prior restraint in preventing the publication of something. If you published something that was considered offensive to the king, you could still be prosecuted and punished for your statements. The early Americans were accustomed to this practice in England, and many assumed that this would still be normal even under the First Amendment.

But others argued that the First Amendment would not allow a person to be punished for what he said or printed. One of the purposes of the First Amendment was to encourage free and open debate, even if it was critical of the government. But if subsequent punishment was allowed, that would discourage anyone from printing anything that might offend those in power.

The American Sedition Act of 1798 was actually used by the Federalist Party (who was in power) as a tool to silence criticism by the opposition Republican Party during the presidential election campaign of 1800. One aspect of the Federalist's campaign strategy was to try to silence the leading Republican leaning newspapers. Four influential Republican journals, as well as several lesser ones, were prosecuted under the Sedition Act. As a result, two Republican newspapers actually went out of business.[6] Matthew Lyon, an outspoken Republican congressman, was convicted under the Sedition Act, and sent to jail. He won reelection to Congress in 1798 while he was in jail. It was not a coincidence that not a single Federalist was ever indicted under the Sedition Act.[7]

During this period, the federal judges proved that they could not be trusted to insure the fair and objective execution of the laws. All of the federal judges were Federalists, and many of them joined with relish the campaign to persecute the Republicans. Justice James Iredell, in his charge to a grand jury in 1799, justified the Sedition Act by saying that, although the government could not prevent the publication, it could punish "any dangerous or offensive writings."[8] Newspaper editor Thomas Cooper was charged under the Sedition Act for criticizing President Adams. Supreme Court Justice Samuel Chase was the presiding judge, and his bias against Cooper was plainly evident throughout the trial. Justice Chase repeatedly refused to allow Cooper to introduce evidence. And in his outrageous charge to the jury, Justice Chase said that "if a man attempts to destroy the confidence of the people in their officers," he saps the very "foundation of the government."[9]

CIVIL WAR

The writ of habeas corpus was fundamental to the Framers of the Constitution. The writ is a judicial mandate directing an official to present an individual held in custody to the court so that it can determine whether his detention is lawful. The Supreme Court has called the writ a "fundamental instrument for safeguarding individual freedom against arbitrary and lawless" government action.[10] Section 9 of Article 1 of the Constitution is entitled "Prohibitions on Congress." In this Section, the second paragraph says "the privilege of the writ of habeas corpus shall not be suspended, unless when in case of rebellion or invasion the public safety may require it." This seems to imply that Congress alone would be the entity that would suspend the writ if that became necessary.

Shortly after the outbreak of the Civil War, there was significant sympathy for the Confederacy in the state of Maryland. Maryland was in a key location, because it surrounded the nation's capital on three sides, and therefore controlled access to Washington from many of the northern states. In 1861, the Sixth Massachusetts Volunteers attempted to march through Baltimore on the way to Washington. A mob of Confederate sympathizers attacked the soldiers causing widespread rioting. On April 27, President Lincoln suspended the writ of habeas corpus and declared martial law in Maryland.

Soon thereafter, Union soldiers arrested a man named John Merryman, and accused him of destroying bridges and telegraph wires during the April riots. Merryman immediately filed a petition for a writ of habeas corpus. Roger B. Taney, chief justice of the United States Supreme Court, heard his petition, and ruled that only Congress was authorized to suspend the writ of habeas corpus, and that Lincoln's suspension was unconstitutional. He also ruled that the ordinary civilian courts, rather than military authority, had jurisdiction over the matter. Taney, therefore, issued a writ of habeas corpus, and commanded General George Cadwalader, who had custody of Merryman, to appear with him before the court.

President Lincoln flatly refused to comply with the writ of habeas corpus. When the US marshal arrived at Fort McHenry to serve the writ on General Cadwalader, he was refused entrance to the fort. All Taney could do was to issue a report to the President explaining the situation and asking the President to "perform his constitutional duty to enforce the laws." Lincoln ignored Taney's report. Given the widespread anxiety over the war, there was no meaningful public opposition to Lincoln's unconstitutional actions. A few weeks later, Lincoln suspended the writ in Florida. Then, in September of 1862, he suspended the writ nationwide. Finally, in 1863, Congress enacted legislation to ratify his actions, and to authorize future suspensions of the writ.[11]

Some of the most egregious violations of freedom of speech came, not from the President or Congress, but from the military commanders. Certainly Lincoln should have done more to restrain his commanders, and to impress upon them the importance of constitutional rights. But as we see repeated over and over again, personal liberties are frequent casualties in the fear, anxiety, and confusion of war. President Lincoln defended the suppression of speech when he said "Must I shoot a simple-minded soldier boy who deserts, while I must not touch a hair of a wily agitator who induces him to desert?"[12]

In March 1863 General Ambrose Burnside was appointed the military commander of the Department of Ohio, which combined all the federal troops in the states of Ohio, Indiana, Michigan, Illinois, and Wisconsin. General Burnside was appalled to discover that the newspapers in Ohio contained much criticism of the way the government was conducting the war. Even public meetings were held in which Lincoln and his generals were denounced. In April, without Lincoln's knowledge or approval, Burnside issued General Order 38, which declared that the habit of declaring sympathies for the enemy will not be allowed in this Department. He declared martial law in some areas, and began trying to suppress dissent.

Clement Vallandigham was an Ohio politician, and a gifted orator who spoke out strongly against the war, the draft, abolitionists, President Lincoln, and the suspension of habeas corpus. In May 1863 at Mount Vernon, Ohio, Vallandigham gave a fiery speech condemning General Order 38, saying his right to speak was based on General Order No. 1—The Constitution of the United States. Burnside was furious, and in a revolting display of force, sent a contingent of more than a hundred soldiers to Vallandigham's home at two thirty in the morning. They broke down his front door and hauled him off to prison in Cincinnati. A military commission found Vallandigham guilty, and recommended imprisonment for the duration of the war.

Many newspapers, including the Chicago Times, were critical of Vallandigham's arrest. In June, General Burnside ordered Union soldiers to close the Chicago Times. As many as 300 newspapers were closed during the war for criticizing the government.[13] At that time, newspapers were circulated primarily by mail, so often the papers were suppressed by revoking their mailing privileges, but occasionally editors were actually arrested. Sometimes these suspensions were effective only for brief periods after the government felt the effects of political or public pressure.

WORLD WAR I

As the United States moved closer and closer to World War I, President Woodrow Wilson was very critical of anyone he considered "disloyal." He insisted that new legislation was needed to restrict "warfare by propaganda."[14] Wilson stated that disloyal individuals "had sacrificed their right to civil liberties." He warned that "if there should be disloyalty, it will be dealt with a firm hand of stern repression."[15] The president proposed to Congress legislation which would, among other things, prohibit the press from publishing anything that the president had decided would be useful to the enemy. Congress rejected this express censorship of the press, but it did enact the Espionage Act of 1917 (amended in 1918), which contained vague and ambiguous prohibitions such as:

- Utter, print, write, or publish any disloyal, profane, scurrilous, of abusive language about the government, Constitution, or the military
- Use any language intended to bring the form of government, Constitution, or military into contempt, scorn, or disrepute
- Making false statements with the intent to interfere with the military success of the United States
- Cause or attempt to cause insubordination, disloyalty, mutiny, or refusal of duty in the military
- Advocate or suggest any of the above acts
- Mailing any publication that contains any matter that is in violation of any of the provisions of this act[16]

Even though the president was disappointed that he didn't get all that he wanted, the administration was still able to twist the language of this law to relentlessly harass, persecute, and censor dissenters. More than two thousand people were prosecuted during the war for allegedly disloyal speech, and over one hundred people were sentenced to jail terms of ten years or more just for statements they had made. Not a single person was convicted for actual spying or sabotage.[17]

An example of the reasoning used to expand the reach of the Espionage Act is found in the case of *Shaffer v. United States*.[18] The defendant was charged with mailing a book containing anti-war passages. The appeals court ruled that:

Printed matter may tend to obstruct the . . . service even if it contains no mention of recruiting or enlistment, and no reference to the military service of the United States . . . The service may be obstructed by . . . undermining the spirit of loyalty . . . the question here . . . is whether the natural and probable tendency and effect of the words . . . are such as are calculated to produce the result condemned by the statute.[19]

So your speech could be seditious even if you don't mention the military and don't advocate any resistance, because your words might have a "tendency" to reduce loyalty. It is easy to see the potential for abuse in this reasoning.

The courts again seemed to go along with this rush to use any excuse to prosecute critical speech. Supreme Court Justice Oliver Wendell Holmes inserted into a Court opinion the statement "when a nation is at war, many things that might be said in time of peace are such a hindrance to its effort that their utterance will not be endured so long as men fight and no Court could regard them as protected by any constitutional right . . ." He also wrote that the government's power to restrict speech is greater in time or war.[20]

- Rose Pastor Stokes was convicted for making a speech before a group of women in which she said "I am for the people and the government is for the profiteers." Even though there were no soldiers in her audience, she was sentenced to ten years in prison because her remarks had the "tendency" to "chill enthusiasm" of mothers, sisters and sweethearts.[21]
- The producer of a movie called "The Spirit of 76" was given ten years in jail because, by showing British atrocities during the American Revolution in the movie, he tended to raise questions about the good faith of America's wartime ally.[22]
- Walter Matthey of Iowa was sentenced to a year in jail for "attending a meeting, listening to an address in which disloyal utterances were made, applauding some of the statements made by the speaker . . . and contributing 25 cents."[23]
- Charles Schenck was the general secretary of the Socialist Party, which had mailed leaflets saying that the draft was a plot by the rich to force the poor to fight in the war. The flyers encouraged readers to petition for the repeal of the conscription law. Schenck was sentenced to prison under the 1917 Espionage Act. His First Amendment challenge went to the Supreme Court, where in 1919 Oliver Wendell Holmes wrote the opinion upholding Schenck's conviction. In the ever

changing world of Supreme Court opinions, Holmes created new criteria for prosecuting dissent. The court found that Schenck had created a "clear and present danger" to the country's ability to raise an army, and that justified overruling his right of free speech guaranteed by the First Amendment.

In this frenzied rush to suppress even the slightest questioning of the war effort, very few judges were willing to speak out against the madness. One of the brave souls who did question the censorship was federal District Judge Learned Hand, who issued a ruling in the case of *Masses Publishing Co. v. Patten*. The Masses was a monthly journal that featured some prominent writers and philosophers. The attractive magazine was filled with political commentary, lively satire, and cartoons, poking fun at contemporary culture. In 1917 Postmaster General Albert Burleson ordered the August issue of the Masses excluded from the mails due to some cartoons and poems, which he said violated the Espionage Act. This was because, Burleson said, the material willfully caused insubordination, disloyalty, or refusal of duty in the military. Judge Hand argued that to read the word "cause" so broadly would involve "necessarily as a consequence the suppression of all hostile criticism, and of all opinion except what encouraged and supported the existing policies." He said that this "would contradict the normal assumption of democratic government" and would be "contrary to the use and wont of our people."[24] Unfortunately, Judge Hand's ruling against the postmaster was promptly reversed by the court of appeals. Hand had been under consideration for promotion to the court of appeals, but in the criticism that followed this ruling he was passed over for this appointment.

Many states passed similar laws. A Minnesota man was sent to prison for saying to patriotic knitters, "No soldier ever sees those socks." One man was sentenced to three years in prison for saying, "this was a Morgan war, and not a war of the people."[25] The University of Virginia fired a journalism professor for making a pacifist speech.[26]

BETWEEN THE WARS

After the end of World War I, organized labor was anxious to flex its muscles. It had tried to maintain peace during the war, but now battles between labor and management erupted in over 1800 strikes in various cities.[27] On top of that, the Russian revolution created anxiety. A new atmosphere of panic and fear was building, and Communists were being blamed. The FBI and some politicians fanned the flames by vowing to combat "radicalism." In November of 1919, about 650 people were arrested on suspicion of radicalism. Of course, many of these people were perfectly innocent. On January 2, 1920, another 4000 suspects were arrested. Eventually about 3000 people were actually deported. Many states also enacted criminal anarchy laws, and at least 1400 people were arrested under state laws. Judge Learned Hand wrote that:

> The merry sport of Red-baiting goes on, and the pack gives tongue more and more shrilly . . . I own a sense of dismay at the increase in all the symptoms of apparent panic. How far people are getting afraid to speak . . . I don't know, but I am sure that the public generally is becoming rapidly demoralized in all its sense of proportion.[28]

Later in 1920, these arrests and deportations were discredited and criticized, but in the meantime many people had to experience major injustices and disruptions to their lives.

During the Depression, President Roosevelt told the FBI to collect information about Nazi and Communist groups. This information was for intelligence purposes only, and not related to an investigation of any specific crime. By 1941, the FBI had expanded its domestic intelligence operations to cover a wide variety of completely legal activities of peaceful groups. Agents were directed to investigate persons of German "sympathies," to identify members of German fraternal societies, and to gather lists of subscribers of German and communist foreign language newspapers. In 1939, the FBI began creating a list of persons to be possibly incarcerated in case of war or national emergency, including persons with strong communist "tendencies." (At its peak in 1955, this list contained 26,000 names, including educators, lawyers, and doctors.) The FBI had been using illegal bugs and wiretaps without warrants or authorization. Then in 1940, President Roosevelt formally directed the Attorney General to permit the FBI to use such tactics. That same year, the FBI also began an illegal program of monitoring and opening first class mail.[29] If anyone sent a message to President Roosevelt expressing disagreement with his foreign policy, that person's name and address might be given to the FBI to be investigated.[30] Guilt by association became national policy, with the enactment of laws denying employment to members of the Communist Party.[31]

In 1938, war in Europe was looking more and more likely. In the United States, fascist organizations such as the German-American Bund were growing. Members of the Bund wore Nazi-style uniforms and published propaganda produced by the Nazi Party in Germany. Concern about these activities prompted the House to create the House Un-American Activities Committee (HUAC) to investigate un-American propaganda activities in the United States. Actually, the committee chairman, Martin Dies, seemed more concerned about exposing Communist influences. The HUAC proceedings were zealous and often irresponsible, searching for Communists everywhere. Its first report named hundreds of organizations as "Communistic," including the Boy Scouts and the Camp Fire Girls. Many government officials and employees wound up on his list of Communist sympathizers. Many people had their reputations damaged by Dies' strategy of public disclosure. When the FBI investigated these accusations, they were generally rejected as unfounded and reckless, but this gave a preview of how much damage can be done to innocent persons by legislative investigating committees.[32]

In 1939, Congress passed the Hatch Act, which banned from federal employment any person who is a member of "any political party or organization" that advocates the "overthrow or our constitutional form of government." The national hysteria about the threat of Communism was intensified by the signing, in 1939, of the Nazi-Soviet nonaggression pact. In 1940, Congress reenacted the Espionage Act of 1917, making some of its provisions applicable in peacetime. Congress also passed the Alien Registration Act of 1940 (the Smith Act) which required all resident aliens to register with the government, and forbade any person to advocate, abet or teach the overthrowing of the government. It even provided that past beliefs or activities, even if discontinued or repudiated, still subjected aliens to deportation.[33] The Smith Act expanded the excuses for deporting aliens to include weapons violations and misuse of heroin.

WORLD WAR II

Most of the states resisted the temptation to search out disloyalty, acquiescing to President Roosevelt's plea to leave that to the federal government. New York, however, passed a law excluding from state employment members of Communist organizations. The Washington legislature refused to seat an elected state senator because he had once been a member of the Communist Party. Fifteen states banned the Communist Party from the ballot.

There is a provision in federal law that allows a person's American citizenship, if it was acquired by naturalization, to be cancelled if it was obtained by fraud. On this basis, the government instituted a series of legal actions during the war to cancel the naturalization of individuals who had indicated by "disloyal" conduct that they were not at the time of naturalization "attached to the principles of the Constitution." By the end of 1943, the United States had issued 146 "decrees of cancellation," most of them for former German nationals. This program was effectively ended by the 1944 Supreme Court case of *Baumgartner v. United States*,[34] which involved a German-born man. He had become a naturalized citizen in 1932, and later embraced some of Hitler's ideas. The Court ruled that an individual could not be denaturalized for speaking "foolishly and without moderation," or for making even "sinister-sounding" statements, "which native-born citizens utter with impunity."[35]

COLD WAR

The so-called Cold War after World War II was a bleak period in the history of free speech in the United States. Fear of Communism spread throughout the country. In the 1946 congressional elections, many Republicans accused their Democratic opponents of Communist sympathies, and the Republicans won significant victories. Since Red-baiting was so successful, it continued even after the elections.

In 1946 President Truman appointed the Temporary Commission on Employee Loyalty. The chairman of this commission stated that the presence of even one disloyal employee in the government would constitute a "serious threat . . . to the security of the United States." Every federal civilian employee had to undergo a loyalty investigation, and if anything "suspicious" was uncovered, he would have a hearing before a "loyalty board." The FBI would produce any evidence they had gathered about his associations, beliefs, sympathies, what books he has read, and what his neighbors thought about him. Much of this information was unsubstantiated gossip and slander, not checked or verified. There was no definition of what constituted "disloyalty."[36]

Criteria included "Membership in . . . or sympathetic association with any . . . group . . . designated by the Attorney

General as totalitarian, Fascist, Communist or subversive." The Attorney General had the broad and arbitrary power to make a list of such organizations. The criteria for being on this list were vague and undisclosed, and an organization had no right to contest its inclusion on this list. In fact, some of the organizations listed had done nothing more subversive than to state opposition to some administration policy. Historian and journalist Alan Barth said that the power of the Attorney General to generate this list was "perhaps the most arbitrary and far-reaching power ever exercised by a single public official in the history of the United States. By virtue of it, the Attorney General may stigmatize, and in effect, proscribe any organization of which he disapproves." The publication of this list by the Administration was apparently an effort to discredit, without hearings or charges, groups that were opposing American foreign policy. The practice of placing organizations on the list without any hearings was eventually held to be unconstitutional by the Supreme Court, but before this happened the use of the list was effective in destroying most of the organizations on the list.[37]

In these "loyalty hearings," the accused was not allowed to confront the witnesses against him or even learn their identity. In many cases, charges were only vague allegations without specifics of time, place or even the actual activity. There was no time limit, so someone might be accused of an "association" which occurred forty years previously.

The object of the loyalty hearings was generally not to identify actual acts of disloyalty, but rather to determine if the subject had any disloyal "thoughts" which at some future time might possibly lead to some undefined disloyal action. No case or even evidence of actual spying or espionage was uncovered. All cases involved accusations of associations or memberships considered "subversive."[38]

Between 1947 and 1956, about 3,900 federal employees were discharged for disloyalty. In addition, about 12,000 federal employees resigned rather than go through the humiliating process.[39]

Alan Barth described the Truman loyalty program as follows:

Any American hearing of a foreign country in which the police were authorized to search out the private lives of law-abiding citizens, in which a government official was authorized to proscribe lawful associations, in which administrative tribunals were authorized to condemn individuals by star-chamber proceedings on the basis of anonymous testimony, for beliefs and associations entailing no criminal conduct, would conclude without hesitation that the country was one in which tyranny prevailed.[40]

In 1946, President Truman, as President Roosevelt had done in 1940, authorized the FBI to install wiretaps in cases involving subversive activities. The FBI also again greatly expanded its domestic political intelligence investigations.[41] The Truman administration made more than a hundred highly publicized deportation arrests in 1948 of prominent aliens who led left-wing unions, or generally opposed government policy. A clear message was sent to noncitizens that they should avoid "dubious" political activities and associations.[42]

Many state legislatures were also caught up in the hysteria, and passed laws outlawing or restricting the Communist Party. Michigan authorized life imprisonment for members of the Communist Party. Tennessee authorized the death penalty. Thirty-five states barred the Communist Party's candidates from the ballot. Hundreds of states and cities required loyalty oaths for public employees. New York required a loyalty oath of all persons getting a fishing license.[43]

One area of special concern was education. The National Education Association opposed the employment of Communist Party members as teachers. In 1953, the Association of American Universities resolved that membership in the Communist Party "extinguishes the right to a university position." In 1958, Congress required that applicants for student loans under the National Defense Education Act swear that they did not belong to or support any organizations advocating the illegal overthrow of the government.[44] At public schools and colleges across the nation, hundreds of teachers were fired because of their actual or suspected, past or present membership in the Communist Party.[45]

The House Un-American Activities Committee rediscovered its mission to unearth Communists. By 1948, it had created a list of over 360,000 persons who had in the past signed a Communist Party election petition.[46] It amassed files on hundreds of thousands of Americans who had done nothing wrong. The primary tactic of the HUAC was public exposure and humiliation, with the intent of getting the subjects fired by their employers. And that is exactly what did happen to many of the targets without any trials or due process.[47] Reputations were ruined and careers destroyed. If one allegedly subversive person belonged to a particular organization, then every member of that organization could be contaminated just by his membership in the group.

Some of the most famous hearings held by the HUAC involved its investigation into Hollywood. Communists had infiltrated the motion picture industry, and thus introduced Communist propaganda into motion pictures, it claimed. Ten writers and actors were called before the committee to testify, and were sent to prison for contempt for refusing to answer the famous question "Are you now or have you ever been a member of the Communist Party?" Around 250 writers, directors, and actors were blacklisted in Hollywood during this period, as well as about 1500 in radio and television. Many people were cowed into submission. The movie studios pledged not to employ anybody who refused to answer the question about being a member of the Communist Party.[48]

In 1950, Senator Joe McCarthy (R-WI) began making outrageous claims that he knew of 200 Communists who were employees of the State Department. His wild accusations resonated with many Americans who were fearful of this new aggressive adversary. His talent for theater and self-promotion garnered a great deal of attention. A senate committee made an investigation of McCarthy's claims, and found them totally without merit. But this had now become a partisan issue, with most of the Republicans supporting McCarthy. So his power and popularity actually grew. Hundreds of innocent people were accused, ridiculed, and humiliated by McCarthy and the other congressional hearings, and had their reputations permanently damaged and their careers destroyed.

In 1950, the McCarran Internal Security Act was passed, which called for the registration of all Communist organizations, and disclosure to the Attorney General of a list of their members. These members were barred by the Act from employment by the government or by defense contractors. The futile efforts of the loyalty program to try to attempt to predict future illegal behavior was extended to the entire population by this act, which provided, whenever war is declared, for the mass round-up of dissidents, and their indefinite detention without trial if the Attorney General believed that they "probably" would engage in future illegal conduct.[49] In 1954, the Communist Control Act was enacted; this law outlawed the Communist Party.[50]

In 1950, President Truman issued an executive order barring any person from seagoing employment unless the "character and habits of life of the applicant are such . . . that the presence of such individual . . . would not be inimical to the security of the United States."[51] The government began in 1951 to seize foreign publications coming into the United States that were accused of being "communist propaganda." This assault on the freedom of the press involved confiscation of publications such as *The London Economist, Pravda* and a book entitled *The Happy Life, Children in the Rumanian People's Republic.*[52]

The State Department also suffered greatly from this atmosphere of repression. Most of the smart, knowledgeable experts on China were purged from the State Department by 1952. Their crime was, in most cases, to have predicted correctly that Chiang Kai-sheck was likely to lose to the Chinese Communists. No one was allowed to say anything good about the Communists, even if it was true, and even if it might be helpful in formulating our foreign policy. This paralysis was still evident years later as we were debating strategy for Vietnam. Honest analysis of the strengths of the Viet Cong and the weakness of South Vietnam was inhibited, not only at the State Department, but even at the White House. It was so dangerous politically to be seen as "soft on communism" that this affected decisions about the Korean War, the Bay of Pigs debacle, and the Vietnam adventure. Shortly after taking office, President Lyndon Johnson told US Ambassador to South Vietnam Henry Cabot Lodge: "I am not going to lose Vietnam. I am not going to be the President who saw Southeast Asia go the way China went."[53]

The Supreme Court did not have a good record of trying to control this hysteria. There were a few good decisions supporting free speech. But there were too many shameful ones:

- In the case of Bailey v. Richardson (1950) the Court agreed that federal employees could be dismissed in loyalty proceedings on the basis of unsworn secret evidence submitted by unnamed persons.
- In 1952, the Court upheld the deportation of an Italian who had come to the United States in 1920, and had belonged to the Communist Party from 1923 to 1929.
- In the case of Adler v. Board of Education (1952), the Court said that teachers could be fired for mere membership in organizations on a list made by the New York State Board of Regents.
- The Court, in 1952, upheld a provision of the Internal Security Act that stated that alien communists could be held indefinitely without bail pending deportation proceedings.

- In 1953, in the case of Shaugnessy v. United States ex rel Mezei, the Supreme Court upheld the indefinite imprisonment of a man who had lived in the United States since 1923, based on confidential information which the Attorney General refused to disclose. This man faced the prospect of unlimited confinement based on executive decree without accusation of a crime, without a jury trial, and with no provision for review or appeal.[54]
- The Supreme Court, in the case of Beilan v. Board of Education (1958), upheld the firing of a Philadelphia school teacher for refusal to answer questions of school officials about his past political affiliations.
- In 1958, the Court, in the case of Lerner v. Casey, upheld the firing of a New York subway conductor for refusing to answer similar questions posed by city officials.[55]
- The Court also upheld the contempt conviction of a college professor who had refused to answer questions from the House Un-American Activities Committee about his political affiliations (Barenblatt v. United States, 1959); upheld the firing of two Los Angeles County employees for refusing to answer HUAC questions (*Nelson and Globe v. Los Angeles*, 1960); and upheld the exclusion on loyalty grounds of a lawyer by the California state bar (*Konigsberg v. State Bar of California*, 1961).[56]

VIETNAM WAR

During the Vietnam War, the anti-war protests were an irritation to President Lyndon Johnson, who directed the FBI to investigate alleged Communist influence. Their investigation revealed that the actual influence of the Communist Party USA (CPUSA) on the anti-war movement was negligible. But the FBI continued to conduct surveillance and monitoring of leftist groups and people. When Richard Nixon took office as president in 1969, he pressed the FBI to expand these efforts. The Nixon administration also enlisted the Internal Revenue Service on a massive scale. The IRS established a special unit called the Special Services Staff to collect information on dissident organizations and people. They used targeted tax audits and tax investigations to strike a blow at these organizations. The IRS also gave confidential tax information on dissidents to the FBI.

This program was kept strictly secret because of its political sensitivity.

The government was so suspicious and fearful of the Communist Party and antiwar activists that serious efforts were made to hinder their activities. Not only were they subject to intense surveillance and unconstitutional censorship, but the government initiated programs to harass and disrupt them. Some of these activities used by the FBI included:

- Sending anonymous or fictional materials to CPUSA members to try to create dissention and cause disruption
- Leaking non-public information to news media
- Advising authorities of CPUSA members' activities to adversely affect their credit standing or get them fired from their jobs
- Using anonymous communications to inform family and groups to which the individuals belonged of their "radical or immoral activity"
- Writing letters to the spouses of activists suggesting that their partners had been engaged in extramarital affairs
- Using FBI informants inside the CPUSA to raise objections and doubts about proposed plans, and promote internal dissention
- Disrupting meetings by causing last minute cancellation of hall rentals
- Planting a document in the car of a leading CPUSA official that made him appear to be an informer
- Sending forged letters to the CPUSA and to organized crime figures to try to set the two groups against each other
- Submitting bogus housing forms to try to disrupt efforts to provide housing for out-of-town demonstrators
- Disabling and burning of cars owned by radicals
- Encouraging local police to harass them for minor offenses
- Stealing of mail from mailboxes of dissidents[57]

The CIA, NSA and Army Intelligence also got involved in surveillance, including opening mail and intercepting phone conversations, and amassed dossiers on thousands of individuals. The CIA was opening mail sent to or from individuals involved in the antiwar movement. The CIA turned over to the FBI information resulting from more than twenty thousand mail openings, including very personal material about individuals involved in antiwar demonstrations, teach-ins, and similar activities. The CIA infiltrated and monitored many antiwar organizations, such as Students for a Democratic Society and the Women's Strike for Peace. Beginning in 1967, President Johnson pressured the CIA to investigate possible Communist or other "subversive" involvement in the antiwar movement. Although they consistently reported that foreign involvement was minimal, Presidents Johnson and Nixon continued to insist on further investigation. The CIA collected large quantities of information on the domestic activities of American citizens, much of which was routinely shared with the FBI.

During this same period, Army Intelligence conducted its own large scale domestic spying operation, assigning fifteen hundred undercover agents to collect information about various groups and individuals. Army Intelligence agents monitored private communications and collected information about the private political, financial, and sex lives of tens of thousands of individuals. This information was shared with the FBI, local police departments, and other government agencies.

There was intensified harassment and arrests of demonstrators in Washington DC. In 1975, a federal judge ruled that there had been massive civil liberties violations and unnecessary police violence during every major demonstration in Washington DC between 1969 and 1975, and ordered all arrest records arising out of those demonstrations erased.[58]

In 1968, the Johnson administration tried and convicted several prominent anti-war activists including the chaplain of Yale University, William Sloane Coffin, and the prominent pediatrician Dr. Benjamin Spock, for conspiracy to counsel, aid and abet violations of the draft. During the trial, the position of the government was that all 28,000 signers of an anti-draft statement, all persons who voiced support or even applauded at rallies where the defendants spoke, and even newsmen who reported the defendants' speeches, could be indicted as members of the conspiracy. This was intended to have a chilling effect on all potential anti-war supporters by making them think that if they sign a petition, express their opinion, or participate in a lawful demonstration, they might someday be charged with a criminal conspiracy.[59] President Johnson asked the FBI for reports on private citizens who sent telegrams to the White House opposing the war.[60]

Chapter Fourteen

Supreme Court

When the Constitution was submitted to the states for ratification, many people were concerned that the federal judiciary would become a real threat to our liberties, because it vested enormous power in a small group of unelected judges. The judges would have an arbitrary power to change the nature of the government. It was also feared that they would "be the principal means of consolidating all power in the general government."[1] One writer said, "If . . . the legislature pass any laws, inconsistent with the sense the judges put upon the constitution, they will declare it void; and therefore in this respect their power is superior to that of the legislature."[2] Another wrote that "we are more in danger of sowing the seeds of arbitrary government in this department [judiciary] than in any other."[3]

But most of the Framers thought that the judicial branch would be the weakest branch, so no checks were needed on their power. For example, in The Federalist No. 78, Alexander Hamilton wrote that

> Whoever attentively considers the different departments of power must perceive that, in a government in which they are separated from each other, the judiciary, from the nature of its functions, will always be the least dangerous to the political rights of the Constitution . . . the judiciary is beyond comparison the weakest of the three departments of power; that it can never attack with success either of the other two.[4]

Soon, however, it became evident how the judiciary was twisting the words of the Constitution to enforce its own prejudices and opinions. Gradually, it became clear to more people the effect of the coup that the Court had perpetrated. Thomas Jefferson said that the Constitution had become "a mere thing of wax in the hands of the judiciary, which they may twist and shape into any form they please."[5] He also wrote:

> You seem . . . to consider the judges as the ultimate arbiters of all constitutional questions; a very dangerous doctrine indeed, and one which would place us under the despotism of an oligarchy. Our judges are as honest as other men, and not more so. They have, with others, the same passions for party, for power, and the privilege of their corps. . . . Their power [is] the more dangerous as they are in office for life, and not responsible, as the other functionaries are, to the elective control.[6]

In the case of *Home Building & Loan Assn. v. Blaisdell*, the Supreme Court admitted that it would be willing to bend the Constitution in order to do what it felt at the time would advance the "common good." The Court saw "the necessity of finding ground for a rational compromise between individual rights and public welfare" which required the "use of reasonable means to safeguard the economic structure upon which the good of all depends." The protection of individual rights was no longer the primary objective of the Constitution, which needed "to be adapted to the various crises of human affairs . . . With a growing recognition of public needs and the relation of individual right to public security . . ."[7] In another case, the Supreme Court again indicated how flexible they could be in sacrificing individual liberty, by stating that "The state is free to adopt whatever economic policy may reasonably be deemed to promote public welfare and to enforce that policy by legislation adapted to its purpose."[8]

Humberto Alvarez-Machain was a physician, and a citizen and resident of Mexico. The United States Drug Enforcement Administration (DEA) thought that Machain was involved in the kidnapping and murder of a DEA special agent. In 1990, the DEA arranged for a group of men to go to Mexico and kidnap Machain, and fly him to El Paso, Texas, by private plane. Upon arrival in Texas, Machain was handed over to the DEA and placed under arrest. Not only did this abduction violate international law, but it also violated the extradition treaty between the United States and Mexico. Despite vigorous protests from the Mexican government, the US Supreme Court ruled[9] that Machain could still be tried in the United States in spite of his illegal abduction from Mexico.[10]

The Supreme Court acknowledged that it has gone far beyond what the Framers intended, when it said "The Federal Government undertakes activities today that would have been unimaginable to the Framers . . . because the Framers would not have believed that the Federal Government, rather than the States, would assume such responsibilities. Yet the powers conferred upon the Federal Government by the Constitution were phrased in language broad enough to allow for the expansion of the Federal Government's role."[11] The Supreme Court is in effect operating as a continuing constitutional convention.

In a letter to Monsieur A. Coray, Thomas Jefferson wrote, on October 31, 1823:

> At the establishment of our constitutions, the judiciary bodies were supposed to be the most helpless and harmless members of the government. Experience, however, soon showed in what way they were to become the most dangerous; that the insufficiency of the means provided for their removal gave them a freehold and irresponsibility in office; that their decisions, seeming to concern individual suitors only, pass silent and unheeded by the public at large; that these decisions, nevertheless, become law by precedent, sapping, by little and little, the foundations of the constitution, and working its change by construction, before any one has perceived that that invisible and helpless worm has been busily employed in consuming its substance. In truth, man is not made to be trusted for life, if secured against all liability to account.[12]

As Supreme Court Justice Benjamin Curtis warned, "When a strict interpretation of the Constitution, according to the fixed rules which govern the interpretation of the laws, is abandoned, and the theoretical opinions of individuals are allowed to control its meaning, we have no longer a Constitution; we are under the government of individual men, who for the time being have the power to declare what the Constitution is, according to their own views of what it ought to mean."[13] Solicitor General Robert H.

Jackson said that "the rule of law is in unsafe hands when courts cease to function as courts and become organs for control of policy."[14] The esteemed constitutional scholar and author Gerald Gunther rejected "the view that courts are authorized to step in when injustices exist and other institutions fail to act. That is a dangerous—and I think illegitimate—prescription for judicial action."[15] Abram Chayes, constitutional law professor at Harvard Law School, observed that recent judicial action "adds up to a radical transformation of the role and function of the judiciary . . . Its chief function now is as a catalyst of social change with judges sitting as planners on a large scale.[16] Supreme Court Justice Owen Roberts was very clear when he said that the Court in constitutional litigation "has only one duty—to lay the article of the Constitution which is invoked beside the statute which is challenged and to decide whether the latter squares with the former."[17]

Charles Evans Hughes, later to be a Supreme Court Chief Justice, was just being honest when he said in 1907 that "the Constitution is what the judges say it is." What is really frightening is that that sounds a lot like the 1936 decree of the Third Reich Commissar of Justice: "A decision of the Fuhrer in the express form of a law or decree may not be scrutinized by a judge." This represents a clear break with the American concept of limited government under the rule of law. That meant that the government and its agents were supposed to be under the law, not above it. But now listen to Justice Felix Frankfurter when, in speaking of the Supreme Court justices, he said that "it is they who speak and not the Constitution." In the case of *Cooper v. Aaron*, the Supreme Court said that "the interpretation of the [Constitution] enunciated by this Court . . . is the supreme law of the land . . ." These statements confirm that the Supreme Court is no longer under law but above it.[18]

Alexander Hamilton eventually admitted: "I am not unaware that the Judiciary career has not corresponded with what was anticipated. At one period, the judges perverted the Bench of Justice into a rostrum for partisan harangues. And lately the Court, by some of its decisions, still more by extrajudicial reasonings and dicta, has manifested a propensity to enlarge the general authority in derogation of the local, and to amplify its own jurisdiction, which has justly incurred the public censure." He suggested that he might consider a constitutional amendment to correct the situation.[19]

When the Supreme Court was usurping all this power, why didn't the system of checks and balances work to correct this situation? The president could have appointed new justices who believed in returning to the correct interpretation of the Constitution. The Senate could have refused to approve nominees who wanted to expand the power of the judiciary. The rise in influence of the Progressive philosophy gives us a clue to the answer. Many liberal politicians in the executive and legislative branches agree with many of the results achieved by the new courts. They realize that their goals for a more liberal America could be accomplished simply through the rulings of the courts rather than by taking the more difficult path of getting new laws passed.

Therefore, rather than acting as a "check and balance" against the Supreme Court, many in Congress decided to support the courts' usurpation of power. The Senate would be glad to approve the nomination of justices who would advance this judicial activism. As the effects of this process became more and more evident, it was obvious that the system of checks and balances was no longer effective.

Liberal congressmen are totally dedicated to this process. A clear example of this came in 1987, following President Reagan's nomination of Robert Bork to be a Supreme Court justice. Bork had been a highly respected judge in the United States Court of Appeals for the District of Columbia Circuit. He had also served as Solicitor General of the United States and had been a professor at Yale Law School. But many liberal senators realized that if Bork was seated on the Supreme Court, he would try to move the Court back to an original interpretation of the Constitution. So they mounted a fierce opposition to his nomination. The Reagan administration was unprepared for the massive public relations campaign that liberal causes launched against the well qualified Judge Bork, and they failed to respond effectively to it. He was defeated in the final vote in the Senate.

THE SUPREME COURT MAKES NEW LAWS

One of the favorite pastimes of some of the Supreme Court justices is discovering new "rights." Dr. Gary L. McDowell, law professor at the University of Richmond, says that:

It cheapens the very idea of rights. Calling an ordinary policy preference a fundamental right does not, because it cannot, make that preference a right in any meaningful, philosophical sense. It only confounds the idea of rights with the power of clever rhetoric. There is yet a deeper problem: the new logic of rights wreaks havoc on the idea of a written constitution . . . these claims rest on the assumption that there is an "unwritten constitution" of un-enumerated rights . . . this un-enumerated right, once discerned and decreed by the Court, became equal in power to those rights that are enumerated. By definition, such a broad and un-enumerated right must depend for its form on judicial decree. What is included and excluded by the right to privacy must remain a matter of judicial discretion on a case-by-case basis . . . Its lines and limits depend not upon any clear textual provision but only upon judicial predilection . . . it was understood that in areas in which the Constitution was silent, the power to deal with issues touching privacy resided with the states where the opinions of the people as to what was moral or immoral, acceptable or unacceptable, would lead to laws reflective of the moral sense of the community. [Now] such laws can no longer reflect the moral sense of the community unless the judge or justice in question happens to agree . . . The judicial arbitrariness . . . raises serious questions about its legitimacy.[20]

One of the most famous examples of this type of abuse is the case of *Roe v. Wade,* in 1973.[21] This decision overturned laws which restricted abortion in most of the states. The justices claimed that they found this right to abortion contained in a "right to privacy" that they saw in the Fourteenth Amendment to the Constitution. The problem is that the Fourteenth Amendment does not say anything about privacy. The Fourteenth Amendment does not say anything about abortion. There is no basis for this new "meaning" that the Court discovered. The primary purpose of the Fourteenth Amendment, passed after the Civil War, was to guarantee that slaves and their descendants would have all the rights of citizens. In fact, at the time the Fourteenth Amendment was enacted, thirty-six states and territories had laws restricting abortion, and nobody saw any conflict at the time.

Law Professor Michael Paulsen called this decision "the most extreme example of judicial activism in the twentieth century. . . . Rarely, if ever, had the Court engaged in such an unashamed, self-consciously activist work of judicial legislation, largely indifferent to constitutional text, structure, and history."[22]

He said that "the Court had simply acted like a legislature and drafted its own abortion-law statute, in complete abandonment of the proper judicial role."[23]

In his dissent to this opinion, Justice Byron White wrote: "I find nothing in the language or history of the Constitution to support the Court's judgment. The Court simply fashions and announces a new constitutional right . . . with scarcely any reason or authority for its action . . . an exercise of raw judicial power."[24] Justice William Rehnquist also dissented, writing, "To reach its result, the Court necessarily has had to find within the scope of the Fourteenth Amendment a right that was apparently completely unknown to the drafters of that Amendment."[25]

There is a strong temptation, especially for a judge, to think about just how much more good he could do if he had more power. Judges are repeatedly faced with situations where the results achieved in their courtrooms do not seem to be the very best possible outcome from the standpoint of fairness and justice. This might be because of some quirk in the way the law was written, or some reason that the law does not apply perfectly to the particular specific situation before the court. In such cases, the judge might think that it would be so nice if he could adjust the law slightly so he could reach what he feels is the right result. But wait, there is a way this could happen. The judge can make a different interpretation of some words in the law or the Constitution, or exploit ambiguities in the language to actually give it a different meaning from what was originally contemplated. If the Court finds that it would like for the Constitution to say something that it doesn't actually say, the Court can claim to have discovered a new "right" in the Constitution. Or it could say that this is its "interpretation" of some part of the Constitution, and suddenly it would become the highest law in the land. The Court discovered that all it had to do was to get five justices to agree, and it could make the Constitution say whatever it wanted it to say. It is, in effect, making new laws. And no one has any authority or control over the Supreme Court. The justices have not been elected by the people, and they have no accountability to anyone, because they are appointed for life.

It makes sense that any legal document, be it a deed or a contract or a law or even our Constitution, should be interpreted based on the intent of the makers in the context of their original thinking. This obvious fact was emphasized by Supreme Court Justice and esteemed constitutional scholar Joseph Story, in his book *Commentaries on the Constitution* (1833), where he wrote,

"The first and fundamental rule in the interpretation of all instruments is, to construe them according to the sense of the terms, and the intention of the parties."[26] Justice Story also said that the Constitution is "to have a fixed, uniform, permanent construction." It should be "not dependent upon the passions or parties of particular times, but the same yesterday, today, and forever."[27] Supreme Court Justice James Wilson agreed that "the first and governing maxim in the interpretation of a statute is to discover the meaning of those who made it."[28] In the case of *South Carolina v. United States* (1905), Justice David Brewer wrote: "The Constitution is a written instrument. As such, its meaning does not alter. That which it meant when adopted, it means now. . . . Any other rule of construction would abrogate the judicial character of this Court and make it the mere reflex of the popular opinion or passion of the day."[29]

The words of the Constitution cannot be constantly redefined to match what someone thinks will better suit modern social conditions. Some say that the Constitution is a "living" document, and its meaning can be rewritten by the courts to satisfy contemporary political agendas. In fact, what is the purpose of a written document if we pretend that it doesn't mean what it says? This philosophy would destroy the Constitution as a durable foundation for our country, and would open the door to all manner of arbitrary activism. The principles of freedom and limited government are timeless, and must not be sacrificed in the search for what some judge thinks is "fair" or "just" on any particular day.

Professor Michael Paulsen observed that many Supreme Court decisions "seemed willfully to misinterpret the Constitution in order to reach results that the justices preferred." The Court frequently "disregarded the language of the Constitution or simply made up nonexistent constitutional language all its own, on order to reach results that the justices liked as a policy matter." The Court was "making its own policies and then reading them into the Constitution."[30] In one case, Professor Paulsen said the Court went so far as "to disregard the language of the Constitution and to substitute instead the accepted, conventional social and moral understandings of the day. . . . It is not the task of courts to tune the Constitution to the times."[31] But Supreme Court Justice William Brennan applauded these trends. In a speech he argued for "the evolution of constitutional doctrine," and said that the "Law has come alive as a living process responsive to changing human needs."[32]

Thomas Jefferson recognized the necessity for a stable interpretation when he said, "The Constitution on which our Union rests, shall be administered by me according to the safe and honest meaning contemplated by the plain understanding of the people of the United States, *at the time of its adoption*."[33] Jefferson also said: "Our peculiar security is in possession of a written Constitution. Let us not make it a blank paper by construction. If [power is boundless] then we have no Constitution. If it has bounds, they can be no other than the definition of the powers which that instrument gives."[34] James Madison said:

> I entirely concur in the propriety of resorting to the sense in which the Constitution was accepted and ratified by the nation. In that sense alone it is the legitimate Constitution. And if that be not the guide in expounding it, there can be no security for a consistent and stable, more than for a faithful exercise of its power. If the meaning of the text be sought in the changeable meaning of the words composing it, it is evident that the shapes and attributes of the Government must partake of the changes to which the words and phrases of all living languages are constantly subject . . . . The language of our Constitution is already undergoing interpretations unknown to its founders.[35]

When the Constitution was submitted to the States for ratification, many were concerned that there was no Bill of Rights specifically protecting certain rights of the people. So when the Constitution was ratified, its supporters promised that it would be amended to add a Bill of Rights. Of course, any listing of rights could only include a limited number of rights. Some people were worried that, if certain rights were listed in the Bill of Rights, then any other rights not listed would be assumed to be subject to the control of the federal government. The Framers wanted to make it clear that there were many more rights, not included in this list, which were retained by the states and the people, and not relinquished to the federal government. A primary purpose of the Constitution was to limit the power of the federal government. So the Ninth and Tenth Amendments were added as a backup to confirm that, just because a right was not listed in the Bill of Rights, that did not mean that that right was relinquished to the federal government. Even those rights not listed would still be retained by the people. The Ninth Amendment to the Constitution reads "The enumeration in the Constitution, of certain rights, shall not be construed to deny or disparage others retained by the people." The Tenth Amendment says "The powers not delegated to the United States by the Constitution, nor prohibited by it to the States, are reserved to the States respectively, or to the people." So only the powers specifically given to the federal government in the Constitution belonged to the federal government. All others were retained by the people.

For example, the right of a person to practice a trade is not mentioned in the Constitution, but this is considered a natural right of each person, so that right is retained by the people. That means the states can pass laws related to this issue, but the federal government does not have the authority to pass laws restricting this right, or to void a state law relating to this subject. Other examples of rights that are not mentioned in the Constitution are the right of parents to control their children's education,[36] the right of travel, the right to life (mentioned in the Declaration of Independence), the right to make decisions about health care, the right to decide what to eat for breakfast, and hundreds more. The federal government has no authority to control these un-enumerated rights of the people. These are totally under the control of the states. That is the meaning of the Ninth Amendment. Or at least that is the way it used to be.

The Supreme Court has decided that, yes, there are some rights that are not listed in the Constitution. But the Court will not accept the original intent that these rights are retained by the states. The federal government has somehow decided that it will assume the responsibility for interpreting and protecting these new rights. So not only can the federal government pass laws in these areas, but it can review and overrule state laws relating to these subjects. This is exactly opposite to what the Ninth Amendment says, so the Supreme Court in its rulings generally ignores the Ninth Amendment. This amendment is rarely ever mentioned in Court opinions. Instead, the Court relies on other phrases like the ambiguous "due process" as an excuse for its distorted pronouncements.

One of the fundamental attributes of the United States was that we were a "nation of laws." The abuses of kings and dictators in other countries were well known, and led to the idea that evens kings and presidents should be under the law. Now the reality is that five unelected people on the Supreme Court can decide what they think is desirable, and can dictate that verdict to control the entire country. This is a system completely different from that designed by the Framers. They set it up so that laws would be made by the people through their elected representatives in Congress. The judges were to have absolutely no role in the process of making laws or amending the Constitution. They were only to interpret the laws, with no influence over making the laws. But now they can both make laws and interpret the laws. This is a dangerous concentration of power that the Framers were trying to avoid.

It is interesting that most of the general public is not aware of this radical shift in the function of the courts. Most people still think that the judiciary is supposed to interpret laws, and make a judgment based on the law and the Constitution. The fact that judicial review is essentially a legislative activity (making new laws) is well known and accepted in the legal profession. But the judiciary does not talk about this very much. They are happy for the public to think that our Constitution still functions as it was originally intended.[37]

JUDICIAL REVIEW

The Supreme Court assumed for itself the authority to declare that a law passed by Congress is void because the Court says it does not comply with their interpretation of the Constitution (*Marbury v. Madison*, 1803). This is known as "judicial review." The Constitution does not explicitly give this power to any branch of the federal government, so according to the Tenth Amendment, it should belong to the people or the States. But since the Supreme Court has assumed this power, this gives the Court the ultimate final authority to decide what the Constitution means, with no accountability to anyone. This means that the federal government (Supreme Court) is allowed to judge the validity of a law enacted by the federal government (Congress). This obviously violates the concept of checks and balances between the federal and state governments.

In the earliest years of this country's history, the concept of judicial review was not universally accepted by everyone. It was denied by several members of the Constitutional Convention, and was referred to as unsettled by several judges. In Vermont, it seems to have been the established doctrine of the period that the judiciary could not disregard a legislative Act. In the preface to I. D. Chipman's (Vermont) Reports, writing of the period of the Vermont constitution of 1777, he says that "No idea was entertained that the judiciary had any power to inquire into the constitutionality of acts of the legislature, or to pronounce them void for any cause, or even to question their validity." In

Zephaniah Swift's *System of the Laws of Connecticut*, published in 1795, the author (later to be chief justice of that state) argues strongly against the power of the judiciary to disregard a legislative enactment, while mentioning that the contrary opinion "is very popular and prevalent." As late as 1808, judges were impeached by the legislature of Ohio for holding acts of that body to be void.[38] The Massachusetts constitution in 1780 said "the judicial shall never exercise the legislative and executive powers or either of them." The constitution of Kentucky, in 1792, had a similar requirement.[39] Supreme Court Justice Hugo Black was convinced that "any broad, unlimited power to hold laws unconstitutional because they offend what this Court conceives to be the [collective] conscience of our people . . . was not given by the Framers, but rather has been bestowed on the Court by the Court."[40]

Former Speaker of the House Newt Gingrich understood the problems caused when one branch of the government claims to be superior to the other two, when he wrote the following:

> In 1958, all nine sitting justices of the Supreme Court . . . asserted that the Supreme Court's interpretation of the Constitution was supreme in importance to the constitutional interpretation of the other two branches of government[41] . . . Following [this decision] . . . the executive and legislative branches have . . . behaved as if they have no choice but to give total deference to Supreme Court decisions, even if the executive and/or legislative branch believes the Supreme Court has seriously erred in its constitutional judgments. . . . Our constitutional framework of three branches exercising their unique powers to check and balance the other two branches was designed to protect individual liberties . . . A judicial branch that is largely unaccountable and not subject to meaningful checks and balances can—and does—routinely issue constitutional rulings that threaten individual liberties, . . . undermine American culture, and ignore the consent of the governed.
>
> The Supreme Court has become a permanent constitutional convention in which the whims of five appointed judges have rewritten the meaning of the Constitution . . . unchecked by the other co-equal branches of government. . . . This power grab by the

Supreme Court is a modern phenomenon and a dramatic break from all previous American history. . . . [The Framers] expected the legislative branch would define the reach of the judicial branch. . . . [But] to use Madison's words, the judiciary has in fact become the invading branch against which the other branches need to exercise some practical security.

Even the occasional Supreme Court justice has recognized that the Court has engaged in the dangerous pattern of judges making law . . . In an 1893 dissent,[42] Justice Stephen Johnson Field wrote: "a supposed unwritten law . . . which has no existence except in the brain of the federal judges . . ." Writing in 1973, Justice Lewis Powell pointed out that "the separation of powers was designed to provide, not for judicial supremacy, but for checks and balances." . . . Thomas Jefferson was quite clear about the absurdity of claims to judicial supremacy: "You seem . . . to consider the judges as the ultimate arbiters of all constitutional questions; a very dangerous doctrine indeed, and one which would place us under the despotism of an oligarchy."[43] . . . President Andrew Jackson [said]: "The opinion of the judges has no more authority over Congress than the opinion of Congress has over the judges, and on that point the President is independent of both."[44] . . . Abraham Lincoln followed through on his refusal to accept judicial supremacy by refusing to treat *Dred Scott* as legally binding on the executive branch. For example, his administration issued US passports to free blacks and treated them as full citizens notwithstanding the Dred Scott Court's refusal to do so. . . . None of Lincoln's actions on behalf of free blacks would have been possible had he accepted judicial supremacy.

The Founding Fathers were well aware that federal judges—like congressmen and presidents—are fallible human beings that can make mistakes. They established a system of checks and balances to ensure that each of the branches of government could correct and balance mistakes by the other branches . . . The speed at which the Court changes its mind . . . shows that it cannot possibly be infallible: If it were, why would the Court constantly find the need to reverse or modify its precedents? The Constitution has not changed much in the last sixty years but constitutional law has changed dramatically during this period: either the Court has been making a lot of mistakes or it is simply making some things up as it goes along. Either way, the decisions of the Supreme Court and the federal courts clearly do not deserve instinctive or uncritical reliance. Rather, we should recognize that judges can and do make mistakes. When serious constitutional mistakes are made, it is the proper role of the legislative and executive branches to correct them.

What then can be done today to bring the Supreme Court and the other federal courts back under the Constitution and respecting the rule of law? . . . The Constitution [gives Congress the power to] limit the jurisdiction of the federal courts through ordinary legislation.[45] This legislation would remove the power of the courts to hear certain types of cases . . . . Abraham Lincoln . . . [said] that in certain circumstances, the holdings of Supreme Court decisions should be limited to the litigants in a case, and not be held to apply as a general controlling standard for similar cases. . . . In very rare circumstances, the executive branch might choose to ignore a court decision.[46]

It is certainly true that if a legislative body enacts a law which is obviously and blatantly contrary to some provision of the Constitution, there needs to be some mechanism to identify that violation, and to declare the law to be void. And on the surface, the judiciary would appear to be the logical body to perform that function. However, our experience has shown that the Supreme Court is doing a very poor job on that account. Congress is continually passing laws in areas where they have not been authorized to act by the Constitution. They use all manner of excuses such as the Commerce Clause, the General Welfare Clause, or sometimes no excuse at all. And the Supreme Court permits this abuse by upholding these laws. At other times, the Court thwarts the clear will of the people by invalidating acts based on mere personal opinion, where the claimed breach of the Constitution is so questionable and controversial that it has no credibility. This insane situation has the Court mired in such a swamp of subjective judgment and arbitrary rulings that any relation to the Constitution is very fragile.

We now have a judiciary that says that whatever it says is the law, and is superior to all the other branches of government, and even the Constitution itself. This is judicial supremacy. Judges have been legislating from the bench, and claiming that their decisions should be binding on all courts in all future decisions. We cannot accept this practice of judges rewriting the Constitution under the pretense of interpreting it. Abraham Lincoln set an example of refusing to accept judicial supremacy. In the *Dred Scott v. Sanford* (1857) decision, the Supreme Court ruled that blacks had no rights and were not even citizens. Lincoln was correct in defying this decision. In his first inaugural address, in 1861, Abraham Lincoln said, "The candid citizen must confess that if the policy of the Government upon vital questions affecting the whole people is to be irrevocably fixed by decisions of the Supreme Court, the instant they are made in ordinary litigation between parties in personal actions, the people will have ceased to be their own rulers, having to that extent practically resigned their Government into the hands of that eminent tribunal."[47]

Actually, there are several layers of checks which should act to thwart a law which is unconstitutional:

1. When a bill is moving through the Senate or the House, if a congressman feels that the bill is not constitutional, his oath to uphold the Constitution will require him to vote "no" so as to try to prevent the bill from ever becoming law.
2. When a bill passes Congress and is presented to the President for his signature, the President could veto the bill if he felt it did not comply with the Constitution.
3. The President also has the right to pardon anyone convicted under the law.
4. Grand juries could refuse to indict under a statute they felt was unconstitutional or unjust.
5. Even the trial juries have the right to acquit a defendant for any reason, including the unconstitutionality of the law.[48]

Unfortunately, these safeguards are not very effective because everyone in the legal system has become accustomed to the understanding that it is the job of only the judiciary to declare a law unconstitutional, and so no one else should even be thinking about that question. For example, President George W. Bush signed the Bipartisan Campaign Reform Act of 2002, even though he knew major parts of it violated the First Amendment. He explained "I expect that the courts will resolve these legitimate legal questions as appropriate under the law."[49]

One tragic consequence of this situation is that the Congress does not give as much attention as it should to the question of a bill conflicting with the Constitution. Our senators and representatives have gotten used to the idea that all questions of Constitutionality will be addressed by the Supreme Court, so they don't have to give that too much thought. The result is a poorer quality of legislation since Congress does not do a thorough job of analysis of the bills it passes. In 2012 Nancy Pelosi, Minority Leader of the House of Representatives, was asked by a reporter what part of the Constitution empowered Congress to pass a certain bill. She responded disdainfully "Are you Serious?"[50]

Chapter Fifteen

What to Do

I have to confess my fear that it may be too late to save this country. The politicians and special interests are so firmly entrenched, and the destructive policies have become so habitual, that there may be no way to stop this train. Many of the steps that it would take to alter course would involve reducing the power of the career politicians. Most of these politicians are so selfish and arrogant that they are not likely to vote for measures that would decrease their power, even if it might help the country as a whole. Therefore, my feeling is that for any meaningful reform to be possible, it will take a tremendous grassroots effort by the people themselves. Nothing less will have any chance of overcoming the deep-rooted power of the politicians, bureaucrats, corporations and special interests that are now running our country.

I am not making any claim that I know what to do to restore our freedoms. The ideas presented here are just ideas. They could be discussed and debated and modified, and I encourage such debate. I am sure that others will have different ideas far superior to mine. But we need to start having this discussion. We need to first recognize the problem—that our freedoms are disintegrating at a rapid rate. Then we need to decide that we are determined to do whatever is necessary to stop the decline, and try to regain what has been lost. Some of the ideas discussed below might even require an amendment to the Constitution. But we have already tried all the standard approaches: register to vote, vote for the good guys, write to your congressmen, etc. And it hasn't worked! Of course, we need to continue to do those things. But presidents and congressmen come and go, and things do not seem to change very much.

Many people are still under the illusion that they have some control over their government because they can vote for presidents and congressmen. But elected officials now have less and less power, because the really effective multitude of decisions that affect every detail of our lives are being made by the army of unelected bureaucrats in Washington, which staff all the agencies and departments, and by the courts. Both political parties say the right words during campaigns, but after the election it is back to business as usual. We have to be willing to move to the next level. We have to be willing to consider more radical ideas, and even recognize that some deep structural changes to our government might be required. If we can find enough people who love their country enough to put it back on the right path, then maybe there is a chance.

Getting an amendment to our Constitution enacted is a very challenging and cumbersome process. The first step is for a supermajority of both houses of Congress to approve it. But it is almost impossible to comprehend that congressmen would vote for a measure to reduce their power. The amendment would then have to be approved by three-fourths of the states, which is another difficult challenge. But it seems inevitable that this will be required to repair our system. For many years, the Supreme Court has been willing to uphold all kinds of laws which transfer power from the states to the federal government, using excuses like the Commerce Clause. In the case of *NLRB v. Jones & Laughlin Steel Corp.*, the Court said "Congress cannot be denied the power to exercise that control."[1] In the *United States v. Darby Lumber Co.*, the Court held that Congress could use its power under the Commerce Clause in any way that did "not infringe some constitutional prohibition."[2] This same idea was repeated in the case of *Heart of Atlanta Motel v. United States*, where the Court said it would not restrict Congress as long as it violates no express constitutional limitation.[3] Our strategy seems clear. If we are going to slow down this out-of-control Congress, we will have to supply the missing "express constitutional limitations."

MONEY, MONEY EVERYWHERE

One of the big problems with our political system is that there is too much money involved. Common sense tells you that it should not take one billion dollars to campaign for president. But that is what has been spent by and for each candidate in recent elections. There are many interests that are willing to "donate" money to a politician in hopes that sometime in the future they can get something in some legislation that will benefit them or their clients. The opportunities for corruption and cronyism are overwhelming. It seems like, even if we do elect a relatively honest person to congress, the longer he stays in Washington, the more he is likely to be seduced by the money and power. In fact, nearly half of our congressmen are millionaires.

Actually, most of the money problems in Washington are not committed by crooks, or even by evil men. These are mostly good men just trying to operate in a corrupted system. They will defend their actions by saying that's just how the system works. You have to do certain things to get anything accomplished. Since they have to raise so much money for their re-election campaign, they have simply become too dependent on the lobbyists and special interests that supply much of that money. They may try to do the right thing, but it is just a fact of human nature that the sources of these funds will get an unequal share of attention and access. There are many subtle ways that money can influence a congressman's actions. The "gifts" from a lobbyist to a congressman are said to be for "building relationships." The lobbyist would say that they are a way to "thank friends," or to "open channels of communication." They produce a subconscious feeling of wanting to "return the favor." Another result is that the congressman is reluctant to disappoint the lobbyist, because the "gifts" may stop coming. So we see a gradual and almost unconscious shifting of the congressman's loyalty from his constituents to his benefactors. The Member of Congress will claim—and may indeed believe—that his decisions are not directly caused by the favors he has received. But it is all part of a complex game of creating a feeling of personal obligation to his funders. And one effect is that the congressman's focus is diverted, to some extent, from the will of the people to the will of his patrons. The public sees all the money and earmarks and influence, and instinctively knows that the system is rotten through and through. The American Bar Association looked at the status of lobbying and stated that a "self-reinforcing cycle of mutual financial dependency has become a deeply troubling source of corruption in our government."[4]

There is no doubt that all this money influences not only elections, but also the shape of legislation between elections. The lobbying industry has exploded over the last few decades. Lobbying expenditures are more than three billion dollars a year—double the amount spent in the year 2000. And why are businesses, labor unions and other organizations willing to spend all this money? Because it works. Research has shown that for every one dollar that an average firm spends on lobbying, the return to the firm is between six and twenty dollars.[5] If a company can have even a small influence on the enormous government spending, grants, regulations, and tax laws, the results can be extremely profitable to the firm.

At one time, we thought that transparency was the answer. If all donations were made public, then people could decide for themselves if they thought that someone was using money to influence legislation or elections. Unfortunately, it turned out that that is not a good approach. One reason was that most people just will not go to the trouble to research the donations and find out who gave what to whom. And even if they did have the information, it didn't really matter that much. For most people, it didn't affect what they did or how they voted. But there was another, even more serious, problem with the idea of making donations public. Suppose Paul donated some money to a particular candidate or political cause. Since that donation would be made public, the people who are opposed to that candidate would know that Paul made that donation. Then Paul would become a target of all the powerful special interests that are opposed to that candidate. Paul might be harassed, threatened, and intimidated. These interests might try to get Paul fired from his job, ruin him financially, or boycott his business. If the current administration was opposed to the candidate, then Paul could find the power of the government itself deployed against him. All this will have the effect of discouraging anyone else who is considering supporting that candidate.

One possible approach would be to not allow any political expenditures by businesses, unions and other special interests. Only individuals would be eligible to donate, and each individual would be limited to donating only some very small amount to a candidate or to a Political Action Committee. The donations would not be required to be made public. But how could a candidate get his message out without all that money? That would not be a problem, because it is very inexpensive for each candidate to post his positions and arguments on the internet, where anyone who is interested would be able to see them. Of course, the average voter will not spend hours and hours researching the positions of each candidate, so we need to make it as easy as possible for a person to become informed. To do this, a system is needed to allow someone to go to a single website where they could easily and quickly find a summary of each candidate's positions on a variety of issues. This website would also contain references to other sources of information for anyone who wants more detailed information on a particular subject. The Supreme Court has been very reluctant to approve limitations on campaign spending, so it would probably require a constitutional amendment to allow Congress and the states to enact these restrictions on expenditures. But the level of corruption in politics is escalating out of control. Something has to be done.

CAREER POLITICIANS

Politics is a permanent career for many congressmen. Many have been in Washington for 20 or 30 years or more. When the founders of this country established the Congress, they did not envision that a person would spend most of his life in Congress. They wanted a person to serve in Congress for a short time and then return to his normal business. In the eighteenth and nineteenth centuries, that was generally what happened. Since the founders recognized that most people preferred to spend only a short term in Congress, and popular sentiment also favored frequent rotation of the members of Congress, they did not think it necessary to put a requirement for term limits in the Constitution. Instead, they provided a very short term of two years for members of the House of Representatives in order to provide more frequent elections.

The founders were aware of some European countries with monarchies, and a somewhat permanent ruling class. They distrusted such a ruling class, and did not want that for America. However, now in the Twenty-first Century, the members of Congress have almost become that permanent ruling class that the founders feared. The system has evolved so that it is very difficult now to defeat an incumbent, for several reasons:

- Each congressman has a staff in Washington and in their home district. This staff is a great help in the congressman to ingratiate himself with his constituents, because they can answer questions, assist people who have problems with the government, do favors for people, contact people, and many other things.
- Members of Congress also have a travel allowance so they can go meet with voters in their home district.
- They can also send postage-free letters to their constituents.
- When an incumbent is campaigning for re-election, many of the things he does, such as town hall meetings, appearing on television, and special events, are

considered part of his job as a congressman, and he gets paid for his time and expenses. His challenger, on the other hand, has to pay his own bills.

- Congressmen typically have much better name recognition, since they have been in Congress for several years and have already waged at least one successful campaign.
- Since he has been through one campaign already, he has valuable experience in running a campaign, and he may still have a campaign organization which he can use again.
- Members of Congress have ready access to the news media.
- A congressman is generally able to raise large amounts of campaign contributions, compared to his challenger.
- If his party controls the state legislature, their gerrymandering is designed to help him get reelected.

Adding a requirement to the Constitution for term limits for congressmen would be one step toward restoring us back to the ideals of our founders. The wisdom of term limits has been recognized for a long time. Some offices in the ancient Roman Republic were limited to a single term of one year. In the early democracy of Athens, a member of the council could not serve two terms in succession, nor could a citizen serve more than twice during his lifetime. Some of the founders of this country, including Thomas Jefferson, Richard Henry Lee, and George Mason, recommended term limits. In recent years, term limits has become very popular with the people, with many states adopting term limits for their governors and state legislatures. But to get term limits for the federal Congress would require that congressmen vote for it, and it is unlikely that many congressmen would vote to reduce their own power.

But there is another possible plan that would destroy the permanent ruling class in Congress. Instead of having the people vote and elect their congressmen, we could send a random sample of ordinary people to Washington and let them vote on legislation directly. To do that, we would first send an inquiry to all the people in a state who were registered to vote, asking if they would be willing to go to Washington and serve in Congress for one term. Then, from the list of people who answered in the affirmative, a random slate of people would be selected to be sent to the House of Representatives for one term.

This would be even better than a requirement for term limits:

- Because the congressmen would be chosen at random, this group would likely be more representative of the general population than is the current congress.
- This would completely eliminate the campaigning that we hate to put up with. It would also eliminate the requirement to raise enormous amounts of money, and all the potential for corruption that comes with that.

This is not a new idea. In the ancient democratic city-state of Athens, Greece, the members of the governing council were chosen by lot.[6] Athens is considered the birthplace of democracy, inventing a new system of government which was an inspiration to other governments, including the American Constitution.

Someone might criticize this plan because these people would be inexperienced, and may not know much about how Congress works. That is no different than the situation we have today, because, even now, sometimes new people are elected to Congress. They have no experience and do not know all the details of the legislative process. As a result, they have to go through an orientation process, and a learning period. Each congressman has a staff of experienced people who will help him or her learn the ropes, and answers questions. The staff will also do research and gather information to help the congressman decide how to vote on each bill.

You might say that we would be asking a lot of a person, to expect him or her to step away from their business and friends for a few years to go to Washington. My answer to that would be to remember what the founders of this country did for us. They were willing to make enormous sacrifices and risks in order to give us the freedoms we have. For what they did, many of those patriots lost their possessions, their families, and even their lives. It is now time for us to do our part. We may be asked to sacrifice and take risks in order to pass our freedom down to future generations. Are we ready to step up and answer the call?

GERRYMANDERING

The game of redrawing congressional districts for partisan advantage has been going on for many years, but in recent decades advances in computer technology and databases have allowed much more precision and sophistication to be utilized.

The architects of these districts have a tremendous amount of statistics available about each street and neighborhood to allow accurate predictions about voting patterns. Powerful computer programs allow party hacks to draw the boundaries of election districts with the primary objective of maximizing the re-election prospects of incumbents. We have seen the results—these impossibly odd shaped and elongated districts. The damage to the political process is substantial. Many races are no longer competitive because it is almost impossible to defeat an incumbent congressman. Also, with these distorted stretched-out districts, congressmen no longer represent cohesive communities.

Many people have tried to change this system over the years, but with very limited results. I think it might be worthwhile to try to pass an amendment to the US Constitution to outlaw gerrymandering. This could apply to both federal and state congressional districts. Many different approaches to redistricting have been suggested, but here are some basic principles that I think many people could agree on. First, take the process out of the hands of the state legislatures, and create an independent, non-political commission to do the job. Next create some logical, objective rules to control the creation and modification of the districts:

- Whenever possible, any political subdivision (e.g., city, county) must be in only one district. If this is impossible, the political entity must be in the minimum number of districts possible.
- It might be worthwhile to encourage portions of a district boundary to correspond to portions of the boundaries of a city or county wherever practical.
- Each district must be contiguous, not in separate unconnected pieces.
- Some people have suggested a rule requiring districts to be as "compact" as possible. There are several ways of mathematically calculating compactness, but I would pick one that is relatively simple and easy to understand. Some realistic tolerance, such as at least fifteen percent, should be allowed. This is probably the least important issue.
- To avoid much of the litigation we have seen in the past, the amendment should state that, as long as the districts met these minimum requirements in this list of rules, they would be immune from challenge in federal courts.

LIMITED FEDERAL GOVERNMENT

The US Constitution gives certain limited defined powers to the federal government. All other powers are reserved to the States and the people. Since the federal government has only limited powers, and the States have undefined and unlimited powers, this implies that the States are sovereign. This is confirmed by the fact that the States ratify amendments to the Constitution. Thomas Jefferson and James Madison, among others, were proponents of this states' rights theory. One of the powers the States must retain is the power to judge when the federal government has exceeded its authority by exercising powers not specifically delegated to it. If the federal government were allowed to be the judge of when it has exceeded its authority, then that would be the same as giving it unlimited power. Unfortunately, this is exactly what has happened. The Supreme Court (part of the federal government) has assumed the authority to be the final judge if a law is constitutional. We can see the result today—the federal government has expanded drastically, until it has tentacles reaching into the tiniest details of every person's daily life.

When our Constitution was being ratified by the state conventions, the extensive debates and discussions clearly prove that it was the universal understanding that one of the primary functions of the Constitution was to limit the powers of the federal government to those plainly enumerated in the document. At the New York Convention, Alexander Hamilton—one of the strongest advocates of a powerful central government—declared that "whatever is not *expressly* given to the Federal Head, is reserved to the members." James Madison declared to the Virginia Convention that the federal government would have "defined and limited objects beyond which it cannot extend its jurisdiction." At the Virginia Convention, Edmund Randolph also affirmed that all rights were declared in the Constitution to be "completely vested in the people, unless *expressly* given away."[7] At the Pennsylvania Convention, James Wilson said that "everything not *expressly* mentioned will be presumed to be purposely omitted." At the North Carolina Convention, Governor Samuel Johnston explained that "Congress cannot assume any other powers than those *expressly* given them, without a palpable violation of the Constitution." The South Carolina Convention was told by Charles Pickney that the federal government could not assume any powers except those that "were *expressly* delegated."[8]

Even after the Constitution was ratified, the same assurances were regularly repeated. Supreme Court Justice Samuel Chase wrote, in the case of *Calder v. Bull* (1798), that "the several State Legislatures retain all the powers of legislation, delegated to them by the State Constitutions; which are not *expressly* taken away by the Constitution of the United States."[9] Roger Sherman, one of the signers of the Constitution, stated that "each State still retains its sovereignty in what concerns its own internal government, and a right to exercise every power of a sovereign State, not *expressly* delegated to the government of the United States." James Madison publicly repeated that the federal government would possess only "*expressly* delegated power."[10] In questioning some federal policies, the Virginia legislature adopted a resolution (drafted by Patrick Henry) complaining that the action "goes to the exercise of a power not *expressly* granted to the General government."[11]

The Tenth Amendment to the Constitution reads: "The powers not delegated to the United States by the Constitution, nor prohibited by it to the States, are reserved to the States respectively, or to the people." In recent history, this has effectively been ignored by Congress and the courts. This is one of the most important keys in our quest to control the size of the federal government. It is imperative that this amendment be restored to the place of honor and respect that it deserves. At the very least, each bill in Congress should be required to include a statement telling exactly which part of the Constitution is being used as the authority for the bill.

It is difficult to craft a way to actually enforce the Tenth Amendment. One approach might be to create a separate independent, objective, bipartisan commission that would review all bills. For a bill to proceed in Congress, it would have to have the certification by this "Tenth Amendment Commission" (10 Comm.) that the bill complied with the Tenth Amendment. Another function of this commission would be to review all existing federal laws and determine if they violated the Tenth Amendment. Those that did would have to be repealed or modified. It would also have the authority to review court decisions for similar usurpations. Upon request by any state, the 10 Comm. would review any specific regulation or executive order. It would be important that this commission have a high level of credibility with the public. It must be perceived as being objective and honest. In order to be independent of the federal bureaucracy, the 10 Comm. must be controlled by the states. Perhaps its members would be appointed by the state legislatures, or through some other system.

The idea of a committee to review laws is not a new idea. In the Continental Congress in 1779, a congressional committee concluded that some state laws violated the rules of the United States, and that such laws therefore "ought to be deemed void."[12] The New York Constitution of 1777 created a committee called the Council of Revision which would have to review and approve all bills passed by the state legislature before they could become law. The constitutions of Pennsylvania (1776) and Vermont (1777) each created a citizen watchdog committed called the Council of Censors, which was to review all the operations of government to ensure that there were no violations of the state constitution.

One way to constrain the runaway growth of our federal government would be a constitutional amendment to try to limit total spending. Of course, there are many ways to approach this. Some possible provisions might include:

1. A budget must be established each year in which federal outlays do not exceed federal revenue. This sounds pretty basic; however this by itself is not foolproof because it would force Congress to rely on estimates of future revenues and outlays, which would be subject to errors and manipulation. So additional stipulations would be required, such as:
2. Spending for each year could not exceed a fixed percentage of the GDP of the previous year.
3. A supermajority vote in Congress would be required to circumvent the first two items in case of some kind of emergency.
4. A supermajority vote in Congress would be required to increase taxes.[13]

Another suggestion is that the total outlays in any fiscal year shall not increase by a percentage greater than the percentage increase in nominal gross national product in the last calendar year.[14] Another indirect method that might have the effect of reducing spending would be to give the president a line-item veto in an appropriations bill. This would allow the president to surgically remove particular projects from a bill, instead of having to accept the entire package on an all-or-nothing basis. Congress passed a line item veto in 1996, but it was declared unconstitutional by the US Supreme Court in a 1998 ruling in the case of *Clinton v. City of New York*,[15] so a constitutional amendment will probably be required to accomplish this.

One factor that makes it so difficult to correct the overreaching of the federal government is that the states have very limited authority to initiate amendments to the Constitution. Article V of the Constitution provides two possible ways to propose amendments to the Constitution:

1. An amendment can be proposed by Congress with a vote of two thirds of both houses.
2. If the legislatures of two thirds of the states request it, a constitutional convention can be called for the purpose of proposing amendments.

The second method has never been used because most people realize that calling a constitutional convention would be a very dangerous proposition. There are no rules to govern this convention, so it would be subject to all manner of fraud, manipulation, confrontation, litigation, and basically political chaos. There is no way to restrict the agenda, so it is certain that powerful, well-funded special interest groups would take advantage of this once-in-a-lifetime opportunity to promote a radical amendment that might drastically change the character of our nation.

Some people have suggested a constitutional amendment to add a third method of adopting amendments. This new method would allow that if a group of at least three-fourths of the states, whose populations total at least two-thirds of the population of the United States, vote for the exact same specific amendment within a six-year period, that amendment would be added to the Constitution without the approval of Congress being required.

There are some other possibilities for constitutional amendments that would help clarify and restrict the power of the federal government. One would be an amendment to prohibit Congress from requiring any positive action by any state. This amendment would read:

Congress shall make no law, nor shall the courts make any ruling, requiring any state to take any action that is not otherwise required expressly and explicitly by this Constitution.

Another way the federal government has tried to control the states is by attaching numerous and varied requirements to money sent from the federal to the state governments. These attached "strings" have become a major source of frustration for the state governments. We need to begin a serious move to gradually eliminate most grants from the federal government to the states. If a state wants a program, it should raise state taxes enough to pay for it. Since the federal government will no longer be paying for that program, it could reduce federal taxes by an offsetting amount, so the taxpayers will not be paying any more. In fact, the taxpayers will be paying less, because they won't have to pay for the bureaucrats in Washington to administer those grants. And the state will have total control over its program, without the meddling from Washington. Another possible approach to reducing this type of abuse would be a constitutional amendment to the effect that "the allocation of resources to states or municipal governments shall not be contingent on the fulfillment of requirements that are not germane to the issue."[16]

NULLIFICATION

In our system of federalism, described in the Constitution, the people gave certain enumerated powers to the federal government. All other powers are, according to the Tenth Amendment, "reserved to the states respectively, or to the people." It is the people and the states that are sovereign, not the federal government. The people gave certain powers to the federal government, so the federal government is acting as an agent of the people.[17] If there is ever a question about an agent's authority, no one would ask the agent to decide if he has exceeded his authority. The sovereign would decide that question. So it is only logical for the people, not the federal government, to decide if the federal government has exceeded its authority. And if the people choose to delegate that job to the states, that is their right. This theory is called Nullification, meaning that a state has the right to nullify any federal law which that state has deemed unconstitutional. This is not a new theory—it was advocated by the third president of the United States, Thomas Jefferson.

There is no question at all that a federal law not authorized by the Constitution is void. The question is who gets to decide this and declare that the law is void. Early in our country's history, the US Supreme Court assumed this power for itself. Over the years, few have questioned this policy, and it is generally accepted today. But there is a serious problem with this procedure. If there is a dispute between a state and the federal government, the US Supreme Court gets to resolve the question. The US Supreme

Court is a branch of the federal government, so you have a branch of the federal government acting as the umpire between itself and a state. There is no way that the Supreme Court could be considered an impartial arbiter in this situation. Experience has shown how poorly this has worked, since the federal government has grown exponentially, and the power of the states has withered. Many unconstitutional federal laws have been passed, and it is now truly rare for the Supreme Court to reject efforts by the federal government to increase the scope of its authority. If the federal government has the exclusive right to judge the extent of its own powers, there will be few limits on its growth.

The Alien and Sedition Acts of 1798 were intended to censor and penalize criticism of the government. Thomas Jefferson thought that these were unconstitutional infringements on the freedom of speech, and wrote a series of resolutions detailing his feelings. These resolutions formed the basis of what was adopted by Kentucky to be known as the Kentucky Resolutions of 1798. One section of these resolutions stated: "Whensoever the general government assumes undelegated powers, its acts are unauthoritative, void, and of no force . . . The government created by this compact was not made the exclusive or final judge of the extent of the powers delegated to itself; since that would have made its discretion, and not the Constitution, the measure of its powers; but that, as in all other cases of compact among powers having no common judge, each party has an equal right to judge for itself." He was saying that the states, as parties to the compact which created the Constitution, have the right to judge when the Constitution has been violated. John Breckinridge, who sponsored the Resolutions in the Kentucky House, explained that when the federal government passed laws that extended beyond its constitutional powers, the people at the state level ought "to make a legislative declaration that, being unconstitutional, they are therefore void and of no effect." He also said, with respect to the Alien and Sedition Acts, "I hesitate not to declare it as my opinion that it is then the right and duty of the several States to nullify those acts, and to protect their citizens from their operation."[18] The next year, Kentucky adopted another set of resolutions as a follow up and in response to some of the criticisms of this theory. The Kentucky Resolutions of 1799 read, in part: "The several states who formed that instrument [the Constitution], being sovereign and independent, have the unquestionable right to judge of its infraction; and that a nullification, by those sovereignties, of all unauthorized acts done under colour of that instrument, is the rightful remedy."[19]

The state of Virginia also passed a set of resolutions, written by James Madison, in 1798, expressing similar concerns, and asking other states to join with Virginia in declaring the Alien and Sedition Acts unconstitutional.[20]

Naturally, the federal government did not like this idea. They did not want the states to have the power to nullify federal laws—they wanted to keep that power for themselves. And so the US Supreme Court has ruled that the states do not have that right.[21] But the logic behind the Nullification theory is indisputable: if the federal government is the exclusive judge of the extent of its powers, that is the definition of despotism.

Some have argued against the principle of Nullification by saying that the "Supremacy Clause" of the Constitution makes the federal government superior to the state governments. What the Supremacy Clause actually says is "this Constitution, and the laws of the United States which shall be made in pursuance thereof . . . shall be the supreme law of the land." The point is that the Supremacy Clause *only* applies to laws made *in pursuance thereof*. Nullification maintains that if a given law is not authorized by the Constitution, then it is not "in pursuance thereof," and, therefore, the Supremacy Clause does not apply. That phrase "in pursuance thereof" is very important because, without it, the Constitution would allow Congress to pass any laws it wanted to, even if they were not constitutional, and these laws would still be supreme.

At various times in our history, some states have embraced the idea of nullification of an unconstitutional law:

- In 1807, President Jefferson, in response to some British and French infringements upon American shipping, instituted an embargo that prevented American merchant ships from traveling to any foreign port. This was devastating to New England's maritime economy, and they claimed that the embargo was unconstitutional. Some state governments refused to cooperate in enforcing the embargo.[22]
- Congress in 1814 enacted a bill regarding the enlistment of minors (18 years old) into the army. Massachusetts and Connecticut declared the law to be unconstitutional, and passed laws designed to hamper its enforcement.[23]
- The Pennsylvania legislature approved a resolution stating that "the general government by this treaty [Constitution] was not constituted the exclusive or final judge of the powers it was to exercise."[24]

- The federal Fugitive Slave Act of 1850 was criticized by some northern states, who attempted to obstruct its enforcement. Laws and procedures were adopted which interfered with the capture and returning of runaway slaves. In Wisconsin, an anti-slavery newspaper editor named Sherman Booth incited a mob of people to force their way into a jail and release a runaway slave. Federal marshals arrested Booth for violation of the Fugitive Slave Act, but the state Supreme Court ordered his release, and then refused to comply with an order of the US Supreme Court to turn Booth over to federal custody.[25]

Of course, as a practical matter, the attempt of just one or two states to nullify a federal law is not going to be effective. The US Supreme Court will inevitably rule against them, and most people will accept that that settles the matter. The only way to make any progress in this direction would be to find a very popular issue with widespread public support, and for several states to unite in opposition to federal control. One place we may be seeing the beginnings of such a movement is medical marijuana. At this writing, two states, Colorado and Washington, have legalized the use of marijuana for medical purposes, and other states are considering the same move. This, of course, conflicts with the federal drug laws. When large numbers of people are determined not to obey a law they consider unconstitutional, that law will not be enforced. In this particular dispute, the United States Department of Justice has already backed down, and has notified these two states that the federal government will not interfere with the state laws. This has happened just as James Madison predicted in The Federalist 46, where he wrote that an "unwarrantable measure of the Federal Government" could be opposed by the states by the "refusal to co-operate with the officers of the Union" and by "the embarrassments created by legislative devices." This, he said, "would present obstructions which the Federal Government would hardly be willing to encounter."[26] This is not strictly following the Nullification doctrine exactly, because they didn't start off declaring that the federal drug laws were unconstitutional. Instead their strategy was to gradually build public support on the issue and encourage some states to adopt defiant measures. As the movement gathers steam and gets more and more support, the federal government will eventually be overwhelmed, and will be forced to abandon or modify the offending drug laws.

One part of the state strategy on some issues will be to pass state laws which prohibit state or local officials from assisting or participating in enforcement of certain federal laws.[27] The reason that this would be effective is that, in many cases, federal enforcement of federal laws depends heavily on state and local law enforcement assistance. The withdrawal of state and local assistance would effectively cripple enforcement of some federal laws. Jon Roland of the Constitution Society[28] has recommended that each state create within that state a commission similar to the "10 Comm." described above, which would review federal laws and regulations for constitutionality. When this state commission finds a law to be unconstitutional, a mandatory edict would be issued requiring that no state or local officials cooperate in the enforcement of that law.

EXISTING PROGRAMS

If we are really serious about reducing the size of the federal government, we are going to have to think about the hundreds of programs currently that are being run by the feds for which they do not have any constitutional authorization. Some of these programs have been around for a long time and are quite popular, especially with those who receive benefits from them. If we could find a way to gradually move these programs out of Washington, this would be a giant step toward our goal of shrinking the government.

One good example is Social Security. This is a very popular program, which many people depend on during their retirement years. No one would ever suggest that we get rid of it completely. However, there is no authority in the Constitution for the federal government to operate a retirement plan. The Supreme Court said that the General Welfare Clause allowed the government to do this.[29] But we have already seen in Chapter 9 that this is a totally bogus interpretation of this clause. Since the federal government is not allowed to operate this program, it must be given to the states. One possibility is that it could be run by an independent national corporation controlled by the states. In this way, a person could keep his retirement account even if he changed jobs or moved to another state. This is the same way that the current Social Security contributions follow a person from job to job.

We have heard how changing demographics are reducing the ratio of workers to retirees. As a result, the Social Security system will soon be taking in less money in taxes than it is paying out in benefits. The system will then be running a deficit, and it will have to make some adjustments by raising taxes, reducing benefits, raising the retirement age, or some combination of these, or else it will go bankrupt. The new system that replaces Social Security should not be this type of pay-as-you-go system, but instead should be a true retirement system, where a person's benefits actually come from the amount he has contributed. Another benefit of that type of system would be that, unlike the current Social Security system, a person would have a legal claim on his own account.

Certainly there would be many problems to be resolved in transferring such a massive system to a new entity. The transition would have to be set up so that current workers and retirees do not lose any of their promised benefits. This would involve a large cost to the government, but the cost would be spread out over many years. What would this new system look like? Where has this been done before? Some other countries have privatized retirement systems, but actually there is one very good model for this type of system in Galveston County, Texas. They have had a private retirement system for their county workers for 30 years, which has been working very well. Just like in Social Security, employees contribute a percent of their income and the county also makes a contribution. Once the county makes its contribution, its financial obligation is satisfied. There are no long-term, unfunded liabilities that have been so disastrous for some other cities and counties. Top rated financial institutions submit competitive bids to manage the money, and they guarantee the worker a certain minimum rate of return. In good years, when their investments do well, workers get a higher rate of return, but their rate will never go below the guaranteed minimum. Over the long term, the rate actually received in the Galveston plan has averaged substantially higher than the minimum. Stock market volatility has always been one of the primary objections to a privatized retirement program. This plan has solved that risk problem.

According to the Galveston plan's financial management company, a worker retiring after spending his entire working career in this plan will have an income higher than he would have if he were in Social Security. And a study by the Cato institute, "Still a Better Deal: Private Investment vs. Social Security," demonstrates that actual investment returns over the past 40 years show that a system of private investment will, in fact, provide significantly higher rates of return than the current Social Security system.[30] It is important to remember that Social Security is in fiscal trouble, and will probably soon have to cut its benefits, so that will make the Galveston plan look even better by comparison. They wanted this plan to be a complete substitute for Social Security, so it also includes survivors, disability, and death benefits. We know that many people do not have the discipline to save money for their retirement, so whatever new plan is adopted should be mandatory—not voluntary. For a national program, there should be participation by multiple financial companies. All the assets for the entire country should not be managed by a single company. Some kind of insurance against the failure of one company would be advisable.

There are obviously many details that could be fine-tuned to try to improve the plan. Social Security currently makes adjustments to increase the retirement benefits for low income workers and decrease benefits for high income workers. That kind of adjustment might be considered for this new plan. Another option would be to allow the worker to set aside a small portion of his account for an investment which might pay a higher return. This would have to be a very conservative investment, such as some kind of index fund.

FOURTEENTH AMENDMENT

The Fourteenth Amendment has been a major source of much of the expansion of the federal power. We need an amendment to the Constitution to effect the following changes:

- The Fourteenth Amendment should be repealed. Much of it relates to the Civil War and is obsolete. The clauses in Section 1 are so vague and have been interpreted so broadly as to cause more trouble than benefits. If it is felt that any of these requirements need to remain in the Constitution, these should be rewritten in more specific and narrow language.
- Even if the entire Fourteenth Amendment is not repealed, a new amendment is certainly needed to establish that a child born to someone who is in the country illegally or temporarily is not considered an American citizen.
- The idea that the federal Bill of Rights applies to the states should be rejected. This would return us to the

original intent of the Founders. When the Bill of Rights was being introduced, one amendment was proposed which would have imposed more restrictions on state governments, but this amendment was rejected by the Senate. So the original intent of the Founders was clearly primarily to limit the federal government.

State constitutions should incorporate language similar to the federal Bill of Rights in order to protect these rights. In most cases, this is already included in the state constitutions.

SEVENTEENTH AMENDMENT

The Founders knew the history of tyranny and abuse of power in the monarchies of Europe. They went to great extremes to develop a system of separation of powers to prevent the concentration of power in a single individual, group, or department. This resulted in the three branches of the federal government, executive, legislative, and judicial. They also divided power between the state and federal governments, with a limited amount of power in certain areas being given to the federal government, and with the states having undefined powers in all other areas. In this way, the states were given the primary responsibility of directly governing the people. This division of powers between the federal and state governments was the basic principle of federalism, which was so central to the thinking of our Founders.

It was recognized that the federal government might someday try to exert excessive power over the states, so to balance this, the states were given some influence on the federal government by having members of the US Senate elected by the state legislatures, while the members of the House of Representatives would be elected by popular vote. The Founders did not think they could trust the federal courts to protect the rights of states. After all, the Supreme Court was a part of the federal government, and so it was natural that it would be expected to be biased in the direction of taking power from the states and giving more power to the federal government. So they incorporated some features into the Constitution to protect the states' interests and rights in the new government. The most important of these features was the election of senators by the state legislatures.

This was done very deliberately, as explained by James Madison, saying that balance would be promoted by "render[ing] them by different modes of election."[31] The Senate, he said, would be "disinclined to invade the rights of the individual states."[32] He also explained that this system was intended to "secure the authority of" the states.[33] Alexander Hamilton also explained that if the states, in their political capacities, had been excluded "from a place in the organization of the national government . . . it would doubtless have been interpreted into an entire dereliction of the federal principle; and would certainly have deprived the State governments of that absolute safeguard which they will enjoy under this provision."[34] This system was intended to protect states' rights and to minimize the influence of special interests.

During the debates regarding the Senate at the Constitutional Convention, George Mason illustrated the prevailing thinking when he said the State Legislatures also ought to have "some means of defending themselves against encroachments of the National Government. . . . And what better means can we provide than the giving them some share in, or rather to make them a constituent part of, the National Government."[35]

During the Connecticut Ratifying Convention, Oliver Wolcott told the delegates that members of "the Senate . . . are appointed by the states, and will secure the rights of the several states."[36] Fisher Ames of Massachusetts referred to senators as "ambassadors of the states."[37]

Understandably, many people in Washington wanted to increase the power of the federal government and to reduce the power of the state governments. One way to do that would be to eliminate the states' control over the US Senate. In the nineteenth century, a movement emerged to change the method of selection of senators, so they would be elected by popular vote. This cause was helped by a few well publicized stories of corruption and bribery in some state legislatures in the selection of senators. Another factor was the emotional feeling by many uninformed citizens, ignorant of the benefits of separation of powers, that having the people vote on something was always the best way to reach a decision. In 1913, the Seventeenth Amendment to the Constitution was enacted, which required the popular election of senators. Under the old system, the two houses of Congress were elected by different methods and had different constituencies. After the adoption of the seventeenth amendment, both houses are now almost identical, elected by popular vote. We have lost a major degree of diversity and balance in Congress, and the states have lost their significant influence in the federal government. The states foolishly gave up this power when they ratified the

Seventeenth Amendment. It is no coincidence that, after this amendment, the federal government has greatly expanded its intrusion into matters previously controlled by the states. The system of federalism, so skillfully crafted by our Founders, has been emasculated.

After this amendment, the Senate now has the same problem as the House—it takes many thousands, or even millions, of dollars to run for election. Much of that money comes from businesses and special interests, who naturally might expect some favors (tax breaks, subsidies, favorable legislation) in return for their donations.

Before this amendment, senators were elected by the state legislatures, so the senators would consult with these legislators about impending federal legislation. Now there is no reason for senators to talk to anyone in the state government. Senators are now very isolated from the people and the states. But you can bet that they get input from the large corporations which direct millions of dollars to their campaigns.

The Seventeenth Amendment must be repealed in order to restore the balance in Congress, to restore some portion of states' rights, and to move back toward our wonderful original system of federalism.

SUPREME COURT

The Supreme Court assumed on its own authority the right to declare a law unconstitutional, and declared that its decision is the supreme law of the land. This is a conflict of interest, because it allows the national government to interpret its own laws. Many years of experience have shown that the Court is abusing its power by twisting the law to try to enforce the Justices' personal opinions and biases, even if this violates the Constitution or the will of the people. Something needs to be done to give some relief from this problem.

Congress has both the power and the duty to curb the power of the judicial supremacists. According to the Constitution, Congress can limit the types of cases that the federal courts and the Supreme Court can hear. This has actually been done several times in the past, and the Supreme Court has held that Congress does have this power. For example, Congress could pass a law stating that federal courts do not have jurisdiction over whether an acknowledgment of God by public officials violates the Establishment Clause of the First Amendment.[38]

Another approach would be to require a supermajority vote on the Supreme Court to overturn any law passed by a legislative body, or by a public referendum. This would ensure that laws are not overturned casually with very weak justification, but only in cases of egregious or flagrant violation of a Constitutional principle. The objective is to restore the appropriate deference to the people's representatives in the legislature. Currently, the constitutions of two states, Nebraska and North Dakota, require a supermajority of state Supreme Court justices in order to exercise judicial review.[39] This idea has been proposed several times in the US Congress, but never adopted.

Another possible strategy for reigning in the power of the courts is based on the foundational principle of our national government, which is the separation into three *equal* branches. Since the branches are supposed to be equal, one does not have any power superior to the other. Therefore, the judiciary does not have the authority to overturn an act of Congress. Yes, someone has to decide if a law is constitutional. But who should do that? The legislature could do that just as well as the judiciary. In fact, it might be more logical for Congress to make that decision, because Congress is subject to the will of the people at the polls. The people have control of Congress, and can correct any legislative errors through the ordinary functions of modifying and repealing laws (and through elections).

Many people agreed with this line of thinking, including some judges. John Gibson was a judge on the Pennsylvania Supreme Court. In the case of *Eakin v. Raub* he wrote a dissent challenging the concept of judicial review. He wrote that "it is the business of the judiciary, to interpret the laws, not scan the authority of the lawgiver." He thought that this task of voiding laws should be left to the people. For the judiciary to do this would be a "usurpation of legislative power." He said, "I am of the opinion, that it [the power to limit Congress] rests with the people, in whom full and absolute sovereign power resides, to correct abuses of legislation, by instructing their representatives to repeal the obnoxious act." He accurately anticipated our current dilemma when he asked, if judges are given this power "where shall it stop? There must be some point of limitation to such an inquiry." He also pointed out that "the judiciary is not infallible," and there must be some way to correct an error by the courts.[40]

Thomas Jefferson touched on this in a letter he wrote to Abigail Adams on September 11, 1804, in which he said: "Nothing in the Constitution has given them [judges] a right to decide for the executive, more than to the executive to decide for them. Both magistrates are equally independent in the sphere of action assigned to them."[41]

James Madison, on June 17, 1789, asked, "Upon what principle it can be contended, that any one department draws from the Constitution greater powers than another, in marking out the limits of the powers of the several departments?"[42]

Still another approach to limiting the courts' abuses would be to give the Congress the veto power over court decisions, similar to the power to override a presidential veto. There are several possible ways to try to restore this balance, but something must be done.

With our normal life expectancy being continuously increased, it is time that the idea of lifetime tenure for federal judges needs to be revisited. Their lifetime appointment and virtually no accountability have helped to produce the current state of arrogance and judicial activism. A new constitutional amendment should provide fixed terms for all federal judges including the Supreme Court. The terms could be in the range of twelve or sixteen years, and they would be staggered so that each president in each presidential term would appoint approximately the same number of justices.[43]

Many important cases have been decided in the Supreme Court by a 5–4 decision. This is unfortunate when this happens, because it indicates a deep difference of opinion. When the court cannot reach a consensus, this tells us that the question at hand is confusing, controversial, and divisive, where honest men may disagree. This, in turn, suggests that the particular law or Constitutional phraseology may be unclear or confusing, and may be subject to varying interpretations. Where such confusion exists, we have to fear that the same issue may arise again and again. Also, the public will recognize this uncertainty, and many will feel that the correct decision was not reached. Whenever there is such a split decision by the Supreme Court, there should be a way to encourage Congress to look at the particular law or Constitutional article in question, and attempt to write new legislation which clarifies the intent. Our goal should always be toward more clarity and better understanding.

COMMERCE CLAUSE

The Commerce Clause has certainly been used as an excuse for tremendous mischief, so a constitutional amendment is absolutely necessary to put a stop to this damage. The new amendment must clarify that the Commerce Clause "shall not be construed to include the power to regulate or prohibit any activity that is confined within a single state, regardless of its effects outside the state." It should say that the Commerce Clause shall not authorize the federal government to do anything that could be done by a state.

Many of the unjust and unnecessary federal laws include the statement that the prohibited conduct is "in or affecting interstate commerce" or a similar phrase. The purpose of this broad and meaningless phrase is to ostensibly bring the activity under the Commerce Clause, even though the law has almost nothing to do with commerce. The amendment must make it clear that laws justified under the Commerce Clause must be primarily related to *interstate commerce*. Even the Supreme Court recognized this requirement when it ruled in *United States v. Lopez* that a certain law could not be justified under the Commerce Clause because "neither the actors nor their conduct has a commercial character."[44]

This approach would leave the federal government without the power to deal with large scale environmental problems. This is really a separate issue from commerce, and should be dealt with in a separate amendment.

AMERICA MUST ACKNOWLEDGE GOD

It is not only the duty of a nation to acknowledge God, it is good public policy, according to our Founders. George Washington wrote in his first Thanksgiving Proclamation, "Whereas it is the duty of all nations to acknowledge the providence of Almighty God, to obey his will, to be grateful for his benefits, and humbly implore His protection and favor . . ."[45] John Adams, our second President, said "Our constitution was made only for a moral and religious people. It is wholly inadequate to the government of any other."[46]

The long history and tradition of this country shows that it was the intent of the original founders to acknowledge and encourage worship of the Judeo-Christian God. This was evident starting with the earliest charters for the original colonies in the seventeenth century, up through the modern customs of prayer in schools, displays of manger scenes and Ten Commandments, and opening of legislative sessions with prayer. These popular traditions endured until they came under attack from the federal judiciary about the middle of the twentieth century.

We must find a balanced approach that guarantees religious freedom to everyone. People of all persuasions should be free to preach in the street, pass out literature, express their views in the workplace and in school, and display religious symbols without fear of punishment. On the other hand, it should not be considered an unconstitutional infringement of someone's rights if he is forced to listen to a prayer before a football game, or if he might see a display of the Ten Commandments at a courthouse. These trivial matters certainly do not constitute the "establishment" of a particular denomination as a "state church," nor are they a serious attack on a person's right to practice his religion. They are merely the acknowledgment that, from its earliest beginnings, this nation was founded as a Christian nation.

This is not a radical idea. Don't forget that we have tried this approach, and it worked just fine. For the first 150 years of this country's history, the government acknowledged and even encouraged Christianity, and no one feared that we were establishing a state religion. We must return to these practices, which were established by the very people who wrote the Constitution and the Bill of Rights.

NOTE FROM THE AUTHOR

Thank you for reading this book. If you have enjoyed it, I would really appreciate you leaving a review on Amazon.com.

Appendix A
Bill of Rights

The first ten amendments to the US Constitution:

Amendment I
Congress shall make no law respecting an establishment of religion, or prohibiting the free exercise thereof; or abridging the freedom of speech, or of the press; or the right of the people peaceably to assemble, and to petition the Government for a redress of grievances.

Amendment II
A well regulated Militia, being necessary to the security of a free State, the right of the people to keep and bear Arms, shall not be infringed.

Amendment III
No Soldier shall, in time of peace be quartered in any house, without the consent of the Owner, nor in time of war, but in a manner to be prescribed by law.

Amendment IV
The right of the people to be secure in their persons, houses, papers, and effects, against unreasonable searches and seizures, shall not be violated, and no Warrants shall issue, but upon probable cause, supported by Oath or affirmation, and particularly describing the place to be searched, and the persons or things to be seized.

Amendment V

No person shall be held to answer for a capital, or otherwise infamous crime, unless on a presentment or indictment of a Grand Jury, except in cases arising in the land or naval forces, or in the Militia, when in actual service in time of War or public danger; nor shall any person be subject for the same offence to be twice put in jeopardy of life or limb; nor shall be compelled in any criminal case to be a witness against himself, nor be deprived of life, liberty, or property, without due process of law; nor shall private property be taken for public use, without just compensation.

Amendment VI

In all criminal prosecutions, the accused shall enjoy the right to a speedy and public trial, by an impartial jury of the State and district wherein the crime shall have been committed, which district shall have been previously ascertained by law, and to be informed of the nature and cause of the accusation; to be confronted with the witnesses against him; to have compulsory process for obtaining witnesses in his favor, and to have the Assistance of Counsel for his defence.

Amendment VII

In Suits at common law, where the value in controversy shall exceed twenty dollars, the right of trial by jury shall be preserved, and no fact tried by a jury, shall be otherwise re-examined in any Court of the United States, than according to the rules of the common law.

Amendment VIII

Excessive bail shall not be required, nor excessive fines imposed, nor cruel and unusual punishments inflicted.

Amendment IX

The enumeration in the Constitution, of certain rights, shall not be construed to deny or disparage others retained by the people.

Amendment X

The powers not delegated to the United States by the Constitution, nor prohibited by it to the States, are reserved to the States respectively, or to the people.

Notes

CHAPTER ONE – LIMITED GOVERNMENT

1. *The United States v. Worrall*, 2 U.S. 384, 393 (1798).

2. John W. Whitehead, *The Second American Revolution* (Westchester, IL: Crossway Books, 1985), 205.

3. Milton and Rose Friedman, *Free to Choose* (New York: Avon Books, 1981), 274.

4. Reinhold Niebuhr, *The Irony of American History* (Chicago: University of Chicago Press, 2008), 23.

5. Merrill D. Peterson, *Thomas Jefferson Writings* (New York: Penguin Books, 1984), 1079.

7. Alexander Hamilton, James Madison, John Jay, *The Federalist Papers* (New York: Bantam Books, 1982), 251.

8. Ronald J. Pestritto and William J. Atto, *American Progressivism* (Lanham, MD: Lexington Books, 2008), 181.

9. Glenn Beck, *Glenn Beck's Common Sense* (New York: Mercury Radio Arts, 2009), 64.

10. Ralph A. Rossum, *Federalism, The Supreme Court, and the Seventeenth Amendment* (Lanham, MD: Lexington Books, 2001), 182.

11. Ronald J. Pestritto and William J. Atto, *American Progressivism* (Lanham, MD: Lexington Books, 2008), 50.

12. Akhil Reed Amar, *The Bill of Rights* (Harrisonburg, VA: R. R. Donnelley & Sons, 1998), 38.

13. Herbert J. Storing, *What the Anti-Federalists Were For* (Chicago: University of Chicago Press, 1981), 11.

14. *Roe v. Wade*, 410 U.S. 113 (1973).

15. *New York v. United States*, 112 S. Ct. 2408, 2431 (1992).

16. *House v. Mayes*, 219 U.S. 270, 282 (1911).

17. Alexander Hamilton, James Madison, John Jay, *The Federalist Papers* (New York: Bantam Books, 1982), 128–129.

18. Ibid., 152.

19. Ibid., 193.

20. Ibid., 199.

21. Ibid., 223.

22. Ibid., 236.

23. Andrew P. Napolitano, *The Constitution in Exile* (Nashville, TN: Thomas Nelson, 2006), 187–188.

24. Ibid., 185

25. Ibid., 190.

26. *South Dakota v. Dole*, 483 U.S. 203, 212 (1987).

27. *Scarborough v. United States*, 431 U.S. 563 (1977).

28. *Fry v. United States*, 421 U.S. 542 (1975).

29. *FERC v. Mississippi*, 456 U.S. 742 (1982).

30. *Hodel v. Virginia Surface Mining and Reclamation Association, Inc.*, 452 U.S. 264 (1981).

31. W. Lucas, *Timely Renewed* (Lexington, KY: Create Space, 2010), 48.

32. *United States v. Darby Lumber Co.*, 312 U.S. 100 (1941).

33. *Garcia v. San Antonio Transit Auth.*, 469 U.S. 528, 572 (1985), Powell dissenting.

34. Christopher Wolfe, *The Rise of Modern Judicial Review* (New York: Basic Books, 1986), 309.

35. *New York v. United States*, 505 U.S. 144, 183 (1992).

36. *New State Ice Co. v. Liebmann*, 285 U.S. 311 (1932), Brandeis dissenting.

37. Robert A. Levy and William Mellor, *The Dirty Dozen* (Washington, DC: Cato Institute, 2009), 184.

38. Thomas Sowell, *A Conflict of Visions* (New York: Basic Books, 2007), 54.

39. Ibid., 134

40. John W. Whitehead, *The Second American Revolution* (Westchester, IL: Crossway Books, 1985), 59.

41. James W. Lucas, *Timely Renewed* (Lexington, KY: Create Space, 2010), 48.

42. John W. Whitehead, *The Second American Revolution* (Westchester, IL: Crossway Books, 1985), 69.

43. Ibid.

44. Wayne Grudem, *Our First Liberty on Trial* (Scottsdale, AZ: Alliance Defense Fund, 2010), 48–70.

45. Walter Isaacson, *Benjamin Franklin* (New York: Simon & Schuster, 2004), 459.

46. Patrick Conley and John Kaminski, *The Bill of Rights and the States* (Madison, WI: Madison House, 1992), 29.

47. Ibid., 57.

48. Ibid., 53.

49. William Bonner, *The Idea of America* (Paris: Les Belles Lettres, 2003), 68–71.

CHAPTER TWO – SPEECH / FIRST AMENDMENT

1. *Whitney v. California*, 274 U.S. 357, 375 (1927), Brandeis concurring.

2. Adam Freedman, *The Naked Constitution* (New York: Broadside Books, 2012), 140.

3. Robert G. Natelson, *The Original Constitution* (Los Angeles: Tenth Amendment Center, 2011), 175–176.

4. *Shaffer v. United States*, 255 F. 886 (9th Cir. 1919).

5. *Brandenburg v. Ohio*, 395 U.S. 444 (1969).

6. *Grayned v. City of Rockford*, 408 U.S. 104 (1972).

7. *Dennis v. United States*, 341 U.S. 494 (1951).

8. *Pickering v. Board of Education*, 391 U.S. 563, 568 (1968).

9. *Mosholder v. Barnhardt*, 679 F. 3d 443, 449 (2012).

10. *Konigsberg v. State Bar of California*, 366 U.S. 36, 61 (1961), Black dissenting.

11. Adam Freedman, *The Naked Constitution* (New York: Broadside Books, 2012), 148.

12. Robert Justin Goldstein, *Political Repression in Modern America From 1870 to 1976* (Chicago: University of Illinois Press, 2001), 496.

13. *United States v. Cleveland*, 128 F. 3d 267 (5th Cir. 1997).

14. Andrew P. Napolitano, *Constitutional Chaos* (Nashville, TN: Thomas Nelson, 2004), 84.

15. *Snyder v. Phelps*, Docket No. 09-751 (2011).

16. Adam Freedman, *The Naked Constitution* (New York: Broadside Books, 2012), 151–152.

17. Phil Bronstein, "Update: Chronicle responds after Obama Administration punishes reporter for using multimedia, then claims they didn't," SFGate.com, April 28, 2011.

18. *New York Times Co. v. United States*, 403 U.S. 713, 714 (1971).

19. *Beauharnais v. Illinois*, 343 U.S. 250 (1952), Black dissenting.

20. *New York Times Co. v. Sullivan*, 376 U.S. 254 (1964), Black concurring.

21. John W. Whitehead, *A Government of Wolves* (New York: Select Books, 2013), 27.

22. Ibid., 26.

23. Vaughan Bell, Peter Halligan and Hadyn Ellis, "Beliefs about Delusions" *The Psychologist*, August 2003, 419.

24. *Chaplinsky v. New Hampshire*, 315 U.S. 568, 572 (1942).

25. David L. Hudson Jr., *Let the Students Speak* (Boston: Beacon Press, 2011), 12.

26. Ibid., 15.

27. Ibid., 39.

28. Ibid., 57.

29. Ibid., 64.

30. David K. Shipler, *Rights at Risk* (New York: Alfred A. Knopf, 2012), 274.

31. *Morse v. Frederick*, 551 U.S. 393 (2007).

32. David L. Hudson Jr., *Let the Students Speak* (Boston: Beacon Press, 2011), 118.

33. *Bethel School District No. 403 v. Fraser*, 478 U.S. 675 (1986).

34. David L. Hudson Jr., *Let the Students Speak* (Boston: Beacon Press, 2011), 92.

35. *Boroff v. Van Wert City Board of Education*, 240 F.3d 465 (6th Cir. 2000).

36. *Harper v. Poway Unified School District*, 04-57037 (9th Cir. 2006).

37. *Denno v. Sch. Bd. of Volusia County*, 218 F. 3d 1267 (11th Cir. 2000).

38. *Hazelwood Sch. Dist. v. Kuhlmeier*, 484 U.S. 260, 288 (1988).

39. *Tinker v. Des Moines Sch. Dist.*, 393 U.S. 503, 508 (1969).

40. *Hazelwood Sch. Dist. v. Kuhlmeier*, 484 U.S. 260 (1988).

41. *Bethel School District No. 403 v. Fraser*, 478 U.S. 675 (1986).

42. *Morse v. Frederick*, 551 U.S. 393 (2007).

43. *LaVine v. Blaine School District*, 279 F. 3d 719 (9th Cir. Jan. 29, 2002).

44. David L. Hudson Jr., *Let the Students Speak* (Boston: Beacon Press, 2011), 137.

45. *LaVine v. Blaine School District*, 279 F. 3d 719 (9th Cir. Jan. 29, 2002).

46. David L. Hudson Jr., *Let the Students Speak* (Boston: Beacon Press, 2011), 133.

47. David K. Shipler, *Rights at Risk* (New York: Alfred A. Knopf, 2012), 298.

48. David L. Hudson Jr., *Let the Students Speak* (Boston: Beacon Press, 2011), 163.

49. Ibid., 172.

50. Ibid., 174.

51. "Spotlight on Speech Codes 2014: The State of Free Speech on Our Nation's Campuses" (Philadelphia: The Foundation For Individual Rights In Education, 2014).

52. Ibid.

53. Eugene Volokh, "What Speech Does 'Hostile Work Environment' Harassment Law Restrict?" 85 *Georgetown Law Journal* 627 (1997).

CHAPTER THREE – RELIGION / FIRST AMENDMENT

1. W. Cleon Skousen, *The 5000 Year Leap* (Malta, ID: National Center for Constitutional Studies, 2006), 98.

2. *Holy Trinity v. United States*, 143 U.S. 457, 471 (1892).

3. John Eidsmoe, *Christianity and the Constitution* (Grand Rapids, MI: Baker Book House, 1987), 33.

4. Ibid., 352.

5. Letter to the Officers of the First Brigade of the Third Division of the Militia of Massachusetts, 11 October 1798.

6. Alexander Hamilton, James Madison, John Jay, *The Federalist Papers* (New York: Bantam Books, 1982), 189.

7. Verna Hall, *Christian History of The Constitution* (San Francisco: The American Christian Constitution Press, 1960), IV.

8. Benjamin F. Morris, *The Christian Life and Character of the Civil Institutions of the United States* (Powder Springs, GA: American Vision, 2007), 309.

9. *Wallace v. Jaffree*, 472 U.S. 38, 105 (1985), Rehnquist dissenting.

10. Robert Flood, *The Rebirth of America* (Philadelphia: Arthur S. DeMoss Foundation, 1986), 32.

11. Barry Adamson, *Freedom of Religion the First Amendment and the Supreme Court* (Gretna, LA: Pelican Publishing Co., 2008), 191.

12. Merrill D. Peterson, *Thomas Jefferson Writings* (New York: Penguin Books, 1984) 289.

13. Barry Adamson, *Freedom of Religion the First Amendment and the Supreme Court* (Gretna, LA: Pelican Publishing Co., 2008), 79.

14. *Wallace v. Jaffree*, 472 U.S. 38, 98 (1985), Rehnquist dissenting.

15. Michael Paulsen and Luke Paulsen, *The Constitution An Introduction* (New York: Basic Books, 2015), 101.

16. Barry Adamson, *Freedom of Religion the First Amendment and the Supreme Court* (Gretna, LA: Pelican Publishing Co., 2008), 152.

17. Newt Gingrich, *God in America* (Nashville, TN: Thomas Nelson, 2006), 31.

18. Robert Flood, *The Rebirth of America* (Philadelphia: Arthur S. DeMoss Foundation, 1986), 39.

19. Newt Gingrich, *God in America* (Nashville, TN: Thomas Nelson, 2006), 46.

20. *Wallace v. Jaffree*, 472 U.S. 38, 103 (1985), Rehnquist dissenting.

21. Merrill D. Peterson, *Thomas Jefferson Writings* (New York: Penguin Books, 1984), 1464.

22. "American Indians And Christianity," *Oklahoma Historical Society's Encyclopedia Of Oklahoma History & Culture,* http://digital.library.okstate.edu/encyclopedia/entries/A/AM011.html.

23. Benjamin F. Morris, *The Christian Life and Character of the Civil Institutions of the United States* (Powder Springs, GA: American Vision, 2007), 386.

24. Dr. Mark A. Beliles & Stephen K. McDowell, *America's Providential History* (Charlottesville, VA: The Providence Foundation, 2010), 176.

25. Newt Gingrich, *God in America* (Nashville, TN: Thomas Nelson, 2006), 121.

26. Ibid., 99–101.

27. Barry Adamson, *Freedom of Religion the First Amendment and the Supreme Court* (Gretna, LA: Pelican Publishing Co., 2008), 153.

28. Ibid., 156.

29. *Marsh v. Chambers* 463 U.S. 783, 792 (1983).

30. Barry Adamson, *Freedom of Religion the First Amendment and the Supreme Court* (Gretna, LA: Pelican Publishing Co., 2008), 154.

31. *McCreary County v. American Civil Liberties Union of Ky.*, 545 U.S. 844 (2005), Scalia dissenting.

32. *Holy Trinity v. United States*, 143 U.S. 457, 471 (1892).

33. *Zorach v. Clauson*, 343 U.S. 306, 313 (1952).

34. *Elk Grove Unified School District v. Newdow*, 542 U.S. 1 (2004), Thomas concurring.

35. *Everson v. Board of Education*, 330 U.S. 1, 15 (1947).

36. Mike Lee, *Our Lost Constitution* (New York: Sentinel, 2015), 97.

37. Ibid., 87.

38. Adam Freedman, *The Naked Constitution* (New York: Broadside Books, 2012), 163.

39. *Board of Education v. Allen*, 392 U.S. 236 (1968); *Lemon v. Kurtzman*, 403 U.S. 602, 612 (1971).

40. *Engel v. Vitale*, 370 U.S. 421 (1962).

41. *School Dist. of Abington Tp. v. Schempp*, 374 U.S. 203, 313 (1963), Stewart dissenting.

42. Michael Paulsen and Luke Paulsen, *The Constitution An Introduction* (New York: Basic Books, 2015), 291.

43. *Santa Fe Independent School District v. Doe* , 530 U.S. 290 (2000), 318 Rehnquist dissenting.

44. *Lee v. Weisman*, 505 US 577, 631–633 (1992), Scalia dissenting.

45. Robert H. Bork, *Coercing Virtue* (Washington, DC: The AEI Press, 2003), 65.

46. Adam Freedman, *The Naked Constitution* (New York: Broadside Books, 2012), 187.

47. John W. Whitehead, *The Second American Revolution* (Westchester, IL: Crossway Books, 1985), 58.

48. Barry Adamson, *Freedom of Religion the First Amendment and the Supreme Court* (Gretna, LA: Pelican Publishing Co., 2008), 150.

49. *Newdow vs. Rio Linda Union School District* (9th Cir. Mar. 12, 2010).

50. *Freedom from Religion Foundation v. Hanover School District* (1st Cir. Nov. 12, 2010).

51. *Aronow v. United States*, 432 F.2d 242, 243 (9th Cir. October 6, 1970).

52. David K. Shipler, *Rights at Risk* (New York: Alfred A. Knopf, 2012), 271.

53. Phyllis Schlafly and George Neumayr, *No Higher Power* (Washington, DC: Regnery Publishing, 2012), 37.

54. Ibid., 38.

55. Ibid., 40.

56. *Whitson v Knox County Board of Education*, No. 10-6240.

57. John W. Whitehead, *The End of Man* (Westchester, IL: Crossway Books, 1986), 29.

CHAPTER FOUR – SECOND AMENDMENT

1. Joyce Lee Malcolm, *To Keep and Bear Arms* (Cambridge, MA: Harvard University Press, 1994), 45.

2. Ibid., 127.

3. Ibid., 129.

4. Ibid., 123.

5. Ibid., 130.

6. Ibid., 166.

7. Ibid., 139.

8. Ibid., 146.

9. Ibid., 159.

10. Ibid., 161.

11. Cesare Beccaria, *An Essay on Crimes & Punishments* (New York: Stephen Gould, 1809), 124-125.

12. Thomas Jefferson, *The Commonplace Book of Thomas Jefferson: A Repertory of His Ideas on Government*, ed. Gilbert Chinard (Baltimore: Johns Hopkins Press, 1926), 314.

13. Joyce Lee Malcolm, *To Keep and Bear Arms* (Cambridge, MA: Harvard University Press, 1994), 164.

14. David Bodenhammer & James Ely, The *Bill of Rights in Modern America* (Bloomington, IN: Indiana University Press, 2008), 98.

15. Alexander Hamilton, James Madison, John Jay, *The Federalist Papers* (New York: Bantam Books, 1982), 242.

16. David Bodenhammer & James Ely, The *Bill of Rights in Modern America* (Bloomington, IN: Indiana University Press, 2008), 95.

17. Ibid., 100.

18. Ibid., 103–105.

19. *District of Columbia v. Heller*, 554 U.S. 570 (2008); also see McDonald v. Chicago, 561 U.S. 3025 (2010).

20. John R. Lott Jr., *More Guns, Less Crime: Understanding Crime and Gun Control Laws* (Chicago: University Of Chicago Press, 2010)

CHAPTER FIVE – FOURTH AMENDMENT

1. *Camara v. Municipal Court*, 387 U.S. 523, 528–529 (1967).

2. *Illinois v. Gates*, 462 U.S. 213 (1983).

3. *Camara v. Municipal Court*, 387 U.S. 523, 528–529 (1967).

4. Gene Healy, *Go Directly to Jail* (Washington, DC: Cato Institute, 2004), 53–55.

5. *Murray's Lessee v. Hoboken Land & Improvement Co.*, 59 U.S. 272 (1856).

6. Charles M. Wetterer, *The Fourth Amendment* (Springfield, NJ: Enslow Publishers, Inc., 1998), 28.

7. *Carroll v. United States*, 267 U.S. 132 (1925).

8. *Oliver v. United States*, 466 U.S. 170 (1984).

9. *California v. Ciraolo*, 476 U.S. 207 (1986).

10. *California v. Greenwood*, 486 U.S. 35 (1988).

11. *United States v. Miller*, 425 U.S. 435 (1976).

12. *United States v. Davis*, 482 F. 2d 893.

13. *Skinner v. Railway Lab. Execs. Ass'n*, 489 U.S. 602 (1989).

14. Ryan Gabrielson," Sobriety Checkpoints Catch Unlicensed Drivers", *New York Times*, February 13, 2010.

15. Gene Healy, *Go Directly to Jail* (Washington, DC: Cato Institute, 2004), 53.

16. *Atwater v. Lago Vista*, 532 U.S. 318, 318 (2001).

17. *Atwater v. Lago Vista*, 532 U.S. 318, 360-372 (2001), O'Connor dissenting.

18. *United States v Sokolow*, 490 U.S. 1 (1989).

19. Cynthia Lee, *The Fourth Amendment Searches and Seizures* (Amherst, NY: Prometheus Books, 2011), 319.

20. *Illinois v. Wardlow*, 528 U.S. 119, 132 (1999), Stevens dissenting.

21. *United States v. Drayton*, 536 U.S. 194 (2002).

22. *Kentucky v. King*, 131 S. Ct. 1849 (2011), Ginsburg dissenting.

23. David Bodenhammer & James Ely, *The Bill of Rights in Modern America* (Bloomington, IN: Indiana University Press, 2008), 159.

24. *Weeks v. United States*, 232 U.S. 383 (1914).

25. *Burdeau v. McDowell*, 256 U.S. 465 (1921).

26. *Nix v. Williams*, 467 US 431 (1984).

27. *United States v. Leon*, 468 U.S. 897 (1984).

28. Cynthia Lee, *The Fourth Amendment Searches and Seizures* (Amherst, NY: Prometheus Books, 2011), 203.

29. *Schmerber v. California*, 384 U.S. 757, 767 (1966).

30. Cynthia Lee, *The Fourth Amendment Searches and Seizures* (Amherst, NY: Prometheus Books, 2011), 307.

31. *Florence v. Board of Chosen Freeholders*, 566 U.S. ___ (2012).

32. *California Bankers Assn. v. Shultz*, 416 U.S. 21 (1974), Douglas dissenting.

33. John Podesta, "USA PATRIOT Act: The Good, the Bad, and the Sunset," American Bar Association, Winter 2002.

34. Naomi Wolf, "JSoc: Obama's Secret Assassins," *The Guardian*, February 2013.

35. James Bamford, *The Shadow Factory* (New York: Anchor Books, 2009), 319.

36. Ibid., 116.

37. John W. Whitehead, *A Government of Wolves* (New York: Select Books, 2013), 110.

38. Ibid., 80.

39. Mike Lee, *Our Lost Constitution* (New York: Sentinel, 2015), 126.

40. Ibid., 127.

41. Geoffrey R. Stone, *Perilous Times* (New York: W. W. Norton & Co., 2004), 394–395.

42. *Osborn v. United States*, 385 U.S. 323, 343 (1966), Douglas dissenting.

43. *Camara v. Municipal Court*, 387 U.S. 523, 528–529 (1967).

CHAPTER SIX – FIFTH AMENDMENT

1. *Green v. United States*, 355 U.S. 184, 187 (1957).

2. *Bartkus v. Illinois*, 359 U.S. 121 (1959), Black dissenting.

3. *Fox v. State of Ohio*, 46 U.S. 410, 439 (1847), McLean dissenting.

4. *Moore v. People*, 55 U.S. 13, 22 (1852), McLean dissenting.

5. *Bartkus v. Illinois*, 359 U.S. 121 (1959), Black dissenting.

6. *Waller v. Florida*, 397 U.S. 387 (1970).

7. *Abbate v. United States*, 359 U.S. 187, 203 (1959), Black dissenting.

8. *United States v. All Assets of G.P.S. Automotive Corp.* 66 F. 3d 483 (2d Cir. 1995).

9. Leonard W. Levy, *Origins of the Fifth Amendment* (New York: Macmillan Publishing Co., 1986), 63.

10. Ibid., 434.

11. Ibid., 107.

12. Ibid., 108.

13. Ibid., 272, 313.

14. *Kastigar v. United States*, 406 U.S. 441 (1972).

15. Ibid., 467, 469.

16. *Ullmann v. United States*, 350 U.S. 422, 445 (1956), Douglas dissenting.

17. *Brown v. Walker*, 161 U.S. 591, 637 (1896), Field dissenting.

18. Leonard W. Levy, *Origins of the Fifth Amendment* (New York: Macmillan Publishing Co., 1986), 428.

19. Gene Healy, *Go Directly to Jail* (Washington, DC: Cato Institute, 2004), 62.

20. Ibid., 63

21. *Miranda v. Arizona*, 384 U.S. 436 (1966).

22. *Berghuis v. Thompkins*, 560 U.S. 370, (2010), Sotomayor dissenting.

23. David K. Shipler, *Rights at Risk* (New York: Alfred A. Knopf, 2012), 38.

24. *Illinois v. Perkins*, 496 U.S. 292 (1990).

25. The Innocence Project is a non-profit legal clinic affiliated with the Benjamin N. Cardozo School of Law at Yeshiva University in New York, dedicated to exonerating wrongfully convicted people through DNA testing. See their website at http://www.innocenceproject.org/.

26. *Bram v. United States*, 168 U.S. 532 (1897).

27. *Arizona v. Fulminante*, 499 U.S. 279 (1991).

28. David K. Shipler, *Rights at Risk* (New York: Alfred A. Knopf, 2012), 53–63, 72.

29. Ibid., 77–79.

30. *Calder v. Bull*, 3 U.S. 386, 388 (1798).

31. *Kelo v. City of New London*, 545 U.S. 469 (2005).

32. Andrew P. Napolitano, *Constitutional Chaos* (Nashville, TN: Thomas Nelson, 2004), 69.

33. *Pumpelly v. Green Bay Company*, 80 U.S. 166 (1871).

34. *Pennsylvania Coal Co. v. Mahon*, 260 U.S. 393, 415 (1922).

35. *Penn Central Transportation Co. v. New York City*, 438 U.S. 104 (1978).

36. Adam Freedman, *The Naked Constitution* (New York: Broadside Books, 2012), 250.

37 Mark R. Levin, *Liberty and Tyranny* (New York: Threshold Editions, 2009), 201.

38. Shaila Dewan, "Law Lets I.R.S. Seize Accounts on Suspicion, No Crime Required," *New York Times*, Oct. 25, 2014.

39. Andrew Schneider and Mary Pat Flaherty, "Drug Law Leaves Trail of Innocents," *Chicago Tribune*, Aug. 11, 1991.

40. Marian R. Williams et al., *Policing for Profit* (Arlington, VA: Institute for Justice, 2010), 18-23.

41. Paul Craig Roberts and Lawrence M. Stratton, *The Tyranny of Good Intentions* (New York: Three Rivers Press, 2008), 128.

42. Marian R. Williams et al., *Policing for Profit* (Arlington, VA: Institute for Justice, 2010), 18-23.

43. John Yoder and Brad Cates, "Government Self-interest Corrupted a Crime-fighting Tool Into an Evil," *Washington Post*, Sept. 18, 2014.

44. *Calero-Toledo v. Pearson Yacht Leasing Co.*, 416 U.S. 663, 693 (1974).

45. Paul Craig Roberts and Lawrence M. Stratton, *The Tyranny of Good Intentions* (New York: Three Rivers Press, 2008), 104–106.

CHAPTER SEVEN – SIXTH AMENDMENT

1. Paul Craig Roberts and Lawrence M. Stratton, *The Tyranny of Good Intentions* (New York: Three Rivers Press, 2008), 131.

2. Ibid.

3. Gene Healy, *Go Directly to Jail* (Washington, DC: Cato Institute, 2004), 116.

4. Akhil Reed Amar, *America's Constitution* (New York: Random House, 2006), 241.

5. Michael Paulsen and Luke Paulsen, *The Constitution An Introduction* (New York: Basic Books, 2015), 111.

6. David K. Shipler, *Rights at Risk* (New York: Alfred A. Knopf, 2012), 107.

7. Ibid., 115–116.

8. Harvey A. Silverglate, *Three Felonies a Day* (New York: Encounter Books, 2009).

9. *United States v. Singleton*, 165 F. 3d 1297 (10th Cir. 1999, en banc).

10. Andrew P. Napolitano, *Constitutional Chaos* (Nashville, TN: Thomas Nelson, 2004), 98.

11. Harvey A. Silverglate, *Three Felonies a Day* (New York: Encounter Books, 2009), 89.

12. The American Bar Association passed a resolution opposing the practice of prosecutors taking into consideration the fact that an organization has provided counsel to an employee in making a determination of whether an organization has been cooperative in the context of a government investigation. (Resolution 302B, August 7, 2006).

13. Harvey A. Silverglate, *Three Felonies a Day* (New York: Encounter Books, 2009), 143.

14. Paul Craig Roberts and Lawrence M. Stratton, *The Tyranny of Good Intentions* (New York: Three Rivers Press, 2008), 82.

15. Paul Craig Roberts and Lawrence M. Stratton, *The Tyranny of Good Intentions* (New York: Three Rivers Press, 2008).

16. *Santobello v. New York*, 404 U.S. 257, 260 (1971).

17. John H. Langbein, "Land Without Plea Bargaining: How the Germans Do It" (1979). *Faculty Scholarship Series*, Paper 534.

18. *Johnson v. Zerbst*, 304 U.S. 458 (1938).

19. *Gideon v. Wainwright*, 372 U.S. 335 (1963).

CHAPTER EIGHT – FOURTEENTH AMENDMENT

1. Section One of The Civil Rights Act of 1866 provides that all citizens "of every race and color" shall have the right "to make and enforce contracts, to sue, be parties, and give evidence, to inherit, purchase, lease, sell, hold, and convey real and personal property, and to full and equal benefit of all laws and proceedings for the security of person and property, as is enjoyed by white citizens, and shall be subject to like punishment."

2. *Griswold v. Connecticut*, 381 U.S. 479 (1965), Black dissenting.

3. Raoul Berger, *Government by Judiciary* (Indianapolis, IN: Liberty Fund, 1997), 50.

4. Ibid., 38.

5. Ibid., 401.

6. Ibid., 32.

7. Ibid., 51.

8. Ibid., 50.

9. Ibid., 36.

10. Ibid., 169.

11. Ibid., 33.

12. Ibid., 51.

13. Ibid., 51.

14. *Adamson v. California*, 332 U.S. 46 (1947), Black dissenting.

15. *Campbell v. Morris*, 3 H. & McH. 535, 554 (Md. 1797); Abbott v. Bayley, 6 Pick. 89, 91 (Mass. 1827).

16. Raoul Berger, *Government by Judiciary* (Indianapolis, IN: Liberty Fund, 1997), 181.

17. Ibid., 37.

18. Ibid.

19. *Baker v. Carr*, 369 U.S. 186 (1962).

20. Raoul Berger, *Government by Judiciary* (Indianapolis, IN: Liberty Fund, 1997), 94.

21. Ibid., 90.

22. Ibid., 95.

23. Ibid., 91.

24. *Baker v. Carr*, 369 U.S. 186, 332–334 (1962), Harlan dissenting.

25. *Baker v. Carr*, 369 U.S. 186, 269–270,280–284 (1962), Frankfurter dissenting.

26. Ibid., 310–311.

27. Ibid., 323.

28. *Carr v. Corning*, 182 F. 2d 14, 17.

29. Raoul Berger, *Government by Judiciary* (Indianapolis, IN: Liberty Fund, 1997), 140.

30. Ibid., 137.

31. Ibid., 147–148.

32. Ibid., 143.

33. *Garnes v. McCann*, 20 Ohio St. 198, 211 (1871).

34. *Stoutmeyer v. Duffy*, 7 Nev. 342, 348 (1872).

35. *Ward v. Flood*, 48 Cal. 36 (1874).

36. *Cory v. Carter*, 48 Ind. 327, 359 (1874).

37. *Bertonneau v. Bd. Of Directors*, 3 F. Cas. 294 (Cir. Ct. D. La. 1878) (No. 1, 361).

38. *Plessy v. Ferguson*, 163 U.S. 537, 544 (1896).

39. Learned Hand, "The Bill of Rights" (1958).

40. *Cooper v. Aaron*, 358 U.S. 1, 15 (1958).

41. Raoul Berger, *Government by Judiciary* (Indianapolis, IN: Liberty Fund, 1997), 399.

42. Ibid., 189.

43. Ibid., 78.

44. Ibid., 189.

45. Ibid., 78.

46. *Slaughterhouse Cases*, 83 U.S. 36, 77–78 (1873).

47. Ibid., 37.

48. Ibid., 78.

49. *Adamson v. California*, 332 U.S. 46, 62–63 (1947), Frankfurter concurring.

50. *Bartkus v. Illinois*, 359 U.S. 121, 124 (1959).

51. *United States v. Cruikshank*, 92 U.S. 542, 552 (1875).

52. *Maxwell v. Dow*, 176 U.S. 581, 586 (1900).

53. *Baldwin v. Missouri*, 281 U.S. 586, 595 (1930).

54. Raoul Berger, *Government by Judiciary* (Indianapolis, IN: Liberty Fund, 1997), 399.

55. *School Dist. of Abington Tp. v. Schempp*, 374 U.S. 203, 309–310 (1963), Stewart dissenting.

56. Stanley Morrison, "Does the Fourteenth Amendment Incorporate the Bill of Rights? The Judicial Interpretation," *2 Stan. L. Rev*, 140 (1949): 143–157.

57. Raoul Berger, *Government by Judiciary* (Indianapolis, IN: Liberty Fund, 1997), 179.

58. Eugene Hickok, *The Bill of Rights Original Meaning and Current Understanding* (Charlottesville, VA: University Press of Virginia, 1991), 13.

59. *Hurtado v. California*, 110 U.S. 516, 534–535 (1884).

60. Raoul Berger, *Government by Judiciary* (Indianapolis, IN: Liberty Fund, 1997), 222.

61. Ibid., 230.

62. *Duncan v. Louisiana*, 391 U.S. 145, 172 (1968), Harlan dissenting.

63. Raoul Berger, *Government by Judiciary* (Indianapolis, IN: Liberty Fund, 1997), 395.

64. Ibid., 231.

65. Ibid., 227.

66. *Hurtado v. California*, 110 U.S. 516, 534–535 (1884).

67. *Adamson v. California*, 332 U.S. 46, 111 (1947), Black dissenting.

68. *Harper v. Virginia Bd. of Elections*, 383 U.S. 663, 675–676 (1966), Black dissenting.

69. *Adamson v. California*, 332 U.S. 46, 79 (1947), Black dissenting.

70. Raoul Berger, *Government by Judiciary* (Indianapolis, IN: Liberty Fund, 1997), 282.

71. *Robinson v. California*, 370 U.S. 660, 689 (1962), White dissenting.

72. John W. Whitehead, *The Second American Revolution* (Westchester, IL: Crossway Books, 1985), 213.

73. *Romer v. Evans*, 517 U.S. 620 (1996).

CHAPTER NINE – CLAUSES

1. Alexander Hamilton, James Madison, John Jay, *The Federalist Papers* (New York: Bantam Books, 1982), 210.

2. Mark R. Levin, *Liberty and Tyranny* (New York: Threshold Editions, 2009), 101.

3. *United States v. Butler,* 297 U.S. 1, 65–66 (1936).

4. *Helvering v. Davis*, 301 U.S. 619, 640 (1937).

5. Alexander Hamilton, James Madison, John Jay, *The Federalist Papers* (New York: Bantam Books, 1982), 55.

6. Robert G. Natelson, "The Enumerated Powers of States," *Nevada Law Journal* 3:469 (2003), 491.

7. *United States v. Alfonso Lopez, Jr.,* 514 U.S. 549, 584 (1995), Thomas concurring.

8. Alexander Hamilton, James Madison, John Jay, *The Federalist Papers* (New York: Bantam Books, 1982), 170.

9. Ibid., 80.

10. Robert G. Natelson. "The Enumerated Powers of States," *Nevada Law Journal* 3 (2003): 469–494.

11. Ibid., 487.

12. Robert G. Natelson, *The Original Constitution* (Los Angeles: Tenth Amendment Center, 2011), 103.

13. Robert G. Natelson, "The Enumerated Powers of States," *Nevada Law Journal* 3:469 (2003), 481–488.

14. *United States v. Dewitt*, 76 U.S. 41, 44 (1869).

15. *Oliver Iron Co. v. Lord*, 262 U.S. 172 (1923).

16. *Carter v. Carter Coal Co.*, 298 U.S. 238 (1936).

17. Alexander Hamilton, James Madison, John Jay, *The Federalist Papers* (New York: Bantam Books, 1982), 112.

18. Randy E. Barnett, "The Original Meaning of the Commerce Clause," 68 *The University of Chicago Law Review*, (2001): 116.

19. *Wickard v. Filburn*, 317 U.S. 111 (1942).

20. *NLRB v. Jones & Laughlin Steel Corp.*, 301 U.S. 1 (1937).

21. *United States v. Rock Royal Cooperative, Inc.*, 307 U.S. 568 (1939).

22. *United States v. Darby Lumber Co.*, 312 U.S. 100 (1941).

23. *Fry v. United States*, 421 U.S. 542 (1975).

24. Robert G. Natelson. "Tempering the Commerce Power," *Montana Law Review* 68:95 (2007), 117.

25. *Scarborough v. United States*, 431 U.S. 563 (1977).

26. *Hodel v. Virginia Surface Mining and Reclamation Association, Inc.*, 452 U.S. 264 (1981).

27. *Hodel v. Indiana*, 452 U.S. 314 (1981).

28. *Gonzales v. Raich*, 545 U.S. 1, 45 (2005), O'Connor dissenting.

29. Ibid., 49.

30. *Gonzales v. Raich*, 545 U.S. 1 (2005), Thomas dissenting.

31. Alexander Hamilton, James Madison, John Jay, *The Federalist Papers* (New York: Bantam Books, 1982), 155.

32. Robert G. Natelson. "Tempering the Commerce Power," *Montana Law Review* 68:95 (2007): 101.

33. Christopher Wolfe, *The Rise of Modern Judicial Review* (New York: Basic Books, 1986), 27.

34. *United States v. Fisher*, 6 U.S. 358, 396(1805).

35. *McCulloch v. Maryland*, 17 U.S. 316 (1819).

36. Adam Freedman, *The Naked Constitution* (New York: Broadside Books, 2012), 242.

37. *Home Building & Loan Association v. Blaisdell*, 290 U.S. 398 (1934).

38. *West Coast Hotel Co. v. Parrish*, 300 U.S. 379, 391 (1937).

39. Richard A. Epstein, "Toward a Revitalization of the Contract Clause," 51 *University of Chicago Law Review* (1984): 703.

40. *West Coast Hotel Co. v. Parrish*, 300 U.S. 379 (1937).

41. *Adkins v. Children's Hosp.*, 261 U.S. 525, 545 (1923).

42. *Allied Structural Steel Co. v. Spannaus*, 438 U.S. 234 (1978).

43. *Energy Reserves Group v. Kansas P. & L. Co.,* 459 U.S. 400, 417 (1983).

44. *Exxon Corp. v. Eagerton*, 462 U.S. 176, 191 (1983).

45. *Collins v. Youngblood*, 497 U.S. 37 (1990).

46. *Calder v. Bull*, 3 U.S. 386 (1798).

47. *Satterlee v. Mathewson*, 27 U.S. 380 (1829), Johnson, concurring.

48. Paul Craig Roberts and Lawrence M. Stratton, *The Tyranny of Good Intentions* (New York: Three Rivers Press, 2008), 65–67.

49. Harold J. Krent, "The Puzzling Boundary Between Criminal and Civil Retroactive Lawmaking," *The Georgetown Law Journal*, 84:2143 (1996): 2164.

50. Paul Craig Roberts and Lawrence M. Stratton, *The Tyranny of Good Intentions* (New York: Three Rivers Press, 2008), 68–75.

51. *Fernandez-Vargas v. Gonzales*, 04-1376 (2006), Stevens dissenting.

CHAPTER TEN – OVERCRIMINALIZATION

1. U.S. Constitution Art. 1, Sec. 1.

2. Mike Lee, *Our Lost Constitution* (New York: Sentinel, 2015), 7.

3. Philip Hamburger, *Is Administrative Law Unlawful?* (Chicago: University of Chicago Press, 2014).

4. *J. W. Hampton, Jr., & Co. v. United States*, 276 U.S. 394, 409, (1928).

5. *National Broadcasting Co., Inc. v. United States*, 319 U.S. 190, 215 (1943).

6. *Mistretta v. United States*, 488 U.S. 361, 372–373 (1989).

7. *Whitman v. American Trucking Assns., Inc.,* 531 U.S. 457 (2001).

8. Robert A. Levy and William Mellor, *The Dirty Dozen* (Washington, DC: Cato Institute, 2009), 75.

9. Milton and Rose Friedman, *Free to Choose* (New York: Avon Books, 1981), 283–285.

10. James W. Lucas, *Timely Renewed* (Lexington, KY: Create Space, 2010), 50–55.

11. Adam Freedman, *The Naked Constitution* (New York: Broadside Books, 2012), 80–81.

12. Paul Craig Roberts and Lawrence M. Stratton, *The Tyranny of Good Intentions* (New York: Three Rivers Press, 2008), 15.

13. *Patterson v. New York*, 432 U.S. 197, 201 (1977).

14. James A. Strazzela, *The Federalization of Criminal Law* (Washington, DC: American Bar Association, 1998), 50.

15. *Perez v. United States*, 402 U.S. 146, 158 (1971), Stewart dissenting.

16. The CATO Institute's National Police Misconduct Reporting Project 2010 Annual Report, The CATO Institute, Washington DC.

17. John W. Whitehead, *A Government of Wolves* (New York: Select Books, 2013), 8.

18. Ibid., 64.

19. Ibid., 64–67.

20. Radley Balko, "Overkill: The Rise of Paramilitary Police Raids in America," The CATO Institute, Washington, DC, 2006, 12.

21. Ibid., 48.

22. John W. Whitehead, *A Government of Wolves* (New York: Select Books, 2013), 60.

23. Jeffrey A. Roth, Christopher S. Koper, "Impact Evaluation of the Public Safety and Recreational Firearms Use Protection Act of 1994", Urban Institute, March 13, 1997; Christopher S. Koper, "An Updated Assessment of the Federal Assault Weapons Ban: Impacts on Gun Markets and Gun Violence, 1994-2003," Report to the National Institute of Justice, June 2004.

24. Russ Siba et al., "Are Zero Tolerance Policies Effective in the Schools?" A report by the American Psychological Association, Adopted August 9, 2006.

25. Georgia Appleseed Center for Law and Justice, *Effective Student Discipline: Keeping Kids in Class*, June 2011.

26. *Kolender v. Lawson*, 461 U.S. 352, 357 (1983).

27. *Grayned v. City of Rockford*, 408 U.S. 104 (1972).

28. *United States v. Weyhrauch*, 548 F. 3d 1237 (2008).

29. Harvey A. Silverglate, *Three Felonies a Day* (New York: Encounter Books, 2009), 117.

30. Ibid., 161–162.

31. Ibid., 119.

32. *Avoyelles Sportsmen's League, Inc. v. Marsh*, 715 F. 2d 897 (5th Cir. 1983).

33. *United States v. Mills*, 817 F. Supp. 1546 (N.D. Fla. 1993).

34. Mike Lee, *Our Lost Constitution* (New York: Sentinel, 2015), 70.

35. *American Mining Congress v. U.S. EPA*, 824 F. 2d 1177, 1189 (1987).

36. This statement is required by the EPA to appear on the product label. See 40 CFR 156.10(i), and the EPA Label Review Manual. This was found on a can of Scrubbing Bubbles Bathroom Cleaner, manufactured by S. C. Johnson & Son, Inc.

37. Alexander Hamilton, James Madison, John Jay, *The Federalist Papers* (New York: Bantam Books, 1982), 317.

38. *Sedima v. Imrex Company, Inc.*, 473 U.S. 479, 499, 105 S. Ct. 3275 (1985).

39. *Scheidler v. National Organization for Women, Inc.*, 04-1244 (2006).

40. 42 U.S.C. § 7413(c)(6); 33 U.S.C. § 1319(c)(6).

41. *United States v. Brittain*, 931 F. 2d 1413 (10th Cir. 1991).

42. *United States v. Park* 421 U.S. 658 (1975).

43. *Bouie v. City of Columbia*, 378 US 347, 351 (1964).

44. *United States v. Bass*, 404 US 336, 347 (1971).

45. *Jerman v. Carlisle*, 08-1200, 130 S. Ct. 1605 (2010).

46. *Estelle v. Williams*, 425 U.S. 501, 503 (1976).

47. *Taylor v. Kentucky*, 436 U.S. 478, 483 (1978).

48. *Morissette v. United States*, 342 U.S. 246, 250–251 (1952).

49. *Utah v. Blue*, 53 Pac. 978, 980 (1898).

50. For actions which are obviously wrongful, such as murder, rape and robbery, it is not necessary to prove intent. The law properly assumes that a person committing these acts would know that they are wrong. But for the thousands of other "regulatory" crimes, which criminalize conduct that is wrongful only because it is prohibited by law, intent is an absolutely essential requirement.

51. Brian W. Walsh and Tiffany M. Joslyn, *Without Intent: How Congress is Eroding the Criminal Intent Requirement in Federal Law* (Washington, DC: Heritage Foundation, 2010), 22.

52. These cases tend to support strict liability:

> *United States v. International Minerals & Chemicals Corp.* 402 U.S. 558 (1971)
>
> *United States v. Park* 421 U.S. 658 (1975)
>
> *United States v. Weitzenhoff* 35 F. 3d 1275 (9th Cir. 1993)
>
> *United States v. Freed* 401 U.S. 601 (1971)

These cases tend to support mens rea requirement:

> *Liparota v. United States* 471 U.S. 419 (1985)
>
> *Ratzlaf v. United States* 510 U.S. 135 (1994)
>
> *Staples v. United States* 511 U.S. 600 (1994)
>
> *Ahmad v. United States* 101 F. 3d 386 (5th Cir. 1996).

53. *Lambert v. California*, 355 U.S. 225, 228 (1957).

54. *Thorpe v. Florida*, 377 So. 2d 221, 223 (1979).

55. *United States v. Rollins*, 706 F. Supp. 742 (1989).

56. Paul Craig Roberts and Lawrence M. Stratton, *The Tyranny of Good Intentions* (New York: Three Rivers Press, 2008), 47–49.

57. *Hanousek v. United States*, 528 U.S. 1102 (2000), Thomas, dissenting from the denial of certiorari).

58. *Bryan v. United States*, 524 U.S. 184, 192 (1998).

59. The default mens rea requirement must apply to all elements of the offense—that is, both the acts that constitute the crime and knowledge of the criminality of the underlying conduct. Also, in writing this new statute, Congress may decide to include the provision that this new default mens rea requirement would apply only to cases that have not yet gone to trial. It might be considered too disruptive to allow this new law to reopen cases where criminal proceedings have already begun.

CHAPTER ELEVEN – INFORMED VOTER

1. Pew Research Center Survey, July 26–29, 2012.

2. NY Times/CBS Survey, April 23–27, 2004.

3. Neil Postman, *Amusing Ourselves to Death* (London: Penguin Books, 2006), 141.

4. David L. Hudson Jr., *Let the Students Speak* (Boston: Beacon Press, 2011), 185–186.

5. Peter Levine, *The Future of Democracy* (Lebanon, NH: University Press of New England, 2007), 125–132.

6. Jonathan Gould, *Guardian of Democracy*: The Civic Mission of Schools, www.civicmissionofschools.org.

7. Sam Dillon, "U.S. Students Remain Poor at History, Tests Show," *New York Times*, 14 June, 2011.

8. Phyllis Schlafly, "What's Happened to Public School Curriculum?", *Phyllis Schlafly Report*, November, 2010.

9. *Minersville Sch. Dist. v. Board of Educ.*, 310 U.S. 586, 599 (1940).

10. Thomas Sowell, "Toxic Teachings Do Harm To America's Schoolkids," *Atlanta Journal-Constitution*, Jan. 8, 2013.

11. Phyllis Schlafly, "What's Happened to Public School Curriculum?", *Phyllis Schlafly Report*, November, 2010.

12. Michael Kazin, "Howard Zinn's History Lessons," *Dissent*, Spring, 2004.

13. Lynne Cheney, "The End of History," *Wall Street Journal*, 20 October, 1994.

14. Gary A. Tobin and Dennis R. Ybarra, *The Trouble With Textbooks* (Lanham, MD: Lexington Books, 2008), 95–101.

15. Phyllis Schlafly, "What's Happened to Public School Curriculum?", *Phyllis Schlafly Report*, November, 2010.

16. Ryan O'Donnell and James Phillips, "Textbook Appeasement: The State Department and the Islamic Saudi Academy," The Heritage Foundation, September 2, 2008.

17. Diane Ravitch, *The Language Police* (New York: Alfred A. Knopf, 2003).

CHAPTER TWELVE – ECONOMIC FREEDOM

1. Terry Miller et al., *2013 Index of Economic Freedom* (Washington, DC: The Heritage Foundation, 2013), 87.

2. Myron Brilliant, "Good Business Demands Good Governance," *2013 Index of Economic Freedom* (Washington, DC: The Heritage Foundation, 2013).

3. James Gwartney et al., *Economic Freedom of the World: 2015 Annual Report* (Canada: The Fraser Institute, 2015). Reprinted with permission. Please refer to their website www.freetheworld.com for more information.

4. Ibid.

5. Terry Miller et al., *2013 Index of Economic Freedom* (Washington, DC: The Heritage Foundation, 2013).

6. Ibid.

7. Horst Feldmann, "Economic Freedom and Unemployment," *Economic Freedom of the World: 2010 Annual Report* (Canada: The Fraser Institute, 2010). Reprinted with permission.   Please   refer   to   their   website www.freetheworld.com for more information.

8. Milton and Rose Friedman, *Free to Choose* (New York: Avon Books, 1981), xvi, 58.

9. Obiageli Ezekwesili, "Fighting Poverty Through Economic Freedom," *2012 Index of Economic Freedom* (Washington, DC: The Heritage Foundation, 2012).

10. Matthew Mitchell, "Economic Freedom and Economic Privilege," *2013 Index of Economic Freedom* (Washington, DC: The Heritage Foundation, 2013).

11. The number and composition of the components of this index will vary across time. This presents a problem similar to that confronted when calculating GDP or a price index over time when the underlying bundle of goods and services is changing from one year to another. In order to correct for this problem and assure comparability across time, the Fraser Institute has done the same thing that statisticians analyzing national income do: they have chain-linked the data.
    The base year for the chain-link index is 2000. Changes in a country's chain-linked index through time are based only on changes in components that were present in adjoining years.
    The chain-linked methodology means that a country's rating will change across time periods only when there is a change in ratings for components present during adjacent years. This is precisely what one would want when making comparisons across time periods.

12. James Gwartney et al., *Economic Freedom of the World: 2015 Annual Report* (Canada: The Fraser Institute, 2015).

13. Milton and Rose Friedman, *Free to Choose* (New York: Avon Books, 1981), 118.

14. James Gwartney et al., *Economic Freedom of the World: 2015 Annual Report* (Canada: The Fraser Institute, 2015).

15. Mike Lee, *Our Lost Constitution* (New York: Sentinel, 2015), 63.

16. Burton Folsom, Jr., *New Deal or Raw Deal* (New York: Threshold Editions, 2009), 56–57.

17. Ibid., 67.

18. Ibid., 69.

19. Mike Lee, *Our Lost Constitution* (New York: Sentinel, 2015), 73.

CHAPTER THIRTEEN – WAR FEVER

1. *Korematsu v. United States*, 584 F. Supp. 1406 (ND Cal. 1984).

2. *Ex parte Milligan*, 71 U.S. (4 Wall.) 2, 120–121 (1866).

3. *Hirabayashi v. United States*, 320 U.S. 81, 110 (1943), Murphy concurring.

4. Geoffrey R. Stone, *Perilous Times* (New York: W. W. Norton & Co., 2004), 37–39.

5. Ibid., 42.

6. Ibid., 48.

7. Ibid., 67.

8. Ibid., 68.

9. Ibid., 59.

10. *Harris v. Nelson*, 394 U.S. 286, 290–291 (1969).

11. Geoffrey R. Stone, *Perilous Times* (New York: W. W. Norton & Co., 2004), 124.

12. Ibid., 111.

13. Ibid., 127.

14. Ibid., 145.

15. Ibid., 137.

16. Ibid., 152–153, 186.

17. Robert Justin Goldstein, *Political Repression in Modern America From 1870 to 1976* (Chicago: University of Illinois Press, 2001), 113.

18. *Shaffer v. United States*, 255 F. 886 (9th Cir. 1919).

19. Geoffrey R. Stone, *Perilous Times* (New York: W. W. Norton & Co., 2004), 171.

20. Ibid., 193.

21. Ibid., 172.

22. Robert Justin Goldstein, *Political Repression in Modern America From 1870 to 1976* (Chicago: University of Illinois Press, 2001), 114.

23. Geoffrey R. Stone, *Perilous Times* (New York: W. W. Norton & Co., 2004), 173.

24. Ibid., 166.

25. Irving Brant, *The Bill of Rights* (New York: Bobbs-Merrill, 1965), 396.

26. Robert Justin Goldstein, *Political Repression in Modern America From 1870 to 1976* (Chicago: University of Illinois Press, 2001), 127.

27. Richard M. Fried, *Nightmare in Red* (New York: Oxford University Press, 1990), 40.

28. Geoffrey R. Stone, *Perilous Times* (New York: W. W. Norton & Co., 2004), 223–224.

29. Robert Justin Goldstein, *Political Repression in Modern America From 1870 to 1976* (Chicago: University of Illinois Press, 2001), 215, 253–254, 324.

30. Ibid., 250.

31. Ibid., 245.

32. Geoffrey R. Stone, *Perilous Times* (New York: W. W. Norton & Co., 2004), 246–248.

33. Ibid., 251.

34. *Baumgartner v. United States*, 322 U.S. 665 (1944).

35. Geoffrey R. Stone, *Perilous Times* (New York: W. W. Norton & Co., 2004), 280.

36. Robert Justin Goldstein, *Political Repression in Modern America From 1870 to 1976* (Chicago: University of Illinois Press, 2001), 300.

37. Ibid., 300, 309, 311, 369.

38. Ibid., 301, 304, 309.

39. Geoffrey R. Stone, *Perilous Times* (New York: W. W. Norton & Co., 2004), 342–351.

40. Robert Justin Goldstein, *Political Repression in Modern America From 1870 to 1976* (Chicago: University of Illinois Press, 2001), 304.

41. Ibid., 294.

42. Geoffrey R. Stone, *Perilous Times* (New York: W. W. Norton & Co., 2004), 327.

43. Ibid., 340.

44. Robert Justin Goldstein, *Political Repression in Modern America From 1870 to 1976* (Chicago: University of Illinois Press, 2001), 363, 409.

45. Geoffrey R. Stone, *Perilous Times* (New York: W. W. Norton & Co., 2004), 422.

46. Ibid., 355.

47. Robert Justin Goldstein, *Political Repression in Modern America From 1870 to 1976* (Chicago: University of Illinois Press, 2001), 344.

48. Geoffrey R. Stone, *Perilous Times* (New York: W. W. Norton & Co., 2004), 365.

49. Robert Justin Goldstein, *Political Repression in Modern America From 1870 to 1976* (Chicago: University of Illinois Press, 2001), 323.

50. Geoffrey R. Stone, *Perilous Times* (New York: W. W. Norton & Co., 2004), 340.

51. Robert Justin Goldstein, *Political Repression in Modern America From 1870 to 1976* (Chicago: University of Illinois Press, 2001), 324.

52. Ibid., 332.

53. Ibid., 387.

54. Ibid., 331, 368–369.

55. Ibid., 411.

56. Ibid., 411–412.

57. Ibid., 407, 448, 460, 471, 481–483.

58. Geoffrey R. Stone, *Perilous Times* (New York: W. W. Norton & Co., 2004), 471, 488–492.

59. Robert Justin Goldstein, *Political Repression in Modern America From 1870 to 1976* (Chicago: University of Illinois Press, 2001), 440.

60. Ibid., 448.

CHAPTER FOURTEEN – SUPREME COURT

1. Ralph A. Rossum, Federalism, *The Supreme Court, and the Seventeenth Amendment* (Lanham, MD: Lexington Books, 2001), 133.

2. Herbert J. Storing, *What the Anti-Federalists Were For* (Chicago: University of Chicago Press, 1981), 50.

3. Ibid.

4. Alexander Hamilton, James Madison, John Jay, *The Federalist Papers* (New York: Bantam Books, 1982), 393–394.

5. Barry Adamson, *Freedom of Religion the First Amendment and the Supreme Court* (Gretna, LA: Pelican Publishing Co., 2008), 216.

6. Thomas Jefferson, Letter to William Jarvis (September 28, 1820), H. A. Washington, *The Writings of Thomas Jefferson*, (New York: Derby & Jackson, 1859) 178.

7. *Home Building & Loan Assn. v. Blaisdell*, 290 U.S. 442–444 (1934).

8. *Nebbia v. New York*, 291 U.S. 502 (1934).

9. *United States v. Alvarez-Machain*, 504 U.S. 655 (1992).

10. Andrew P. Napolitano, *Constitutional Chaos* (Nashville, TN: Thomas Nelson, 2004), 4.

11. New *York v. United States, 505* U.S. 144, 157 (1992).

12. Thomas Jefferson, letter to Monsieur A. Coray, October 31, 1823. Andrew A. Lipscomb, *The Writings of Thomas Jefferson, vol. 15* (Washington, Thomas Jefferson Memorial Association of the U.S., 1903).

13. *Scott v. Sandford*, 60 U.S. 393, 621 (1856), Curtis dissenting.

14. Raoul Berger, *Government by Judiciary* (Indianapolis, IN: Liberty Fund, 1997), 319.

15. Ibid., 390.

16. Ibid., 397.

17. *United States v. Butler*, 297 U.S. 1, 62 (1936).

18. John W. Whitehead, *The Second American Revolution* (Westchester, IL: Crossway Books, 1985), 20.

19. Barry Adamson, *Freedom of Religion the First Amendment and the Supreme Court* (Gretna, LA: Pelican Publishing Co., 2008), 217.

20. David Bodenhammer & James Ely, *The Bill of Rights in Modern America* (Bloomington, IN: Indiana University Press, 2008), 26–32.

21. *Roe v. Wade, 410* U.S. 113 (1973).

22. Michael Paulsen and Luke Paulsen, *The Constitution An Introduction* (New York: Basic Books, 2015), 270.

23. Ibid., 274.

24. *Doe v. Bolton*, 410 U.S. 179, 221–222 (1973), White dissenting.

25. *Roe v. Wade*, 410 U.S. 113, 174 (1973), Rehnquist dissenting.

26. John Eidsmoe, *Christianity and the Constitution* (Grand Rapids, MI: Baker Book House, 1987), 393.

27. Raoul Berger, *Government by Judiciary* (Indianapolis, IN: Liberty Fund, 1997), 381.

28. Ibid., 405.

29. *South Carolina v. United States*, 199 U.S. 437, 448–449 (1905).

30. Michael Paulsen and Luke Paulsen, *The Constitution An Introduction* (New York: Basic Books, 2015), 187.

31. Ibid., 194.

32. Phyllis Schlafly, *The Supremacists: The Tyranny of Judges and How to Stop It* (Dallas: Spence Publishing Company, 2006), 8.

33. John Eidsmoe, *Christianity and the Constitution* (Grand Rapids, MI: Baker Book House, 1987), 392.

34. Raoul Berger, *Government by Judiciary* (Indianapolis, IN: Liberty Fund, 1997), 357.

35. Buckner F. Melton, Jr., *The Quotable Founding Fathers* (New York: Fall River Press, 2008), 58.

36. *Pierce v. Society of Sisters*, 268 U.S. 510, 534–535 (1925). This Supreme Court ruling said that it was unreasonable to interfere "with the liberty of parents and guardians to direct the upbringing and education of children under their control . . . The child is not the mere creature of the State; those who nurture him and direct his destiny have the right, coupled with the high duty, to recognize and prepare him for additional obligations."

37. Christopher Wolfe, *The Rise of Modern Judicial Review* (New York: Basic Books, 1986), 10.

38. James B. *Thayer*, "The Origin and Scope of the American Doctrine of Constitutional Law," *Harvard Law Review 7* (October 25, 1893): 133-134

39. James Bradley *Thayer, The Origin and Scope of The American Doctrine of Constitutional La*w (Boston: Little, Brown, and Company, 1893).

40. *Griswold v. Connecticut*, 381 U.S. 479, 520 (1965), Black dissenting.

41. *Cooper v. Aaron*, 358 U.S. 1, 18 (1958).

42. *Baltimore & Ohio R. Co. v. Baugh*, 149 U.S. 368, 403 (1893), Field dissenting.

43. Thomas Jefferson, Letter to William Jarvis (September 28, 1820), H. A. Washington, *The Writings of Thomas Jefferson,* (New York: Derby & Jackson, 1859) 178.

44. President Andrew Jackson's Veto Message Regarding the Bank of the United States; July 10, 1832.

45. Article 3, Section 2, Paragraph 2 of the Constitution says, "The Supreme Court shall have appellate jurisdiction . . . under such regulations as the Congress shall make."

46. Newt Gingrich, "Bringing the Courts Back Under the Constitution" *Whistleblower*, Jan. 2012, 18.

47. Barry Adamson, *Freedom of Religion the First Amendment and the Supreme Court* (Gretna, LA: Pelican Publishing Co., 2008), 215.

48. Akhil Reed Amar, *America's Constitution* (New York: Random House, 2006), 60.

49. Mike Lee, *Our Lost Constitution* (New York: Sentinel, 2015), 11.

50. Peter Baker, "Supporters Slow to Grasp Health Law's Legal Risks," *New York Times*, June 23, 2012.

CHAPTER FIFTEEN - WHAT TO DO?

1. *NLRB v. Jones & Laughlin Steel Corp.*, 301 U.S. 1 (1937).

2. *United States v. Darby Lumber Co.*, 312 U.S. 100 (1941).

3. *Heart of Atlanta Motel, Inc. v. United States*, 379 U.S. 241, 255 (1964). Also see Gibbons v. Ogden, 22 U.S. 9, 196 (1824).

4. Lawrence Lessig, *Republic, Lost* (New York: Twelve, 2011), 119.

5. Ibid., 117.

6. Aristotle, *The Athenian Constitution* (New York: Penguin Books, 1984), 89.

7. Thomas E. Woods Jr., *Nullification* (Washington, DC: Regnery Publishing, Inc., 2010), 105.

8. Ibid., 33–34.

9. *Calder v. Bull*, 3 U.S. 3 Dall. 386 386, 387 (1798).

10. Thomas E. Woods Jr., *Nullification* (Washington, DC: Regnery Publishing, Inc., 2010), 34–37.

11. Ibid., 107.

12. *Journal of Continental Congress* 13 (Feb. 2, 1779): 1 36.

13. Mike Lee, *The Freedom Agenda* (Washington, DC: Regnery Publishing Co., 2011), 66–76.

14. Milton and Rose Friedman, *Free to Choose* (New York: Avon Books, 1981), 301.

15. *Clinton v. City of New York*, 524 U.S. 417 (1998).

16. Suggested by John H. Sununu, governor of New Hampshire.

17. James Madison said in The Federalist No. 46 "The Federal and State Governments are in fact but different agents and trustees of the people."

18. Thomas E. Woods Jr., *Nullification* (Washington, DC: Regnery Publishing, Inc., 2010), 49.

19. Ibid., 50.

20. Ibid., 52.

21. *Ableman v. Booth*, 62 U.S. 506 (1859).

22. Thomas E. Woods Jr., *Nullification* (Washington, DC: Regnery Publishing, Inc., 2010), 62–64.

23. Ibid., 71.

24. Ibid., 73.

25. Ibid., 80.

26. Alexander Hamilton, James Madison, John Jay, *The Federalist Papers* (New York: Bantam Books, 1982), 240–241.

27. This is a well-established legal principle known as the anti-commandeering doctrine, stating that the federal government cannot force state governments to enforce federal laws. See *Printz v. United States* (95-1478), 521 U.S. 898 (1997).

28. The Constitution Society is an organization that does research and public education on the principles of constitutional republican government. For more information, see their website at http://constitution.org/

29. *Helvering v. Davis*, 301 U.S. 619, 640 (1937).

30. Michael Tanner, "Still a Better Deal, Private Investment vs. Social Security," Cato Institute, February 13, 2012.

31. James Madison, "The Federalist No. 51," in *The Federalist Papers,* ed. Garry Wills, 263 (New York: Bantam Books, 1982).

32. James Madison, "The Federalist No. 46," in *The Federalist Papers,* ed. Garry Wills, 240 (New York: Bantam Books, 1982).

33. James Madison, "The Federalist No. 62," in *The Federalist Papers,* ed. Garry Wills, 313 (New York: Bantam Books, 1982).

34. Alexander Hamilton, "The Federalist No. 59," in *The Federalist Papers,* ed. Garry Wills, 301 (New York: Bantam Books, 1982).

35. Ralph A. Rossum, *Federalism, The Supreme Court, and the Seventeenth Amendment* (Lanham, MD: Lexington Books, 2001), 94.

36. Ralph A. Rossum, *Federalism, The Supreme Court, and the Seventeenth Amendment* (Lanham, MD: Lexington Books, 2001), 103.

37. Thomas E. Woods Jr., *Nullification* (Washington, DC: Regnery Publishing, Inc., 2010), 127.

38. Phyllis Schlafly, *The Supremacists: The Tyranny of Judges and How to Stop It* (Dallas: Spence Publishing Company, 2006), 161–169.

39. Sanford Levinson, "Our Imbecilic Constitution," *New York Times*, May 28, 2012.

40. *Eakin v. Raub*, 12 Sargent & Rawle 330 (Pa. 1825), Gibson dissenting.

41. Christopher Wolfe, *The Rise of Modern Judicial Review* (New York: Basic Books, 1986), 94.

42. Ibid., 95.

43. James W. Lucas, *Timely Renewed* (Lexington, KY: Create Space, 2010), 202.

44. *United States v. Lopez*, 514 U.S. 549, 580 (1995), Kennedy concurring.

45. Robert Flood, *The Rebirth of America* (Philadelphia: Arthur S. DeMoss Foundation, 1986), 32.

46. Letter to the Officers of the First Brigade of the Third Division of the Militia of Massachusetts, 11 October 1798.

INDEX

INDEX OF COURT CASES